C0-APP-805

KETO DIET FOR BEGINNERS
2020-2021

Turbocharge Your Weight Loss Journey without Restrictions. 550 Recipes to Get You Fit as a Fiddle + Full Low Carb List Guide

By

KATHY JENSEN

Copyright @2020. All rights reserved.

No part of this book may be reproduced, stored in a retrieval system, or transmitted in any form or by any means (mechanically, electronically, photocopying, recording, etc) without the prior written permission of the publisher.

Additionally, the purchase of this material entitles the buyer to reproduce worksheets for home or classroom use only - not for commercial resale. Reproduction of this book for an entire school is highly prohibited.

Printed in the U.S.A.

Table of Contents

Introduction

A fascinating twist to the Ketogenic diet – the Dirty keto diet is becoming more popular, thanks to the possibility of losing weight without the rules and restrictions of counting calories or preparing whole food dishes. It is increasingly becoming an effective option for people who want to lose weight fast – since processed and store-bought food items are very much more convenient and easier to stick with on the keto diet.

So, its' more realistic and sustainable and much more in tune with our modern lifestyle than – sourcing for whole food options in a fast, busy lifestyle. Since weight loss is the goal, the principle basically remains the same – high fats and low carb (ideally, the majority of your carbs should be replaced by fats and these fats should be about 80% of your total calorie intake. Carbs should be about 5% while proteins should be about 20%.)

Why Should Dirty Keto Work for You?

If you're a beginner to the Keto diet and simply wants to lose weight, this option will be great for you. It can be tough transitioning from the Standard American Diet (SAD) which is so high on carbs. If you have a very busy lifestyle, or lack motivation or don't just know where to begin, this is the go-to diet for you.

The dirty keto has helped countless people lose weight without the hassle of sourcing for fresh food produce from off-city farmers' markets, and the deep pockets for expensive and assorted "healthy" food options. And if you're on budget, Dirty keto can help you lose weight fast.

The Keto diet has become a popular diet option for improving health and more importantly, shedding excess weight. The Keto diet is a high-fat, low-carb and moderate protein diet, research has shown that it can also improve cognitive decline, type 2 diabetes and similar health conditions.

Basics of the Keto diet

The majority of your carbs should be replaced by fats and these fats should be about 80% of your total calorie intake. Carbs should be about 5% while proteins should be about 20%. Your body will be under Ketosis because you are forcing your body to utilize fats for energy production rather than glucose which is mainly sourced from carbs. Your body utilizes Ketones as an alternate fuel source when in Ketosis. Ketones are molecules produced from fats in the liver when there is a limit in glucose.

Most people avoid fat due to its high calorie content, but evidence has proven that the Keto diet and not low-fat diets are effective for promoting weight loss. Keto diet is also very filling and reduces hunger pangs which is important when you intend to lose weight. It is not difficult to switch to and stick to a Keto diet. What is actually difficult is adhering to strict rules and guidelines. As long as you maintain the Fats : Protein : Carbs ratio, you'll lose weight fast. It's a no-brainer. And quite unbecoming that many have deviated from this core principle of the Keto diet.

Everyone's weight loss needs are different. That is why we have included a Low Carb Reference List Guide for you to make careful choices with a variety of the best Low carb food options - the rules can wait! All you need do is monitor your carb intake. You can substitute or even customize recipes to make losing weight even easier and fun for you!

In the next chapter is the Low carb list Reference guide. This comes listed with all possibly known low carb foods and its carb content per gram serving. With this, you'll unlock your personal weight loss journey for a more targeted, bespoke approach. So, your eating habits, or low carb food preferences do not have to suffer.

The simple formula is to increase the fat and protein content in your meals and snacks while reducing your carb intake. You must restrict your carb intake to reach and remain in Ketosis. Different people achieve Ketosis with varying amounts of carb intake. Generally, it is easy to reach and stay in Ketosis when you decrease your carb intake to not more than 20grams.

Chapter 1
KETO LOW CARB FOOD LIST

DAIRY & EGGS LOW CARB LIST

A Four-ounce cottage cheese contains about 7g carbs and 18g protein, while the same amount of plain Greek yogurt (in gram) contains 5g carbs and 11g protein. When consumed without being combined with other foods both of them promote feelings of fullness. However, you can prepare a quick and easy Keto treat by combining plain Greek yogurt and cottage cheese with chopped nuts, cinnamon, and any low carb sweetener.

LOW CARB EGG & DAIRY

FOOD ITEM	SERVING SIZE	NET CARBS (G)
Eggs	1 egg (56g)	0
Cheese, blue	1 ounce (28.3g)	0-1.5
Cheese, brie	1 ounce (28.3g)	0-1.5
Cheese, cheddar	1 ounce (28.3g)	0-1.5
Cheese, feta	1 ounce (28.3g)	0-1.5
Cheese, parmesan	1 ounce (28.3g)	0-1.5
Cheese, mozzarella	1 ounce (28.3g)	0-1.5
Cheese, goat	1 ounce (28.3g)	0-1.5
Cheese, jack Colby	1 ounce (28.3g)	0-1.5
Cheese, swiss	1 ounce (28.3g)	0-1.5
Cheese, gouda	1 ounce (28.3g)	0-1.5
Cheese, dubliner	1 ounce (28.3g)	0-1.5
Cheese, gruyere	1 ounce (28.3g)	0-1.5
Cheese, gorgonzola	1 ounce (28.3g)	0-1.5
Heavy cream	1 tablespoon(14g)	0.4
Mascarpone cheese	2 tablespoons (28.3g)	0.6
Sour cream	1 tablespoon (11g)	0.6
Half & half	1 tablespoon (14g)	0.7
Cream cheese	1 tablespoon (14.5g)	0.8
Coconut cream	1 tablespoon (14g)	1.7
Whole milk ricotta cheese	1/2 cup (62g)	3.7
Whole Greek yogurt	1 cup (100 grams)	4
Whole cottage cheese	1/2 cup (105g)	7.2

FATS LOW CARB LIST

Fats and Oils are one of the best sources of fats on the Keto diet. Asides weight loss, these fats have been shown to help with general health. For example, Olive oil, which is rich in oleic acid, has been proven to decrease the risk of heart disease. Olive oil is a pure source of fat and does not contain any carbs. Oils in Keto can be used in many ways, including use as salad dressings and as addition to Keto smoothies and drinks.

If you want a healthier substitute for mayo, you can use oils as a healthy mayonnaise. Although, many oils like Olive oils are not stable at high temperatures, it is best you add to already cooked foods.

LOW CARB FATS

FOOD ITEM	SERVING SIZE	NET CARBS (G)
Avocado oil	1 tablespoon (14g)	0
Butter	1 tablespoon (14g)	0
Cocoa butter	1 tablespoon (13.8g)	0
Coconut oil	1 tablespoon (13.8g)	0
Ghee	1 tablespoon (13g)	0
Lard	1 tablespoon (12.8g)	0
MCT oil	1 tablespoon (14.5g)	0
Olive oil	1 tablespoon (13.4g)	0
Other seed & nut oils	1 tablespoon (~13.4g)	0

POULTRY & MEAT LOW CARB LIST

LOW CARB MEAT AND POULTRY

FOOD ITEM	SERVING SIZE	NET CARBS (G)
POULTRY		
Chicken	4 ounces (114g)	0
Duck	4 ounces (114g)	0
Quail	4 ounces (114g)	0
Turkey	4 ounces (114g)	0
MEAT & MEAT PRODUCTS	4 ounces (114g)	0
Bacon	4 ounces (114g)	0
Ground beef	4 ounces (114g)	0
Roast	4 ounces (114g)	0
Sausage	4 ounces (114g)	0
Steak	4 ounces (114g)	0
Veal	4 ounces (114g)	0

FOOD ITEM	SERVING SIZE	NET CARBS (G)

GAME MEATS

Food Item	Serving Size	Net Carbs (g)
Bison	4 ounces (114g)	0
Venison	4 ounces (114g)	0

LAMB

Food Item	Serving Size	Net Carbs (g)
Chops	4 ounces (114g)	0
Ground	4 ounces (114g)	0

PORK

Food Item	Serving Size	Net Carbs (g)
Ground Pork	4 ounces (114g)	0
Ham	4 ounces (114g)	0
Loin	4 ounces (114g)	0
Pork chops	4 ounces (114g)	0

ORGAN MEATS

Food Item	Serving Size	Net Carbs (g)
Heart	4 ounces (114g)	0-0.5
Kidney	4 ounces (114g)	0-0.5
Liver	4 ounces (114g)	0-0.5
Other organ meats	4 ounces (114g)	0-0.5
Sweetbread	4 ounces (114g)	0-0.5
Tongue	4 ounces (114g)	0-0.5

DELI MEATS

Food Item	Serving Size	Net Carbs (g)
Beef (W/O added sugar)	4 ounces (114g)	0-1
Chicken (W/O added sugar)	4 ounces (114g)	0-1
Ham (W/O added sugar)	4 ounces (114g)	0-1
Others	4 ounces (114g)	0-1
Turkey (W/O added sugar)	4 ounces (114g)	0-1

FISH AND SEAFOOD LOW CARB LIST

Fatty fish, salmon, shellfish, mackerel, and sardines are amongst Keto-friendly fish and seafood. Try to consume a minimum of two fish/seafood servings per week but be on the lookout for carbs in shellfish - which can contain significantly higher amounts of carbs than from other seafood sources. Also, aside being relatively low in carbs, Fish and seafood provide excellent sources of vital nutrients such as selenium and omega-3 fats.

LOW CARB FISH AND SEAFOOD

FOOD ITEM	SERVING SIZE	NET CARBS (G)
FISH		
Cod	4 ounces (114g)	0
Flounder	4 ounces (114g)	0
Halibut	4 ounces (114g)	0
Herring	4 ounces (114g)	0
Mackerel	4 ounces (114g)	0
Mahi-Mahi	4 ounces (114g)	0
Sardines	4 ounces (114g)	0
Sea Bass	4 ounces (114g)	0
Snapper	4 ounces (114g)	0
Tilapia	4 ounces (114g)	0
Trout	4 ounces (114g)	0
Tuna	4 ounces (114g)	0
Wild Salmon	4 ounces (114g)	0
SHELLFISH		
Clams	4 ounces (114g)	0-4
Crab	4 ounces (114g)	0-4
Lobster	4 ounces (114g)	0-4
Mussels	4 ounces (114g)	0-4
Octopus	4 ounces (114g)	0-4
Oysters	4 ounces (114g)	0-4
Scallops	4 ounces (114g)	0-3
Shrimp	4 ounces (114g)	0-4
Squid	4 ounces (114g)	0-4

FRUITS LOW CARB LIST

It is best to enjoy fruits in moderation on the Keto Diet. Although most fruits we have around are very much high carb, there are still quite a handful of low carb keto fruits. The below listed fruits are the best low carb options for a Keto diet. Serving sizes vary but for accurate measurement, use weight.

LOW CARB FRUITS

FOOD ITEM	SERVING SIZE	NET CARBS (G)
Avocados, fruit	1/2 fruit (110g)	1.8
Blackberries	1/2 cup (70g)	3.1
Blueberries	1/2 cup (72g)	8.9
Flesh of Coconuts	1/2 cup (42g)	2.5
Cranberries	1/2 cup (56g)	4.6
Currants	1/2 cup (55g)	5.3
Lemons	1 lemon (56g)	5.4
Limes	1 lime (68g)	5.2
Olives	1/2 cup (68g)	2.2
Raspberries	1/2 cup (64g)	3.3
Strawberries	1/2 cup (78g)	4.3
Tomatoes	1 cup (186g)	4.8
Watermelon	1/2 cup (78g)	5.5

VEGETABLE LOW CARB LIST

Cruciferous vegetables such as broccoli, cauliflower, and kale are low carb. Non-starchy vegetables usually have a maximum of 8g to 9g net carbs per cup. They also have a high concentration of minerals, antioxidants, vitamin, and fiber.

LOW CARB VEGETABLES

FOOD ITEM	SERVING SIZE	NET CARBS (G)
Artichokes	1/2 cup (86g)	5.2
Asparagus	1 cup (135g)	2.4
Bamboo shoots	1 cup (149g)	4.6
Bell peppers	1 cup (91g)	3.6
Broccoli	1 cup (90g)	3.6
Brussels sprouts	1 cup (90g)	4.6
Cauliflower	1 cup (104g)	3.2
Celeriac	1/2 cup (79g)	5.8
Celery	1 cup (102g)	1.4

Chili peppers	1 pepper (1.4g)	1
Cucumbers	1/2 cup (55g)	1.6
Eggplant	1 cup (83g)	2.3
Fennel	1 cup (89g)	3.7
Garlic	1 clove (3.2g)	0.9
Green beans	1 cup (104g)	4.3
Jalapeno peppers	1 pepper (13g)	0.5
Jicama	1 cup (128g)	5.1
Kelp noodles	4 ounces. (111 g)	2
Leeks	1/2 cup (47g)	5.5
Mushrooms	1 cup (87g)	2.2
Okra	1 cup (102g)	4.3
Onions	1/2 cup (58g)	4.3
Pickles	1 large (135g)	1.9
Poblano peppers	1	1.9
Pumpkins	1 cup (110g)	6.9
Radishes	1 cup (110g)	2
Rhubarb	1 cup (123g)	2
Rutabagas	1 cup (138g)	8.9
Scallions (green onions)	1 cup (102g)	4.7
Shallots	1 cup (11g)	1.4
Shirataki noodles	1 cup	4.7
Snow peas	1 cup (100g)	4.9
Spaghetti squash	1 cup (102g)	5.5
Turnips	1 cup (128g)	6.1
Yellow squash	1 cup (112g)	2.6
Zucchini	1 cup (112g)	2.4

LEAFY GREENS LOW CARB LIST

Leafy greens are the primary source of fiber and vegetables in a low carb diet. They are very low in carbs and calories, and are also very filling, and packed with fiber and nutrients.

LOW CARB LEAFY GREENS

FOOD ITEM	SERVING SIZE	NET CARBS (G)
Arugula	1 cup (22g)	0.4
Beet greens	1 cup (39g)	0.2
Bibb lettuce	1 cup (56g)	0.6
Bok choy	1 cup (69g)	0.8
Broccoli rabe	1 cup (38g)	0.0
Butter lettuce	1 cup (40g)	0.5
Cabbage	1 cup (90g)	3.0
Chard	1 cup (38g)	0.8
Collard greens	1 cup (252g)	3.9
Endive	1 cup (52g)	0.1
Iceberg lettuce	1 cup (56g)	1.2
Kale	1 cup (68g)	3.4
Mustard greens	1 cup (57g)	0.8
Romaine	1 cup (48g)	0.6
Spinach	1 cup (28g)	0.4
Sprouts	1 cup (32g)	0.1
Watercress	1 cup (32g)	0.2

NUTS & SEEDS LOW CARB LIST

Nuts and seeds make awesome snacks and are a great source of fats and proteins on Keto. Enjoy seeds in moderate amounts on Keto. They are convenient and can be easy to snack on during lazy afternoons or tired nights.

LOW CARB NUTS AND SEEDS FOODS

FOOD ITEM	SERVING SIZE	NET CARBS (G)
Almond butter	2 tablespoon (32g)	2.7
Almonds	1/4 cup (28.3g)	3
Brazil Nuts	1/4 cup (36g)	1
Brazil nuts	1/4 cup (33g)	1.4
Cashews	1/4 cup (31g)	8
Chia Seeds	1/4 cup (36g)	1
Chia seeds	1 ounce (28.35g)	2.1
Coconut flakes	3 tablespoons (22.5g)	3
Flax seeds	2 tablespoons (20.6g)	0.4

Hazelnuts	1/4 cup (34g)	2.3
Hemp seeds	3 tablespoon (30g)	1.4
Macadamia nuts	1/4 cup (33g)	1.7
Nut butters – macadamia, hazelnut, walnut, pecan, etc.	2 tablespoons (~32g)	0.5-3
Peanut butter	2 tablespoon (32g)	4
Peanuts	1/4 cup (36g)	2.8
Pecans	1/4 cup (36g)	1
Pine nuts	1/4 cup (36g)	3.2
Pistachios	1/4 cup (31g)	5
Poppy seeds	1 tablespoon (8.8g)	0.8
Pumpkin seeds	1/4 cup (32g)	1.6
Sesame seeds	1 tablespoon (9g)	1
Sunflower seed butter	2 tablespoon (32g)	5.7
Sunflower seeds	1/4 cup (11.5g)	1.3
Walnuts	1/4 cup (30g)	2

BEVERAGES LOW CARB LIST

Unsweetened Tea and Coffee both contain caffeine which can improve your mood, physical performance and body metabolism. Aside weight loss, consumption of tea and coffee has also been shown to reduce susceptibility to diabetes. Bear in mind that you shouldn't consume tea lattes and "light" coffee because they contain high-carb flavors since they are prepared with non-fat milk.

LOW CARB BEVERAGE FOODS

FOOD ITEM	SERVING SIZE	NET CARBS (G)
Almond milk, unsweetened	1 cup (240ml)	1.5
Beef broth	1 cup (240g)	0
Bone broth	1 cup (240g)	0
Chicken broth	1 cup (240g)	0
Coconut milk, unsweetened canned,	1/2 cup (114g)	3.2
Coconut milk, unsweetened carton	1 cup (240ml)	1
Coffee, unsweetened	1 cup (250g)	0.5
Hard liquor	1 fl. oz (28g)	0

Food Item	Serving Size	Net Carbs (g)
Red Wine	5 fl. oz (148g)	3.1-3.7
Tea, unsweetened	1 cup (240g)	0
Vegetable broth	1 cup (220g)	2
Water	1 cup (236ml)	0
White Wine, dry	5 fl. oz (148g)	3.1-3.7

BAKING LOW CARB LIST
LOW CARB BAKING INGREDIENTS

FOOD ITEM	SERVING SIZE	NET CARBS (G)
Almond flour	1/4 cup (29g)	3
Chocolate, baker's	1 ounce (28g)	2.9-3.4
Chocolate, unsweetened	1 ounce (28g)	2.9-3.4
Cocoa/cacao powder	1 tablespoon (5.5g)	1.1
Coconut flour	2 tablespoon (15g)	4
Collagen protein powder	1 scoop (32g)	0
Flax seed meal, golden	2 tablespoon (12g)	0
Flax seed meal, plain	2 tablespoon (12g)	0
Gelatin	1 tablespoon (6g)	0
Glucomannan	1/2 tsp (2g)	0
Hazelnut flour	1/4 cup (30g)	2
Macadamia nut flour	1/4 cup (29g)	2.9
Peanut flour	1/4 cup (15g)	2.8
Pork rinds	1/2 oz (15g)	0
Psyllium husk powder	1 teaspoon (4g)	0
Pure extracts - vanilla, fruit	1 teaspoon (4g)	0.1
Sunflower seed meal	1/4 cup (29g)	4
Whey protein powder	1 scoop (~32g)	0
Xanthan gum	1/2 tsp (0.8g)	0

SWEETENERS LOW CARB LIST

Below, is a list of the best low carb sweeteners. Serving sizes will depend a lot on the brand, or concentration.

LOW CARB SWEETENERS FOODS

FOOD ITEM	SERVING SIZE	NET CARBS (G)
Monk fruit	1 teaspoon (2.3g)	0
Erythritol	1 teaspoon (4g)	0
Stevia	1 teaspoon (4g)	0
Xylitol	1 teaspoon (4g)	0
Chicory root	1/2 cup (45g)	0

SPICES & SEASONINGS LOW CARB LIST

LOW CARB SPICES & SEASONINGS

FOOD ITEM	SERVING SIZE	NET CARBS (G)
Allspice, ground	1 teaspoon (1.9g)	1
Black pepper	1 teaspoon (2.3g)	0.9
Cardamom	1 teaspoon (2g)	0.8
Cayenne pepper	1/4 tsp (0.5g)	0.2
Celery seed	1 teaspoon (2g)	0.6
Chili powder	1 tablespoon (8g)	1.2
Cinnamon, ground	1 teaspoon (2.6g)	0.7
Cream of tartar	1 teaspoon (3g)	1.8
Cumin, ground	1 teaspoon (2.8g)	0
Curry powder	1 teaspoon (2g)	0
Fennel seed	1 tablespoon (5.8g)	0.7
Garlic powder	1 teaspoon (3.1g)	2
Ginger, ground	1 teaspoon (1.8g)	1
Mustard, ground	1 teaspoon (2g)	0.4
Nutmeg, ground	1 teaspoon (2.2g)	0.6
Onion powder	1 teaspoon (2.4g)	1.5
Paprika (regular or smoked)	1 teaspoon (2.3g)	0.4
Red pepper, ground	1 teaspoon (2g)	0
Salt (sea salt)	1 teaspoon (6g)	0

FOOD ITEM	SERVING SIZE	NET CARBS (G)
Turmeric	1 teaspoon (3g)	1.3

CONDIMENTS LOW CARB LIST

FOOD ITEM	SERVING SIZE	NET CARBS (G)
Apple Cider (ACV)	1 tablespoon (15ml)	0
Vinegar – white	1 tablespoon (15ml)	0
DRESSINGS		
Blue Cheese	2 tablespoons (~30g)	0-2
Caesar	2 tablespoons (~30g)	0-2
Chimichurri sauce	1 tablespoon	1
Horseradish	1 teaspoon (5.6g)	0.5
Mayonnaise	1 tablespoon (13.8g)	0.1
Mustard	1 teaspoon (5g)	0.1
Ranch	2 tablespoons (~30g)	0-2
HOT SAUCE		
Buffalo	1 teaspoon (6.5g)	1.2
Red Pepper Sauce	1 teaspoon (6.5g)	1.2
Sriracha	1 teaspoon (6.5g)	1.2
Coconut aminos	1 tablespoon (15ml)	6
Dressings, oil	2 tablespoons (~30g)	2-3
Dressings, vinaigrette	2 tablespoons (~30g)	2-3
Lemon juice	2 tablespoon (31g)	2/2.5
Lime juice	2 tablespoon (31g)	2/2.5
Marinara sauce	1/2 cup (132g)	7.4
Pesto sauce	1/4 cup (61g)	2.8
Salsa	2 tablespoon (36g)	1.7
Vinegar – balsamic	1 tablespoon (16g)	2.7

HERBS LOW CARB LIST

The below listed herbs are based on chopped "fresh" herbs. If using dried herbs, the conversion rate is 3:1, i.e. 1 tablespoon fresh = 1 teaspoon dried OR 1 tablespoon fresh = 3 teaspoons dried

FOOD ITEM	SERVING SIZE	NET CARBS (G)
FRESH HERBS		
Basil	2 tablespoons (5.3g)	0
Bay leaves	1 tablespoon (0.6g)	0.3
Chives	1 tablespoon (3g)	0.1
Cilantro	1 tablespoon (1g)	0.1
Dill	1 tablespoon (0.6g)	0.1
Marjoram	1 tablespoon (0.6g)	0.2
Mint	1 tablespoon (1.6g)	0.1
Oregano	1 tablespoon (3g)	0.3
Parsley	1 tablespoon (3.8g)	0.1
Rosemary	1 tablespoon (1.7g)	0.2
Sage	1 tablespoon (0.7g)	0.1
Savory	1 tablespoon (1.4g)	0.4
Tarragon	1 tablespoon (0.6g)	0.3
Thyme	1 tablespoon (2.4g)	0.3

The list below is based on "dried" herbs. If using dried herbs, the conversion is 3:1 from fresh herbs above. 1 tablespoon fresh = 1 teaspoon dried.

Basil	2 tsp	0
Bay leaves	1 teaspoon	0.3
Chives	1 teaspoon	0.1
Cilantro	1 teaspoon	0.1
Dill	1 teaspoon	0.1
Marjoram	1 teaspoon	0.2
Mint	1 teaspoon	0.1
Oregano	1 teaspoon	0.3
Parsley	1 teaspoon	0.1
Rosemary	1 teaspoon	0.2
Sage	1 teaspoon	0.1
Savory	1 teaspoon	0.4
Tarragon	1 teaspoon	0.3
Thyme	1 teaspoon	0.3

Poultry and Eggs

1 – Egg Butter

Serves: 2; Preparation: 5 minutes; Cook time: 0 minutes;
Nutrition facts: 159 Calories; 16.5 g Fats; 3 g Protein; 0.2 g Net Carb; 0 g Fiber;
Ingredients

- 2 large eggs, hard-boiled
- 3-ounce unsalted butter
- ½ tsp dried oregano
- ½ tsp dried basil
- 2 leaves of iceberg lettuce

Seasoning:

- ½ tsp of sea salt
- ¼ tsp ground black pepper

How to Prepare:

1. Peel the eggs, then chop them finely and place in a medium bowl.
2. Add remaining ingredients and stir well.
3. Serve egg butter wrapped in a lettuce leaf.

2 – Omelet

Serves: 2; Preparation: 5 minutes; Cook time: 10 minutes;
Nutrition facts: 114.5 Calories; 9.3 g Fats; 4 g Protein; 1 g Net Carb; 0.2 g Fiber;
Ingredients

- 2 eggs
- 2 tbsp shredded parmesan cheese, divided
- 1 tbsp unsalted butter
- 2 slices of turkey bacon, diced

Seasoning:

- ¼ tsp salt
- 1/8 tsp ground black pepper

How to Prepare:

1. Crack eggs in a bowl, add salt and black pepper, whisk well until fluffy and then whisk in 1 tbsp cheese until combined.
2. Take a medium skillet pan, add bacon slices on it, cook for 3 minutes until sauté, then pour in the egg mixture and cook for 4 minutes or until the omelet is almost firm.
3. Lower heat to medium-low level, sprinkle remaining cheese on top of the omelet, then fold the omelet and cook for 1 minute.
4. Slide the omelet to a plate, cut it in half, and serve immediately.

3 – Classic Deviled Eggs

Serves: 2; Preparation: 5 minutes; Cook time: 0 minutes;
Nutrition facts: 145 Calories; 12.8 g Fats; 6.9 g Protein; 0.7 g Net Carb; 0.1 g Fiber;
Ingredients

- 2 eggs, boiled
- 1 1/3 tbsp mayonnaise
- 1/3 tsp mustard paste
- ¼ tsp apple cider vinegar
- 1/8 tsp paprika

Seasoning:

- 1/8 tsp salt
- 1/8 tsp ground black pepper

How to Prepare:

1. Peel the boiled eggs, then slice in half lengthwise and transfer egg yolks to a medium bowl by using a spoon.
2. Mash the egg yolk, add remaining ingredients except for paprika and stir until well combined.
3. Pipe the egg yolk mixture into egg whites, then sprinkle with paprika and serve.

4 – Green Buttered Eggs

Serves: 2; Preparation: 5 minutes; Cook time: 5 minutes;
Nutrition facts: 165 Calories; 14.4 g Fats; 7.3 g Protein; 0.9 g Net Carb; 0.4 g Fiber;
Ingredients

- ¼ cup cilantro leaves, chopped
- 1/2 tsp minced garlic
- ¼ cup parsley, chopped
- 1 tsp thyme leaves
- 2 eggs

Seasoning:

- ¼ tsp salt
- ¼ tsp cayenne pepper
- 1 tbsp butter, unsalted
- 1/2 tbsp avocado oil

How to Prepare:

1. Take a medium skillet pan, place it over low heat, add oil and butter and when the butter melts, add garlic and cook for 1 minute until fragrant.
2. Add thyme, cook for 30 seconds until it begins to brown, then add cilantro and parsley, switch heat to medium level and then cook for 2 minutes until crisp.
3. Cracks eggs on top of herbs, cover with a lid, then switch heat to the low level and cook for 2 to 3 minutes until yolks are set and cooked to the desired level.
4. Serve.

5 – Egg Salad

Serves: 2; Preparation: 5 minutes; Cook time: 0 minutes
Nutrition facts: 240.3 Calories; 22 g Fats; 10.8 g Protein; 0 g Net Carb; 0 g Fiber;
Ingredients

- 2 tbsp mayonnaise
- 1 tsp lemon juice
- 2 large eggs, hard-boiled
- 2 slices of bacon, cooked, crumbled

Seasoning:

- 1/8 tsp cracked black pepper
- ¼ tsp salt

How to Prepare:

1. Peel the eggs, then dice them and place them in a bowl.
2. Add remaining ingredients except for bacon and stir until well mixed.
3. Top with bacon and serve.

6 – Pesto Scramble

Serves: 2; Preparation: 5 minutes; Cook time: 5 minutes
Nutrition facts: 159.5 Calories; 14.5 g Fats; 7 g Protein; 0.4 g Net Carb; 0.1 g Fiber;
Ingredients

- 2 eggs
- 2 tbsp grated cheddar cheese
- 1 tbsp unsalted butter
- 1 tbsp basil pesto

Seasoning:

- 1/8 tsp salt
- 1/8 tsp ground black pepper

How to Prepare:

1. Crack eggs in a bowl, add cheese, black pepper, salt, and pesto and whisk until combined.
2. Take a skillet pan, place it over medium heat, add butter and when it melts, pour in the egg mixture, and cook for 3 to 5 minutes until eggs have scrambled to the desired level.
3. Serve.

7 – Fried Eggs

Serves: 2; Preparation: 5 minutes; Cook time: 8 minutes
Nutrition facts: 179 Calories; 16.5 g Fats; 7.6 g Protein; 0 g Net Carb; 0 g Fiber;
Ingredients
- 2 eggs
- 2 tbsp unsalted butter

Seasoning:
- ¼ tsp salt
- 1/8 tsp ground black pepper

How to Prepare:
1. Take a skillet pan, place it over medium heat, add butter and when it has melted, crack eggs in the pan.
2. Cook eggs for 3 to 5 minutes until fried to the desired level, then transfer the eggs to serving plates and sprinkle with salt and black pepper.

8 – Chicken and Bacon Pancake

Serves: 2; Preparation: 5 minutes; Cook time: 8 minutes
Nutrition facts: 222 Calories; 17 g Fats; 16.5 g Protein; 0 g Net Carb; 0 g Fiber;
Ingredients
- 1 chicken thigh, debone
- 2 slices of bacon
- 1 egg
- 2 tbsp coconut oil

Seasoning:
- ¼ tsp salt
- 1/8 tsp ground black pepper

How to Prepare:
1. Cut chicken into bite-size pieces, place them in a food processor, add bacon, egg, salt, and black pepper and process until well combined.
2. Take a frying pan, place it over medium heat, add 1 tbsp oil and when hot, scoop chicken mixture in the pan, shape each scoop into a round pancake and cook for 4 minutes per side until brown and cooked. When done, transfer pancakes into a plate, drizzle with remaining oil.

9 – Egg and Cheese Breakfast

Serves: 2; Preparation: 20 minutes; Cook time: 5 minutes
Nutrition facts: 271 Calories; 21.5 g Fats; 17.6 g Protein; 1.1 g Net Carb; 0 g Fiber;
Ingredients
- 2 large eggs
- 2 blocks of cheddar cheese, each about 1-ounce

How to Prepare:
1. Take a medium saucepan, half full with water, add eggs in it, then place the pan over medium heat and bring to boil, covering with the lid.
2. When water starts boiling, remove the pan from heat and let it rest until eggs have cooked to the desired level, 4 minutes for the runny center, 6 minutes for the semi-soft center, 10 minutes for medium, and 16 minutes for hard-boiled.
3. Then drain the eggs, rinse it under cold water until cooled, and then peel them. Serve eggs with cheese.

10 – Eggs in Clouds

Serves: 2; Preparation: 5 minutes; Cook time: 5 minutes
Nutrition facts: 101 Calories; 7.1 g Fats; 8.6 g Protein; 0.8 g Net Carb; 0 g Fiber;
Ingredients
- 2 eggs
- 2 tbsp chopped bacon, cooked

Seasoning:
- ¼ tsp salt
- 1/8 tsp ground black pepper

How to Prepare:
1. Turn on the oven, then set it to 350 degrees F and let it preheat.
2. Separate egg whites and yolks between two bowls, and then beat the egg whites until stiff peaks form.
3. Add bacon, fold until mixed, scoop the mixture into two mounds onto a baking sheet lined with parchment paper.
4. Make a small well in the middle of each mound by using a small bowl, bake for 3 minutes, then add an egg yolk into each well and continue baking for 2 minutes. Season eggs with salt and black pepper and then serve.

11 – Buttery Scrambled Eggs

Serves: 2; Preparation: 5 minutes; Cook time: 6 minutes
Nutrition facts: 81.5 Calories; 3.75 g Fats; 3.75 g Protein; 0.25 g Net Carb; 0 g Fiber;
Ingredients
- 3 eggs
- ¼ tsp salt
- 1/8 tsp ground black pepper
- 2 tbsp chopped unsalted butter, cold
- 1 tbsp unsalted butter, softened

How to Prepare:
1. Take a bowl, cracked eggs in it, whisk until well combined, and then stir in chopped cold butter until mixed.
2. Take a skillet pan, place it over medium-low heat, add butter and when it melts, pour in the egg mixture and cook for 1 minute, don't stir.
3. Then stir the omelet and cook for 1 to 2 minutes until thoroughly cooked and scramble to the desired level.
4. Season scramble eggs with salt and black pepper and then serve.

12 – Cream Cheese Pancakes

Serves: 2; Preparation: 5 minutes; Cook time: 5 minutes
Nutrition facts: 97.8 Calories; 8.4 g Fats; 4.4 g Protein; 1 g Net Carb; 0.2 g Fiber;
Ingredients
- 2 oz cream cheese
- 2 eggs
- ½ tsp cinnamon
- 1 tsp unsalted butter

How to Prepare:
1. Place cream cheese in a blender, add eggs and cinnamon, pulse for 1 minute or until smooth, and then let the batter rest for 5 minutes.
2. Take a skillet pan, place it over medium heat, add butter and when it melts, drop one-fourth of the batter into the pan, spread evenly, and cook the pancakes for 2 minutes per side until done. Transfer pancakes to a plate and serve.

13 – Sheet Pan Eggs with Bell Pepper and Chives

Serves: 2; Preparation: 5 minutes; Cook time: 8 minutes
Nutrition facts: 87 Calories; 5.4 g Fats; 7.2 g Protein; 1.7 g Net Carb; 0.7 g Fiber;
Ingredients
- ½ of medium red bell pepper, chopped
- 2 tbsp chopped chives
- 2 eggs

Seasoning:
- ¼ tsp salt
- 1/8 tsp ground black pepper

How to Prepare:
1. Turn on the oven, then set it to 350 degrees F and let it preheat.
2. Meanwhile, crack eggs in a bowl, add remaining ingredients and whisk until combined.
3. Take a small heatproof dish, pour in egg mixture, and bake for 5 to 8 minutes until set.
4. When done, cut it into two squares and then serve.

14 – Crepe

Serves: 2; Preparation: 5 minutes; Cook time: 9 minutes
Nutrition facts: 118 Calories; 9.4 g Fats; 6.5 g Protein; 1 g Net Carb; 0.9 g Fiber;
Ingredients
- 2/3 tbsp psyllium husk
- 1 1/3 tbsp cream cheese
- 2 eggs
- 1 egg white
- 1 tbsp unsalted butter

How to Prepare:
1. Prepare the batter and for this, place all the ingredients in a bowl, except for butter, and then whisk by using a stick blender until smooth and very liquid.
2. Take a skillet pan, place it over medium heat, add ½ tbsp butter and when it melts, pour in half of the batter, spread evenly, and cook until the top has firmed.
3. Carefully flip the crepe, then continue cooking for 2 minutes until cooked and then transfer it to a plate.
4. Add remaining butter and when it melts, cook another crepe in the same manner and then serve.

15 – Omelet with Meat

Serves: 2; Preparation: 5 minutes; Cook time: 12 minutes
Nutrition facts: 126.3 Calories; 8.6 g Fats; 10.7 g Protein; 1.5 g Net Carb; 0 g Fiber;
Ingredients
- 2 oz ground turkey
- 1 tbsp chopped spinach
- 1 tbsp whipped topping
- 2 eggs
- 2 tbsp grated mozzarella cheese

Seasoning:
- ¼ tsp salt
- 1/8 tsp ground black pepper

How to Prepare:
1. Take a skillet pan, place it over medium heat, add ground turkey and cook for 5 minutes until cooked through.
2. Meanwhile, crack eggs in a bowl, add whipped topping and spinach and whisk until combined.
3. When the meat is cooked, transfer it to a plate, then switch heat to the low level and pour in the egg mixture.
4. Cook the eggs for 3 minutes until the bottom is firm, then flip it and cook for 3 minutes until the omelet is firmed, covering the pan.
5. Sprinkle cheese on the omelet, cook for 1 minute until cheese has melted, and then slide omelet to a plate.
6. Spread ground meat on the omelet, roll it, then cut it in half and serve.

16 – Pancakes

Serves: 2; Preparation: 5 minutes; Cook time: 6 minutes
Nutrition facts: 166.8 Calories; 15 g Fats; 5.8 g Protein; 1.8 g Net Carb; 0.8 g Fiber;
Ingredients
- ¼ cup almond flour
- 1 ½ tbsp unsalted butter
- 2 oz cream cheese, softened
- 2 eggs

How to Prepare:
1. Take a bowl, crack eggs in it, whisk well until fluffy, and then whisk in flour and cream cheese until well combined.
2. Take a skillet pan, place it over medium heat, add butter and when it melts, drop pancake batter in four sections, spread it evenly, and cook for 2 minutes per side until brown. Serve.

17 – Cheese Roll-Ups

Serves: 2; Preparation: 5 minutes; Cook time: 0 minutes;
Nutrition facts: 166 Calories; 15 g Fats; 6.5 g Protein; 2 g Net Carb; 0 g Fiber;
Ingredients
- 2 oz mozzarella cheese, sliced, full-fat
- 1-ounce butter, unsalted

How to Prepare:
1. Cut cheese into slices and then cut butter into thin slices.
2. Top each cheese slice with a slice of butter, roll it and then serve.

18 – Scrambled Eggs with Spinach and Cheese

Serves: 2; Preparation: 5 minutes; Cook time: 5 minutes;
Nutrition facts: 171 Calories; 14 g Fats; 9.2 g Protein; 1.1 g Net Carb; 1.7 g Fiber;
Ingredients
- 2 oz spinach
- 2 eggs
- 1 tbsp coconut oil
- 2 tbsp grated mozzarella cheese, full-fat

Seasoning:
- ¼ tsp salt
- 1/8 tsp ground black pepper
- 1/8 tsp red pepper flakes

How to Prepare:
1. Take a medium bowl, crack eggs in it, add salt and black pepper and whisk until combined.
2. Take a medium skillet pan, place it over medium heat, add oil and when hot, add spinach and cook for 1 minute until leaves wilt.
3. Pour eggs over spinach, stir and cook for 1 minute until just set.
4. Stir in cheese, then remove the pan from heat and sprinkle red pepper flakes on top. Serve.

19 – Cheese Omelet

Serves: 2; Preparation: 5 minutes; Cook time: 10 minutes;
Nutrition facts: 275 Calories; 25.7 g Fats; 10.3 g Protein; 0.7 g Net Carb; 0 g Fiber;
Ingredients

- 1.5 oz butter, unsalted
- 2 eggs
- 1 ounce shredded mozzarella cheese, full-fat

Seasoning:

- ¼ tsp salt
- 1/8 tsp ground black pepper

How to Prepare:
1. Take a medium bowl, crack eggs in it, whisk until blended and then whisk in half of the cheese, salt, and black pepper.
2. Take a frying pan, place it over medium heat, add butter and when it melts, pour in egg mixture, spread it evenly and let it cook for 2 minutes until set.
3. Switch heat to the low level, continue cooking for 2 minutes until thoroughly cooked, and then top with remaining cheese.
4. Fold the omelet, slide it to a plate, cut it in half, and then serve.

20 – Egg Wraps

Serves: 2; Preparation: 5 minutes; Cook time: 5 minutes;
Nutrition facts: 68 Calories; 4.7 g Fats; 5.5 g Protein; 0.5 g Net Carb; 0 g Fiber;
Ingredients

- 2 eggs
- 1 tbsp coconut oil

Seasoning:

- ¼ tsp salt
- 1/8 tsp ground black pepper

How to Prepare:
1. Take a medium bowl, crack eggs in it, add salt and black pepper, and then whisk until blended.
2. Take a frying pan, place it over medium-low heat, add coconut oil and when it melts, pour in half of the egg, spread it evenly into a thin layer by rotating the pan and cook for 2 minutes.
3. Then flip the pan, cook for 1 minute, and transfer to a plate. Repeat with the remaining egg to make another wrap, then roll each egg wrap. Serve.

21 – Chaffles with Poached Eggs

Serves: 2; Preparation: 5 minutes; Cook time: 10 minutes;
Nutrition facts: 265 Calories; 18.5 g Fats; 17.6 g Protein; 3.4 g Net Carb; 6 g Fiber;
Ingredients

- 2 tsp coconut flour
- ½ cup shredded cheddar cheese, full-fat
- 3 eggs

Seasoning:

- ¼ tsp salt
- 1/8 tsp ground black pepper

How to Prepare:
1. Switch on a mini waffle maker and let it preheat for 5 minutes.
2. Meanwhile, take a medium bowl, place all the ingredients in it, reserving 2 eggs and then mix by using an immersion blender until smooth.
3. Ladle the batter evenly into the waffle maker, shut with lid, and let it cook for 3 to 4 minutes until firm and golden brown.
4. Meanwhile, prepare poached eggs, and for this, take a medium bowl half full with water, place it over medium heat and bring it to a boil.
5. Then crack an egg in a ramekin, carefully pour it into the boiling water and cook for 3 minutes.
6. Transfer egg to a plate lined with paper towels by using a slotted spoon and repeat with the other egg.
7. Top chaffles with poached eggs, season with salt and black pepper, and then serve.

22 – Chaffle with Scrambled Eggs

Serves: 2; Preparation: 5 minutes; Cook time: 10 minutes;
Nutrition facts: 265 Calories; 18.5 g Fats; 17.6 g Protein; 3.4 g Net Carb; 6 g Fiber;
Ingredients
- 2 tsp coconut flour
- ½ cup shredded cheddar cheese, full-fat
- 3 eggs
- 1-ounce butter, unsalted

Seasoning:
- ¼ tsp salt
- 1/8 tsp ground black pepper
- 1/8 tsp dried oregano

How to Prepare:
1. Switch on a mini waffle maker and let it preheat for 5 minutes.
2. Meanwhile, take a medium bowl, place all the ingredients in it, reserving 2 eggs and then mix by using an immersion blender until smooth.
3. Ladle the batter evenly into the waffle maker, shut with lid, and let it cook for 3 to 4 minutes until firm and golden brown.
4. Meanwhile, prepare scrambled eggs and for this, take a medium bowl, crack the eggs in it and whisk them with a fork until frothy, and then season with salt and black pepper.
5. Take a medium skillet pan, place it over medium heat, add butter and when it melts, pour in eggs and cook for 2 minutes until creamy, stirring continuously. Top chaffles with scrambled eggs, sprinkle with oregano, and then serve.

23 – Sheet Pan Eggs with Mushrooms and Spinach

Serves: 2; Preparation: 5 minutes; Cook time: 12 minutes;
Nutrition facts: 165 Calories; 10.7 g Fats; 14 g Protein; 1.5 g Net Carb; 0.5 g Fiber;
Ingredients
- 2 eggs
- 1 tsp chopped jalapeno pepper
- 1 tbsp chopped mushrooms
- 1 tbsp chopped spinach
- 1 tbsp chopped chard

Seasoning:
- 1/3 tsp salt
- 1/4 tsp ground black pepper

How to Prepare:
1. Turn on the oven, then set it to 350 degrees F and let it preheat.
2. Take a medium bowl, crack eggs in it, add salt and black pepper, then add all the vegetables and stir until combined.
3. Take a medium sheet ball or rimmed baking sheet, grease it with oil, pour prepared egg batter on it, and then bake for 10 to 12 minutes until done. Cut egg into two squares and then serve.

24 – No Bread Breakfast Sandwich

Serves: 2; Preparation: 10 minutes; Cook time: 15 minutes;
Nutrition facts: 180 Calories; 15 g Fats; 10 g Protein; 1 g Net Carb; 0 g Fiber;
Ingredients
- 2 slices of ham
- 4 eggs
- 1 tsp tabasco sauce
- 3 tbsp butter, unsalted
- 2 tsp grated mozzarella cheese

Seasoning:
- ¼ tsp salt
- 1/8 tsp ground black pepper

How to Prepare:

1. Take a frying pan, place it over medium heat, add butter and when it melt, crack an egg in it and fry for 2 to 3 minutes until cooked to desired level.
2. Transfer fried egg to a plate, fry remaining eggs in the same manner and when done, season eggs with salt and black pepper.
3. Prepare the sandwich and for this, use a fried egg as a base for sandwich, then top with a ham slice, sprinkle with a tsp of ham and cover with another fried egg.
4. Place egg into the pan, return it over low heat and let it cook until cheese melts. Prepare another sandwich in the same manner and then serve.

25 – Scrambled Eggs with Basil and Butter

Serves: 2; Preparation: 5 minutes; Cook time: 5 minutes;
Nutrition facts: 320 Calories; 29 g Fats; 13 g Protein; 1.5 g Net Carb; 0 g Fiber;
Ingredients
- 1 tbsp chopped basil leaves
- 2 tbsp butter, unsalted
- 2 tbsp grated cheddar cheese
- 2 eggs
- 2 tbsp whipping cream
Seasoning:
- 1/8 tsp salt
- 1/8 tsp ground black pepper
How to Prepare:
1. Take a medium bowl, crack eggs in it, add salt, black pepper, cheese and cream and whisk until combined.
2. Take a medium pan, place it over low heat, add butter and when it melts, pour in the egg mixture and cook for 2 to 3 minutes until eggs have scrambled to the desired level.
3. When done, distribute scrambled eggs between two plates, top with basil leaves and then serve.

26 – Scrambled Eggs

Serves: 2; Preparation: 5 minutes; Cook time: 5 minutes;
Nutrition facts: 163.5 Calories; 15.5 g Fats; 5.5 g Protein; 0.5 g Net Carb; 0 g Fiber;
Ingredients
- 1-ounce unsalted butter
- 2 large eggs
- 1/8 tsp salt
- 1/8 tsp cracked black pepper
How to Prepare:
1. Take a medium bowl, crack the eggs in it and whisk them with a fork until frothy, and then season with salt and black pepper.
2. Take a medium skillet pan, place it over medium heat, add butter and when it melts, pour in eggs and cook for 2 minutes until creamy, stirring continuously. Divide the eggs evenly between two plates and serve.

27 – Bacon, and Eggs

Serves: 2; Preparation: 5 minutes; Cook time: 10 minutes;
Nutrition facts: 136 Calories; 11 g Fats; 7.5 g Protein; 1 g Net Carb; 0 g Fiber;
Ingredients
- 2 eggs
- 4 slices of turkey bacon
- ¼ tsp salt
- ¼ tsp ground black pepper
How to Prepare:
1. Take a skillet pan, place it over medium heat, add bacon slices in it and cook for 5 minutes until crispy.
2. Transfer bacon slices to a plate and set aside until required, reserving the fat in the pan.

3. Cook the egg in the pan one at a time, and for this, crack an egg in the pan and cook for 2 to 3 minutes or more until the egg has cooked to desire level.
4. Transfer egg to a plate and cook the other egg in the same manner. Season eggs with salt and black pepper and then serve with cooked bacon.

28 – Boiled Eggs

Serves: 2; Preparation: 5 minutes; Cook time: 10 minutes;
Nutrition facts: 112 Calories; 9.5 g Fats; 5.5 g Protein; 1 g Net Carb; 0 g Fiber;
Ingredients
- 2 eggs
- ½ of a medium avocado

Seasoning:
- ¼ tsp salt
- ¼ tsp ground black pepper

How to Prepare:
1. Place a medium pot over medium heat, fill it half full with water and bring it to boil.
2. Then carefully place the eggs in the boiling water and boil the eggs for 5 minutes until soft-boiled, 8 minutes for medium-boiled, and 10 minutes for hard-boiled.
3. When eggs have boiled, transfer them to a bowl containing chilled water and let them rest for 5 minutes.
4. Then crack the eggs with a spoon and peel them.
5. Cut each egg into slices, season with salt and black pepper, and serve with diced avocado.

29 – Eggs on the Go

Serves: 2; Preparation: 5 minutes; Cook time: 10 minutes;
Nutrition facts: 150 Calories; 10.4 g Fats; 11.2 g Protein; 1.3 g Net Carb; 0.2 g Fiber;
Ingredients
- 2 tbsp sliced mushrooms
- 2 eggs
- 2 slices of bacon, chopped
- ¼ tsp salt
- 1/8 tsp ground black pepper

How to Prepare:
1. Turn on the oven, then set it to 400 degrees F and let it preheat.
2. Take two muffin tins, crack an egg in it, add mushrooms and bacon and then season with salt and black pepper.
3. Bake the eggs for 10 to 15 minutes until thoroughly cooked and then serve.

30 – Cottage Cheese Pancake

Serves: 2; Preparation: 5 minutes; Cook time: 20 minutes;
Nutrition facts: 166 Calories; 14 g Fats; 8 g Protein; 2 g Net Carb; 2 g Fiber;
Ingredients
- 2 tbsp almond flour
- ½ tbsp erythritol sweetener
- ½ tsp vanilla extract, unsweetened
- 1 egg
- 2 ¾ tbsp cottage cheese

Seasoning:
- ½ tbsp butter, unsalted, melted
- ½ tsp baking powder

How to Prepare:
1. Take a medium bowl, place all the ingredients in it except for butter and blend by using an immersion blender until smooth.
2. Take a medium skillet pan, place it over medium heat, add butter and when it melts, pour in one-fourth of the batter, spread it even to shape it like a pancake and then cook for 2 minutes per side until golden brown and cooked.
3. Transfer pancake to a plate and then repeat with the remaining batter. Serve.

31 – Egg, Cheddar and Bacon Sandwich

Serves: 2; Preparation: 10 minutes; Cook time: 0 minutes;
Nutrition facts: 191 Calories; 13.6 g Fats; 14.4 g Protein; 1.4 g Net Carb; 0 g Fiber;
Ingredients

- 2 eggs, boiled
- 2 slices of bacon, cooked
- 2 slices of cheddar cheese
- ¼ tsp salt
- ¼ tsp ground black pepper

How to Prepare:
1. Peel the eggs and then cut them in half lengthwise.
1. Slightly cut off egg white from two halves to make them stand and then top each with a cheese slice and bacon slice.
2. Cover the top with the other egg halves, secure by inserting a tooth pick and then season with salt and black pepper. Serve.

32 – Cream Cheese and Spinach Omelet

Serves: 2; Preparation: 5 minutes; Cook time: 5 minutes;
Nutrition facts: 405 Calories; 36 g Fats; 15 g Protein; 4.4 g Net Carb; 0.6 g Fiber;
Ingredients

- 2 oz spinach
- 2 slices of bacon, chopped, cooked
- 3 oz cream cheese
- 1 tbsp sour cream
- 2 eggs
Seasoning:
- ¼ tsp salt
- 1/8 tsp ground black pepper
- ½ tsp dried rosemary
- 2 tbsp butter, unsalted

How to Prepare:
1. Take a medium skillet pan, place it over medium heat, add 1 tbsp butter and when it melts, add spinach and cook for 2 minutes until wilted and moisture evaporated completely.
2. Transfer spinach to a plate, wipe clean the pan, return it over medium heat, add the remaining butter in it and wait until it melts.
3. Crack eggs in a bowl, add sour cream, salt, black pepper and rosemary in it, whisk until blended, then pour eggs into the pan and cook for 1 minute.
4. Spread spinach on one side of the egg, top with cream cheese and bacon, cover the other side of the egg, switch off the heat, cover the pan with the lid and let it rest for 5 minutes. Serve.

33 – Egg Muffin

Serves: 2; Preparation: 5 minutes; Cook time: 12 minutes;
Nutrition facts: 68.5 Calories; 27 g Fats; 3 g Protein; 0.5 g Net Carb; 0 g Fiber;
Ingredients

- 2 large eggs
- ¼ tsp of sea salt
- 1/8 tsp cracked black pepper
- 1/8 tsp dried thyme
- 1/8 tsp garlic powder

How to Prepare:
1. Turn on the oven, then set it to 400 degrees F, and let preheat.
2. Take a medium bowl, crack eggs in it, add remaining ingredients, and then whisk until well blended.
3. Take two silicone muffin cups, line them with muffin liners, and evenly pour in egg mixture.
4. Bake the muffins for 10 to 12 minutes until muffins have set, and the top is nicely golden brown and then take out muffins from the silicone cups. Serve.

34 – Keto Bread

Serves: 2; Preparation: 5 minutes; Cook time: 10 minutes
Nutrition facts: 235 Calories; 20 g Fats; 8 g Protein; 3.7 g Net Carb; 3 g Fiber;
Ingredients
- 2 2/3 tbsp coconut flour
- 2 tbsp avocado oil
- 1 tsp baking powder
- 2 eggs
- 1/8 tsp salt

How to Prepare:
1. Turn on the oven, then set it to 375 degrees F and let it preheat.
2. Meanwhile, prepare the batter for this, add all the ingredients in a bowl and then whisk until well combined.
3. Take a 4 by 4 inches heatproof baking pan, grease it with oil, pour in the prepared batter and bake 10 minutes until bread is firm.
4. When done, let the bread cool in the pan for 5 minutes, then transfer it to a wire rack and cool for 20 minutes. Slice the bread and serve.

35 – Shredded Chicken in a Lettuce Wrap

Serves: 2; Preparation: 5 minutes; Cook time: 15 minutes;
Nutrition facts: 143.5 Calories; 1.4 g Fats; 21.7 g Protein; 3.4 g Net Carb; 0.7 g Fiber;
Ingredients
- 2 leaves of iceberg lettuce
- 2 large chicken thigh
- 2 tbsp shredded cheddar cheese
- 3 cups hot water
- 4 tbsp tomato sauce

Seasoning:
- 1 tbsp soy sauce
- 1 tbsp red chili powder
- ¾ tsp salt
- ½ tsp cracked black pepper

How to Prepare:
1. Turn on the instant pot, place chicken thighs in it, and add remaining ingredients except for lettuce.
2. Stir until just mixed, shut the instant pot with a lid and cook for 15 minutes at high pressure and when done, release the pressure naturally.
3. Then open the instant pot, transfer chicken to a cutting board and shred with two forks.
4. Evenly divide the chicken between two lettuce leaves, and drizzle with some of the cooking liquid, reserving the remaining cooking liquid for later use as chicken broth. Serve.

36 – Cider Chicken

Serves: 2; Preparation: 10 minutes; Cook time: 18 minutes
Nutrition facts: 182.5 Calories; 107.5 g Fats; 15.5 g Protein; 2.5 g Net Carb; 0 g Fiber;
Ingredients
- 2 chicken thighs
- ¼ cup apple cider vinegar
- 1 tsp liquid stevia

Seasoning:
- ½ tbsp coconut oil
- 1/3 tsp salt
- ¼ tsp ground black pepper

How to Prepare:
1. Turn on the oven, then set it to 450 degrees F and let it preheat.
2. Meanwhile, place chicken in a bowl, drizzle with oil and then season with salt and black pepper
3. Take a baking sheet, place prepared chicken thighs on it, and bake for 10 to 15 minutes or until its internal temperature reaches 165 degrees F.
4. In the meantime, take a small saucepan, place it over medium heat, pour in vinegar, stir in stevia and bring the mixture to boil.

5. Then switch heat to the low level and simmer sauce for 3 to 5 minutes until reduced by half, set aside until required.
6. When the chicken has roasted, brush it generously with prepared cider sauce, then Turn on the broiler and bake the chicken for 3 minutes until golden brown.
7. Serve.

37 – Bacon Wrapped Chicken Bites

Serves: 2
Preparation: 10 minutes; Cook time: 20 minutes
Nutrition facts: 153 Calories; 8.7 g Fats; 15 g Protein; 2.7 g Net Carb; 0.7 g Fiber;
Ingredients
- 1 chicken thigh, debone, cut into small pieces
- 4 slices of bacon, cut into thirds
- 2 tbsp garlic powder

Seasoning:
- ¼ tsp salt
- 1/8 tsp ground black pepper

How to Prepare:
1. Turn on the oven, then set it to 400 degrees F and let it preheat.
2. Cut chicken into small pieces, then place them in a bowl, add salt, garlic powder, and black pepper and toss until well coated.
3. Wrap each chicken piece with a bacon strip, place in a baking dish and bake for 15 to 20 minutes until crispy, turning carefully every 5 minutes.
4. Serve.

38 – Cheesy Bacon Wrapped Chicken

Serves: 2
Preparation: 5 minutes; Cook time: 25 minutes
Nutrition facts: 172.5 Calories; 11.5 g Fats; 14.5 g Protein; 0.5 g Net Carb; 0 g Fiber;
Ingredients
- 2 chicken thighs, boneless
- 2 strips of bacon
- 2 tbsp shredded cheddar cheese

Seasoning:
- 1/3 tsp salt
- 2/3 tsp paprika
- 1/4 tsp garlic powder

How to Prepare:
1. Turn on the oven, then set it to 400 degrees F and let it preheat.
2. Meanwhile, season chicken thighs with salt, paprika, and garlic on both sides, and then place them onto a baking sheet greased with oil.
3. Top each chicken thighs with a bacon strip and then bake for 15 to 20 minutes until the chicken has cooked through, and bacon has crispy.
4. When done, sprinkle cheese over chicken, continue baking for 5 minutes until cheese has melted and golden, and then serve.

39 – Beans and Sausage

Serves: 2
Preparation: 5 minutes; Cook time: 6 minutes
Nutrition facts: 151 Calories; 9.4 g Fats; 11.7 g Protein; 3.4 g Net Carb; 1.6 g Fiber;
Ingredients
- 4 oz green beans
- 4 oz chicken sausage, sliced
- ½ tsp dried basil
- ½ tsp dried oregano
- 1/3 cup chicken broth, from chicken sausage

Seasoning:
- 1 tbsp avocado oil
- ¼ tsp salt
- 1/8 tsp ground black pepper

How to Prepare:
1. Turn on the instant pot, place all the ingredients in its inner pot and shut with lid, in the sealed position.
2. Press the "manual" button, cook for 6 minutes at high-pressure settings and, when done, do quick pressure release.
3. Serve immediately.

40 – Paprika Rubbed Chicken

Serves: 2
Preparation: 5 minutes; Cook time: 25 minutes
Nutrition facts: 102.3 Calories; 8 g Fats; 7.2 g Protein; 0.3 g Net Carb; 0.3 g Fiber;
Ingredients
- 2 chicken thighs, boneless
- ¼ tbsp fennel seeds, ground
- ½ tsp hot paprika
- ¼ tsp smoked paprika
- ½ tsp minced garlic

Seasoning:
- ¼ tsp salt
- 2 tbsp avocado oil

How to Prepare:
1. Turn on the oven, then set it to 325 degrees F and let it preheat.
2. Prepare the spice mix and for this, take a small bowl, add all the ingredients in it, except for chicken, and stir until well mixed.
3. Brush the mixture on all sides of the chicken, rub it well into the meat, then place chicken onto a baking sheet and roast for 15 to 25 minutes until thoroughly cooked, basting every 10 minutes with the drippings.
4. Serve.

41 – Teriyaki Chicken

Serves: 2
Preparation: 5 minutes; Cook time: 18 minutes
Nutrition facts: 150 Calories; 9 g Fats; 17.3 g Protein; 0 g Net Carb; 0 g Fiber;
Ingredients
- 2 chicken thighs, boneless
- 2 tbsp soy sauce
- 1 tbsp swerve sweetener
- 1 tbsp avocado oil

How to Prepare:
1. Take a skillet pan, place it over medium heat, add oil and when hot, add chicken thighs and cook for 5 minutes per side until seared.
2. Then sprinkle sugar over chicken thighs, drizzle with soy sauce and bring the sauce to boil.
3. Switch heat to medium-low level, continue cooking for 3 minutes until chicken is evenly glazed, and then transfer to a plate.
4. Serve chicken with cauliflower rice.

42 – Chili Lime Chicken with Coleslaw

Serves: 2
Preparation: 35 minutes; Cook time: 8 minutes
Nutrition facts: 157.3 Calories; 12.8 g Fats; 9 g Protein; 1 g Net Carb; 0.5 g Fiber;
Ingredients
- 1 chicken thigh, boneless
- 2 oz coleslaw
- ¼ tsp minced garlic
- ¾ tbsp apple cider vinegar
- ½ of a lime, juiced, zested

Seasoning:
- ¼ tsp paprika
- ¼ tsp salt
- 2 tbsp avocado oil
- 1 tbsp unsalted butter

How to Prepare:

1. Prepare the marinade and for this, take a medium bowl, add vinegar, oil, garlic, paprika, salt, lime juice, and zest and stir until well mixed.
2. Cut chicken thighs into bite-size pieces, toss until well mixed, and marinate it in the refrigerator for 30 minutes.
3. Then take a skillet pan, place it over medium-high heat, add butter and marinated chicken pieces and cook for 8 minutes until golden brown and thoroughly cooked.
4. Serve chicken with coleslaw.

43 – Beans and Sausage

Serves: 2
Preparation: 5 minutes; Cook time: 4 minutes
Nutrition facts: 182 Calories; 13.3 g Fats; 10.9 g Protein; 3.5 g Net Carb; 1.6 g Fiber;
Ingredients

- 4 oz chicken sausage, sliced
- 4 oz green beans
- ¼ tsp dried oregano
- 1 tbsp avocado oil
- 1 cup of water

Seasoning:

- ½ tsp salt
- ½ tsp ground black pepper
- ¼ tsp dried basil

How to Prepare:

1. Turn on the instant pot, place all the ingredients in the inner pot, stir and shut with lid.
2. Press the manual button, cook for 4 minutes at high-pressure setting, and, when done, do quick pressure release.
3. Serve.

44 – Meat and Feta Cheese Plate

Serves: 2; Preparation: 5 minutes; Cook time: 10 minutes;
Nutrition facts: 536 Calories; 47 g Fats; 25 g Protein; 1.9 g Net Carb; 0.8 g Fiber;
Ingredients

- 2 chicken thighs
- 2 oz feta cheese, full-fat
- ½ cup shredded cabbage
- 8 green olives
- 1/3 cup avocado oil

Seasoning:

- 1/2 tsp salt
- 1/2 tsp ground black pepper

How to Prepare:

1. Take a frying pan, place it over medium heat, add 1 tbsp oil and wait until it melts.
2. Season chicken with ¼ tsp salt and black pepper, add to the frying pan, and cook for 5 minutes per side until thoroughly cooked.
3. While the chicken cooked, shred the cabbage and then cut feta cheese into cubes.
4. Distribute chicken between two plates, add cabbage, olives and feta cheese and then season with remaining salt and black pepper.
5. Serve with remaining avocado oil.

45 – Lime Garlic Chicken Thighs

Serves: 2; Preparation: 35 minutes; Cook time: 15 minutes;
Nutrition facts: 260 Calories; 15.6 g Fats; 26.8 g Protein; 1.3 g Net Carb; 0.6 g Fiber;
Ingredients

- 2 boneless chicken thighs, skinless

- ¾ tsp garlic powder
- 1 ½ tsp all-purpose seasoning
- ½ of lime, juiced, zested
- 1 ½ tbsp avocado oil

How to Prepare:
1. Take a medium bowl, place chicken in it, and sprinkle with garlic powder, all-purpose seasoning, and lime zest.
2. Drizzle with lime juice, toss until well coated and let chicken thighs marinate for 30 minutes.
3. Then take a medium skillet pan, place it over medium heat, add oil and when hot, place marinated chicken thighs in it and cook for 5 to 7 minutes per side until thoroughly cooked. Serve.

46 – Egg McMuffin Sandwich

Serves: 2; Preparation: 10 minutes; Cook time: 5 minutes;
Nutrition facts: 400 Calories; 37.4 g Fats; 11 g Protein; 4 g Net Carb; 0 g Fiber;
Ingredients
- 2 eggs, yolks and egg whites separated
- 1/3 cup grated parmesan cheese
- 4 oz cream cheese, softened
- 1 tsp avocado oil
- 2 tbsp mayonnaise

Seasoning:
- 2/3 tsp salt

How to Prepare:
1. Take a medium bowl, place egg yolks in it, add cream cheese, parmesan, and salt and whisk by using an electric blender until smooth.
2. Take another medium bowl, add egg whites, beat until stiff peaks form and then fold egg whites into egg yolk mixture until combined.
3. Take a skillet pan, place it over medium heat, add oil and when hot, add one-fourth of the batter, spread it into a 1-inch thick pancake, and then fry got 2 minutes per side until golden brown. When done, let sandwiches cool for 5 minutes, then spread mayonnaise on one side of each sandwich and then serve as desired.

47 – Deviled Eggs with Avocado and Mozzarella

Serves: 2; Preparation: 5 minutes; Cook time: 0 minutes;
Nutrition facts: 99.3 Calories; 8.2 g Fats; 6 g Protein; 0 g Net Carb; 0 g Fiber;
Ingredients
- 2 eggs, boiled
- ¼ of an avocado, mashed
- 1 tsp grated mozzarella cheese
- ½ tsp mustard paste
- 1 ½ tsp mayonnaise

Seasoning:
- ¼ tsp salt
- 1/8 tsp cayenne pepper

How to Prepare:
1. Peel the boiled eggs, then slice in half lengthwise and transfer egg yolks to a medium bowl by using a spoon.
2. Mash the egg yolk, add remaining ingredients and stir until well combined.
3. Pipe the egg yolk mixture into egg whites, then sprinkle with some cayenne pepper and serve.

48 – Eggs with Green Onions

Serves: 2; Preparation: 5 minutes; Cook time: 5 minutes;
Nutrition facts: 145 Calories; 9.5 g Fats; 12.7 g Protein; 1 g Net Carb; 0.2 g Fiber;
Ingredients
- 1 green onion, sliced
- ½ tbsp chopped jalapeno pepper
- 2 eggs
- 1 tsp avocado oil

Seasoning:
- ¼ tsp salt
- 1/8 tsp ground black pepper

How to Prepare:
1. Crack eggs in a bowl, add jalapeno, salt, and black pepper and whisk until combined.
2. Take a frying pan, place it over medium-low heat, add oil and when hot, add green onions and cook for 30 seconds until fried.
3. Add beaten eggs, stir until mixed, and then cook for 1 to 2 minutes until eggs have cooked to the desired level.
4. Serve.

49 – Jalapeno Deviled Eggs

Serves: 2; Preparation: 5 minutes; Cook time: 0 minutes;
Nutrition facts: 210 Calories; 16.5 g Fats; 10.7 g Protein; 0.8 g Net Carb; 0.2 g Fiber;
Ingredients

- 2 eggs, boiled
- 1 ½ tbsp mayonnaise
- 2 tsp grated mozzarella cheese
- 2 tsp chopped jalapeno pepper
- 1 tbsp chopped cilantro
Seasoning:
- ¼ tsp salt
- 1/8 tsp ground black pepper
How to Prepare:
1. Peel the boiled eggs, then slice in half lengthwise and transfer egg yolks to a medium bowl by using a spoon.
2. Mash the egg yolk, add remaining ingredients except for cilantro and stir until well combined.
3. Pipe the egg yolk mixture into egg whites, then sprinkle with cilantro and serve.

50 – Bacon Ranch Deviled Eggs

Serves: 2; Preparation: 5 minutes; Cook time: 0 minutes;
Nutrition facts: 260 Calories; 24 g Fats; 8.9 g Protein; 0.6 g Net Carb; 0.1 g Fiber;
Ingredients

- 1 slice of bacon, chopped, cooked
- 2/3 tsp ranch dressing
- 1 1/2 tbsp mayonnaise
- 1/3 tsp mustard paste
- 2 eggs, boiled
Seasoning:
- ¼ tsp paprika
How to Prepare:
1. Peel the boiled eggs, then slice in half lengthwise and transfer egg yolks to a medium bowl by using a spoon.
2. Mash the egg yolk, add remaining ingredients, except for bacon and paprika and stir until well combined.
3. Pipe the egg yolk mixture into egg whites, sprinkle with bacon and paprika, and then serve.

51 – Deviled Eggs with Mushrooms

Serves: 2; Preparation: 5 minutes; Cook time: 0 minutes;
Nutrition facts: 130.5 Calories; 10.9 g Fats; 7.1 g Protein; 0.6 g Net Carb; 0.1 g Fiber;
Ingredients

- 1 tbsp chopped mushroom
- 2 tsp mayonnaise
- ½ tsp apple cider vinegar
- 1 tsp butter, unsalted
- 2 eggs, boiled
Seasoning:
- ¼ tsp salt
- 1/8 tsp ground black pepper
- ¼ tsp dried parsley
How to Prepare:
1. Peel the boiled eggs, then slice in half lengthwise and transfer egg yolks to a medium bowl by using a spoon.
2. Mash the egg yolk, add remaining ingredients and stir until well combined.

3. Pipe the egg yolk mixture into egg whites, sprinkle with black pepper, and then serve.

52 – Deviled Eggs with Tomato and Feta Cheese

Serves: 2; Preparation: 5 minutes; Cook time: 0 minutes;
Nutrition facts: 168 Calories; 14.4 g Fats; 7.9 g Protein; 1.1 g Net Carb; 0.1 g Fiber;
Ingredients
- 2 eggs, boiled
- 2 tsp crumbled feta cheese
- 1 tbsp diced tomato
- 1 tbsp mayonnaise
- 1 tbsp whipped topping
- ¼ tsp salt
- 1/8 tsp ground black pepper
- 1 tsp apple cider vinegar

How to Prepare:
1. Peel the boiled eggs, then slice in half lengthwise and transfer egg yolks to a medium bowl by using a spoon.
2. Mash the egg yolk, add remaining ingredients and stir until well combined.
3. Pipe the egg yolk mixture into egg whites, sprinkle with black pepper, and then serve.

53 – Citrusy Deviled Eggs

Serves: 2; Preparation: 10 minutes; Cook time: 0 minutes;
Nutrition facts: 180 Calories; 13.1 g Fats; 10.5 g Protein; 1.4 g Net Carb; 2.5 g Fiber;
Ingredients
- ½ of avocado, mashed
- 2 slices of bacon, chopped, cooked
- 2 boiled eggs
- ¼ of lime, juiced, zested
- ¼ tsp salt
- ¼ tsp cayenne pepper
- 1/8 tsp ground black pepper

How to Prepare:
1. Peel the boiled eggs, then slice in half lengthwise and transfer egg yolks to a medium bowl by using a spoon.
2. Mash the egg yolk, add remaining ingredients except for bacon and stir until well combined.
3. Spoon the egg yolk mixture into egg whites, sprinkle with bacon and some more cayenne pepper, and then serve.

54 – Mexican Keto Deviled Eggs

Serves: 2; Preparation: 5 minutes; Cook time: 10 minutes;
Nutrition facts: 145 Calories; 11.2 g Fats; 8.5 g Protein; 1.3 g Net Carb; 0.5 g Fiber;
Ingredients
- 1 slice of bacon, chopped cooked
- 2 ¾ tbsp diced tomato
- 2/3 tbsp avocado flesh
- 2 eggs, boiled
- 2/3 tbsp mayonnaise
- ¼ tsp taco seasoning
- 1/8 tsp cayenne pepper
- 1 tsp chopped cilantro

How to Prepare:
1. Peel the boiled eggs, then slice in half lengthwise and transfer egg yolks to a medium bowl by using a spoon.
2. Mash the egg yolk, add remaining ingredients, reserving cilantro and half of tomato and bacon and mash until smooth and well combined.
3. Spoon the egg yolk mixture into egg whites, top with remaining bacon pieces and tomato, sprinkle with cilantro and then serve.

55 – Yogurt Deviled Eggs

Serves: 2; Preparation: 10 minutes; Cook time: 0 minutes;
Nutrition facts: 95 Calories; 6 g Fats; 7.6 g Protein; 1.2 g Net Carb; 0.1 g Fiber;
Ingredients

- 2 eggs, boiled
- 1/8 tsp paprika
- 1 tsp mustard paste
- 1 tsp soy sauce
- 2 tbsp yogurt

Seasoning:

- ¼ tsp salt
- 1/8 tsp ground black pepper

How to Prepare:

1. Peel the boiled eggs, then slice in half lengthwise and transfer egg yolks to a medium bowl by using a spoon.
2. Mash the egg yolk, add remaining ingredients and mash until smooth and well combined.
3. Spoon the egg yolk mixture into egg whites, sprinkle with some more paprika and then serve.

56 – Deviled Green Eggs

Serves: 2; Preparation: 10 minutes; Cook time: 0 minutes;
Nutrition facts: 163 Calories; 12.1 g Fats; 10.8 g Protein; 1.4 g Net Carb; 0.6 g Fiber;
Ingredients

- 2 eggs, boiled
- 1 tbsp mashed avocado
- 2/3 tbsp mayonnaise
- 1 slice of bacon, chopped cooked
- 2 tbsp chopped ham

Seasoning:

- 1 green onion, chopped
- ¼ tsp salt
- 1/8 tsp cayenne pepper
- 1/8 tsp apple cider vinegar

How to Prepare:

1. Peel the boiled eggs, then slice in half lengthwise and transfer egg yolks to a medium bowl by using a spoon.
2. Mash the egg yolk, add remaining ingredients and mash until smooth and well combined.
3. Spoon the egg yolk mixture into egg whites, sprinkle with some more cayenne pepper and then serve.

57 – Pesto Deviled Eggs

Serves: 2; Preparation: 5 minutes; Cook time: 0 minutes;
Nutrition facts: 220 Calories; 19.2 g Fats; 8.1 g Protein; 1.7 g Net Carb; 1 g Fiber;
Ingredients

- 2 eggs, boiled
- 2 tbsp basil pesto
- 1 tbsp avocado oil

How to Prepare:

1. Peel the boiled eggs, then slice in half lengthwise and transfer egg yolks to a medium bowl by using a spoon.
2. Mash the egg yolk, add remaining ingredients and stir until well combined.
3. Pipe the egg yolk mixture into egg whites and then serve.

58 – Hot Deviled Egg with Chicken

Serves: 2; Preparation: 5 minutes; Cook time: 0 minutes;
Nutrition facts: 260 Calories; 19.1 g Fats; 20.5 g Protein; 0.6 g Net Carb; 0 g Fiber;
Ingredients

- 2 eggs, boiled
- 1 chicken thigh, boneless, cooked, chopped
- 2 tbsp mayonnaise

- 1 tsp apple cider vinegar
- 1 tbsp hot sauce

Seasoning:
- 1/3 tsp salt
- ½ tsp paprika
- ¼ tsp cayenne pepper

How to Prepare:
1. Peel the boiled eggs, then slice in half lengthwise and transfer egg yolks to a medium bowl by using a spoon.
2. Mash the egg yolk, add remaining ingredients and stir until well combined.
3. Spoon the egg yolk mixture into egg whites, sprinkle with some more paprika, and then serve.

59 – Deviled Eggs with Sour Cream and Bacon

Serves: 2; Preparation: 10 minutes; Cook time: 0 minutes;
Nutrition facts: 131 Calories; 10 g Fats; 7 g Protein; 0 g Net Carb; 0 g Fiber;
Ingredients
- 2 eggs, boiled
- 1 slice of bacon, cooked, crumbled
- 1 tbsp sour cream
- 1 ½ tsp mustard paste
- 1 tbsp shredded cheddar cheese

Seasoning:
- 1/8 tsp garlic powder
- 1/8 tsp salt
- 1/8 tsp ground black pepper

How to Prepare:
1. Peel the boiled eggs, then slice in half lengthwise and transfer egg yolks to a medium bowl by using a spoon.
2. Mash the egg yolk, add remaining ingredients and stir until well combined. Spoon the egg yolk mixture into egg whites and then serve.

60 – Southwestern Deviled Eggs

Serves: 2; Preparation: 10 minutes; Cook time: 0 minutes;
Nutrition facts: 176 Calories; 12.3 g Fats; 15 g Protein; 1.2 g Net Carb; 0.1 g Fiber;
Ingredients
- 2 boiled eggs
- 1/3 tsp chopped jalapeno
- 1/3 tsp mustard
- ¼ tsp lime juice
- 2 tsp grated cheddar cheese

Seasoning:
- 1/16 tsp paprika
- 1/3 tsp hot sauce

How to Prepare:
1. Peel the boiled eggs, then slice in half lengthwise and transfer egg yolks to a medium bowl by using a spoon.
2. Mash the egg yolk, add remaining ingredients and stir until well combined. Spoon the egg yolk mixture into egg whites and then serve.

61 – Chipotle and Marinara Deviled Eggs

Serves: 2; Preparation: 10 minutes; Cook time: 0 minutes;
Nutrition facts: 91 Calories; 6 g Fats; 7.1 g Protein; 1.5 g Net Carb; 0.6 g Fiber;
Ingredients
- 2 eggs, boiled
- ¼ of lime, juiced
- 1/8 tsp ground black pepper
- 1 tbsp chipotle hot sauce

- 2 tbsp marinara sauce

How to Prepare:
1. Peel the boiled eggs, then slice in half lengthwise and transfer egg yolks to a medium bowl by using a spoon.
2. Mash the egg yolk, add remaining ingredients and stir until well combined. Spoon the egg yolk mixture into egg whites and then serve.

62 – Jalapeno Egg Sandwich

Serves: 2; Preparation: 5 minutes; Cook time: 15 minutes;
Nutrition facts: 450 Calories; 34.3 g Fats; 25.4 g Protein; 7 g Net Carb; 0.8 g Fiber;
Ingredients
- 1 tbsp diced tomato
- 1 tsp chopped jalapeno
- 3 eggs
- 1/3 cup grated parmesan cheese
- 2 oz softened cream cheese

Seasoning:
- 2/3 tsp salt
- 3 tsp avocado oil

How to Prepare:
1. Take two medium bowl, and separate egg yolks and whites in them.
2. Add the cream cheese in the egg yolks, parmesan, and ½ tsp salt and whisk by using an electric blender until smooth.
3. Take another medium bowl, add egg whites, beat until stiff peaks form and then fold egg whites into egg yolk mixture until combined.
4. Take a skillet pan, place it over medium heat, add 1 tsp oil and when hot, add one-fourth of the batter, spread it into a 1-inch thick pancake, and then fry got 2 minutes per side until golden brown.
5. When done, transfer pancake to a plate and repeat with the remaining batter; use 1 tsp avocado oil.
6. Then take a medium bowl, crack eggs in it, add tomato, jalapeno and salt and stir until blended.
7. Add remaining oil in the pan and when hot, pour egg mixture in it and then scramble for 1 to 2 minutes until cooked.
8. When eggs have cooked, distribute them evenly between two sandwich bread and then cover the top. Serve.

63 – Spicy Chili Deviled Eggs

Serves: 2; Preparation: 10 minutes; Cook time: 0 minutes;
Nutrition facts: 82 Calories; 5.3 g Fats; 7 g Protein; 0.4 g Net Carb; 0 g Fiber;
Ingredients
- ¼ of lime, juiced
- 2 eggs, boiled
- 2 tsp chili garlic sauce
- ½ tsp paprika
- 1/8 tsp ground black pepper

How to Prepare:
1. Peel the boiled eggs, then slice in half lengthwise and transfer egg yolks to a medium bowl by using a spoon.
2. Mash the egg yolk, add remaining ingredients and stir until well combined. Spoon the egg yolk mixture into egg whites and then serve.

64 – Deviled Egg with Bacon and Cheddar Cheese

Serves: 2; Preparation: 10 minutes; Cook time: 0 minutes;
Nutrition facts: 161 Calories; 13.1 g Fats; 8.7 g Protein; 1.1 g Net Carb; 0.1 g Fiber;
Ingredients
- 2 eggs, boiled
- 2 slices of bacon, chopped, cooked
- 1 tsp mustard paste
- 1 tbsp grated cheddar cheese
- 1 tbsp mayonnaise

Seasoning:

- ¼ tsp salt
- ¼ tsp paprika
- 1/8 tsp ground black pepper

How to Prepare:
1. Peel the boiled eggs, then slice in half lengthwise and transfer egg yolks to a medium bowl by using a spoon.
2. Mash the egg yolk, add remaining ingredients and stir until well combined. Spoon the egg yolk mixture into egg whites and then serve.

65 – Dill Pickle Deviled Eggs

Serves: 2; Preparation: 10 minutes; Cook time: 0 minutes;
Nutrition facts: 81 Calories; 5.4 g Fats; 7 g Protein; 0.5 g Net Carb; 0.1 g Fiber;
Ingredients
- 2 eggs, boiled
- 1/3 tsp mustard paste
- 1/8 tsp ground black pepper
- 2/3 tsp minced dill pickle

How to Prepare:
1. Peel the boiled eggs, then slice in half lengthwise and transfer egg yolks to a medium bowl by using a spoon.
2. Mash the egg yolk, add remaining ingredients and stir until well combined. Spoon the egg yolk mixture into egg whites and then serve.

66 – Smoky Deviled Egg

Serves: 2; Preparation: 10 minutes; Cook time: 0 minutes;
Nutrition facts: 120 Calories; 9.3 g Fats; 7.3 g Protein; 0.5 g Net Carb; 0.7 g Fiber;
Ingredients
- 2 eggs, boiled
- 1 1/3 tsp paprika
- ½ tsp red chili powder
- 1/3 tsp mustard paste
- 2 tsp mayonnaise

How to Prepare:
1. Peel the boiled eggs, then slice in half lengthwise and transfer egg yolks to a medium bowl by using a spoon.
2. Mash the egg yolk, add remaining ingredients and stir until well combined. Spoon the egg yolk mixture into egg whites and then serve.

67 – Buffalo Deviled Eggs

Serves: 2; Preparation: 5 minutes; Cook time: 0 minutes;
Nutrition facts: 280 Calories; 24 g Fats; 14 g Protein; 2 g Net Carb; 0 g Fiber;
Ingredients
- 2 eggs, boiled
- 1/8 tsp salt
- 1 tbsp cream cheese, softened
- 1 tbsp mayonnaise
- 1/3 tbsp hot sauce

How to Prepare:
1. Peel the boiled eggs, then slice in half lengthwise and transfer egg yolks to a medium bowl by using a spoon.
2. Mash the egg yolk, add remaining ingredients and stir until well combined. Spoon the egg yolk mixture into egg whites and then serve.

68 – Chicken Nuggets

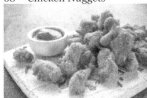

Serves: 2; Preparation: 15 minutes; Cook time: 10 minutes;
Nutrition facts: 196 Calories; 17 g Fats; 9 g Protein; 1 g Net Carb; 2 g Fiber;

Ingredients
- 2 chicken thighs, boneless
- 2 oz almond flour
- 1 tbsp mayonnaise
- ¼ tsp apple cider vinegar
- 1 tbsp avocado oil

Seasoning:
- 1 tbsp and ¼ tsp salt
- 1/8 tsp ground black pepper

How to Prepare:
1. Take a medium bowl, fill it half full with water, stir in 1 tbsp water, then add chicken thighs and let it soak for 10 minutes.
2. Then drain the chicken, pat dry, and cut into nugget size pieces.
3. Take a small bowl, place mayonnaise in it, and then stir in vinegar until mixed.
4. Take a shallow dish, place almond flour in it, add remaining salt and black pepper, and stir until mixed.
5. Prepare chicken nuggets and for this, coat each chicken piece with mayonnaise mixture and then dredge with almond flour mixture until evenly coated on all sides.
6. Take a medium skillet pan, place it over medium heat, add oil and when hot, add chicken nuggets and cook for 4 to 5 minutes per side until nicely browned and cooked. Serve.

69 – Curried Deviled Eggs

Serves: 2; Preparation: 5 minutes; Cook time: 0 minutes;
Nutrition facts: 91 Calories; 5.7 g Fats; 7.4 g Protein; 0.8 g Net Carb; 0 g Fiber;
Ingredients
- 2 eggs, boiled
- ¼ tsp curry powder
- 1/8 tsp cayenne pepper
- ½ tsp mustard paste
- 1 ½ tbsp yogurt

Seasoning:
- 1/8 tsp salt

How to Prepare:
1. Peel the boiled eggs, then slice in half lengthwise and transfer egg yolks to a medium bowl by using a spoon.
2. Mash the egg yolk, add remaining ingredients and stir until well combined. Spoon the egg yolk mixture into egg whites and then serve.

70 – Truffled Deviled Eggs

Serves: 2; Preparation: 5 minutes; Cook time: 0 minutes;
Nutrition facts: 211 Calories; 18.9 g Fats; 8.9 g Protein; 1 g Net Carb; 0.1 g Fiber;
Ingredients
- 2 eggs, boiled
- 1 slice of bacon, chopped, cooked
- ¼ tsp mustard paste
- 1 ½ tbsp mayonnaise
- ½ tbsp white truffle oil

Seasoning:
- ¼ tsp salt
- 1/8 tsp ground black pepper

How to Prepare:
1. Peel the boiled eggs, then slice in half lengthwise and transfer egg yolks to a medium bowl by using a spoon.
2. Take a medium skillet pan, place it over medium heat and when hot, add bacon and cook for 2 to 3 minutes until crisp.
3. Transfer bacon along with bacon dripping into the bowl containing egg yolks, add remaining ingredients, and then mash until smooth and well combined.
4. Spoon the egg yolk mixture into egg whites and then serve.

71 – Curried Eggs

Serves: 2; Preparation: 5 minutes; Cook time: 6 minutes;
Nutrition facts: 120 Calories; 9.2 g Fats; 5.4 g Protein; 0.8 g Net Carb; 0.1 g Fiber;
Ingredients
- 2 eggs, boiled

- ½ tsp garlic powder
- ½ tbsp curry powder
- 1 tsp hot sauce
- 1 tbsp avocado oil

How to Prepare:
1. Peel the eggs and then make few slits in them.
2. Take a frying pan, place it over medium heat, add oil and when hot, add eggs in it, sprinkle with curry powder and garlic powder until evenly coated, and then fry for 3 minutes per side until golden brown. Serve.

72 – Sour Cream and Sriracha Deviled Eggs

Serves: 2; Preparation: 5 minutes; Cook time: 10 minutes;
Nutrition facts: 109 Calories; 8 g Fats; 7.2 g Protein; 1.3 g Net Carb; 0 g Fiber;
Ingredients
- 2 eggs, boiled
- ¼ tsp Sriracha sauce
- ¼ tsp mustard paste
- 2 tbsp sour cream
- 1/8 tsp salt

Seasoning:
- 1/8 tsp ground black pepper

How to Prepare:
1. Peel the boiled eggs, then slice in half lengthwise and transfer egg yolks to a medium bowl by using a spoon.
2. Mash the egg yolk, add remaining ingredients and stir until well combined. Pipe the egg yolk mixture into egg whites, and then serve.

73 – Cajun Style Deviled Eggs

Serves: 2; Preparation: 5 minutes; Cook time: 0 minutes;
Nutrition facts: 131 Calories; 10.8 g Fats; 7.1 g Protein; 1 g Net Carb; 0 g Fiber;
Ingredients
- 2 eggs, boiled
- ½ tsp minced garlic
- ½ tsp Cajun seasoning
- ½ tsp paprika
- 1 tbsp mayonnaise

Seasoning:
- ½ tsp cayenne pepper

How to Prepare:
1. Peel the boiled eggs, then slice in half lengthwise and transfer egg yolks to a medium bowl by using a spoon.
2. Mash the egg yolk, add remaining ingredients and stir until well combined. Spoon the egg yolk mixture into egg whites, and then serve.

74 – Chicken and Peanut Stir-Fry

Serves: 2; Preparation: 5 minutes; Cook time: 10 minutes;
Nutrition facts: 266 Calories; 19 g Fats; 18.5 g Protein; 4 g Net Carb; 2.5 g Fiber;
Ingredients
- 2 chicken thighs, cubed
- ½ cup broccoli florets
- ¼ cup peanuts
- 1 tbsp sesame oil
- 1 ½ tbsp soy sauce

Seasoning:
- ½ tsp garlic powder

How to Prepare:
1. Take a skillet pan, place it over medium heat, add ½ tbsp oil and when hot, add chicken cubes and cook for 4 minutes until browned on all sides.

2. Then add broccoli florets and continue cooking for 2 minutes until tender-crisp.
3. Add remaining ingredients, stir well and cook for another 2 minutes. Serve.

75 – Garlic Cheddar Chicken Thighs

Serves: 2; Preparation: 5 minutes; Cook time: 25 minutes;
Nutrition facts: 128.5 Calories; 9.5 g Fats; 9 g Protein; 0.2 g Net Carb; 0.05 g Fiber;
Ingredients
- 2 chicken thighs
- 1/3 tsp garlic powder
- 1/3 tbsp dried basil
- 1/3 tbsp grated cheddar cheese
- ½ tsp coconut oil

Seasoning:
- 1/8 tsp salt
- 1/3 tsp ground black pepper

How to Prepare:
1. Turn on the oven, then set it to 450 degrees F, and let preheat.
2. Meanwhile, prepare the herb mix and for this, stir together ¼ tsp oil, salt, black pepper, cheese, and basil until combined.
3. Create a pocket into each chicken thigh and then stuff it with half of the prepared herb mix and spread the remaining herb mix evenly on chicken thighs.
4. Take a skillet pan, place it over medium-high heat, add remaining oil and when hot, place stuffed chicken thighs in it and cook for 4 minutes.
5. Then flip the chicken thighs, cook for 5 to 7 minutes until chicken is no longer pink and then roast the chicken thighs for 10 to 12 minutes until a meat thermometer inserted into the thickest part of thighs read 160 degrees F. Let chicken thighs rest for 5 minutes and then serve.

76 – Chicken Thighs with Green Beans

Serves: 2; Preparation: 5 minutes; Cook time: 10 minutes;
Nutrition facts: 393 Calories; 33.5 g Fats; 20 g Protein; 4.1 g Net Carb; 0.5 g Fiber;
Ingredients
- 2 chicken thighs
- 6-ounce green beans
- ¼ of a lemon, juiced, zested
- 2-ounce unsalted butter
- 1 tbsp coconut oil

Seasoning:
- ¾ tsp salt
- 1 tsp garlic powder
- 1 tsp dried basil
- 1 tsp dried thyme

How to Prepare:
1. Prepare the chicken thighs, and for this, pat dry with paper towels and season with ½ tsp salt.
2. Take a medium skillet pan, place it over medium heat, add oil and half of butter and when butter melt, add chicken thighs and cook for 5 minutes per side until thoroughly cooked.
3. Meanwhile, prepare the sauce, and for this, whisk together lemon juice and zest, remaining salt, garlic, thyme, and oregano.
4. Transfer cooked chicken thighs to a plate and set aside.
5. Add green beans into the pan, cook them for 2 minutes, then pour in the sauce along with remaining butter, stir well until coated, and continue cooking for 2 minutes until beans have become tender-crisp. Increase heat to medium-high level, return chicken into the pan, and cook for 3 minutes. Serve.

77 – Chicken and Cauliflower Stir-Fry

Serves: 2; Preparation: 5 minutes; Cook time: 10 minutes;
Nutrition facts: 202 Calories; 12.3 g Fats; 18.3 g Protein; 2.6 g Net Carb; 0.9 g Fiber;
Ingredients
- 2 chicken thighs, boneless, diced
- 1 green onion, sliced
- 2 oz cauliflower florets

- ½ tsp minced garlic
- 2 tbsp chicken broth

Seasoning:
- 1 tbsp avocado oil
- 1/3 tsp salt
- 1/4 tsp ground black pepper
- 1 tbsp soy sauce

How to Prepare:
1. Place cauliflower florets in a heatproof bowl, cover with a plastic wrap, and then microwave for 2 to 3 minutes until blanched.
2. Take a medium skillet pan, place it over medium heat, add oil and when hot, add chicken pieces and cook for 2 to 3 minutes per side until golden brown on all sides.
3. Add scallions, stir in garlic and then cook for 1 minute.
4. Drain the florets, add to the pan, add remaining ingredients, stir until well mixed and then cook for 1 to 2 minutes until done. Taste to adjust seasoning and serve.

78 – Lemon Chicken Thighs

Serves: 2; Preparation: 10 minutes; Cook time: 10 minutes
Nutrition facts: 281.5 Calories; 19.1 g Fats; 26.7 g Protein; 0.3 g Net Carb; 0.4 g Fiber;
Ingredients
- 2 chicken thighs
- ½ tsp garlic powder
- ½ tsp dried thyme
- ½ of lemon, juiced, zested
- 1 cup of water

Seasoning:
- 2 tbsp coconut oil
- ¼ tsp salt
- 1/8 tsp ground black pepper

How to Prepare:
1. Prepare spice rub and for this, stir together garlic, thyme, lemon zest, garlic, salt, and black pepper.
2. Prepare chicken and for this, brush chicken with oil and then season with the lemon-thyme mixture until evenly coated.
3. Turn on the instant pot, grease it with oil, press the saute button, and when hot, add seasoned chicken thighs and cook for 3 minutes per side until golden brown.
4. Then remove chicken thighs from the instant pot, pour in water, add lemon juice, and insert a trivet stand.
5. Place chicken on trivet stand, shut instant pot with lid, and cook at high pressure for 5 minutes.
6. When done, let quick pressure release, open the instant pot, and transfer chicken thighs to a plate, reserving the broth for later use. Serve.

79 – Slow Cooked Korean Pulled Chicken

Serves: 2; Preparation: 5 minutes; Cook time: 4 hours
Nutrition facts: 225 Calories; 12.3 g Fats; 27.6 g Protein; 1 g Net Carb; 0.2 g Fiber;
Ingredients
- 2 chicken thighs
- ½ tsp garlic powder
- 1 tbsp stevia
- 2 tbsp soy sauce
- ½ cup of water

Seasoning:
- 1 tbsp coconut oil
- ¼ tsp salt

How to Prepare:
1. Grease the bottom and inner sides of a 4-quart slow cooker with a non-stick cooking spray.
2. Then season chicken on all sides with 1/2 tsp salt and place in a slow cooker.
3. Whisk together remaining ingredients until combined and then pour this mixture over chicken.
4. Cover and seal with its lid, then plugin and adjust the cooking timer for 4 hours and let cook at high heat setting.
5. When done, shred chicken with forks, then garnish with green onion and serve.

80 – Cinnamon Chicken Thighs

Serves: 2; Preparation: 10 minutes; Cook time: 20 minutes
Nutrition facts: 288 Calories; 22 g Fats; 18 g Protein; 1 g Net Carb; 0 g Fiber;
Ingredients
- 2 chicken thighs
- 1 tsp ground cinnamon
- 1 tsp chopped parsley
- 1/3 tsp dried basil
- 1/3 cup chicken broth

Seasoning:
- 1/3 tsp salt

How to Prepare:
1. Turn on the oven, then set it to 425 degrees F, and let it preheat.
2. Meanwhile, prepare spice mix and for this, place cinnamon, basil, salt, and parsley in a bowl and stir until mixed.
3. Take a casserole dish, pour in chicken broth from lemon chicken, add half of the spice mix and stir until mixed.
4. Coat chicken thighs with remaining spice mix, place them into the casserole dish and bake for 20 to 30 minutes until done, basting the chicken every 5 minutes with its sauce. Serve.

81 – Chicken with Cauliflower

Serves: 2; Preparation: 5 minutes; Cook time: 20 minutes
Nutrition facts: 304 Calories; 25 g Fats; 16.3 g Protein; 1 g Net Carb; 1.25 g Fiber;
Ingredients
- 2 chicken thighs, boneless
- 6 oz cauliflower florets
- 1 tsp ginger powder
- 2 tbsp coconut oil
- ¼ cup mayonnaise

Seasoning:
- ¾ tsp salt
- ¼ tsp ground black pepper
- 1/8 tsp cayenne pepper

How to Prepare:
1. Turn on the oven, then set it to 400 degrees F, and let it preheat.
2. Meanwhile, brush chicken with oil and then season with ginger, ½ tsp salt, and cayenne pepper on both sides.
3. Place chicken on a baking dish and bake for 20 to 25 minutes until chicken is no longer pink and nicely golden.
4. While chicken is cooking, take a saucepan half full with salted water, place it over medium heat, bring it to boil, then add cauliflower florets and cook for 3 minutes or until slightly softened.
5. Drain cauliflower florets, transfer them to a bowl, add mayonnaise, season with remaining salt and black pepper, and stir until well mixed.
6. Serve chicken thighs with cauliflower.

82 – Garlic Chicken with Lemon

Serves: 2; Preparation: 10 minutes; Cook time: 20 minutes
Nutrition facts: 136 Calories; 9.7 g Fats; 10.5 g Protein; 0.8 g Net Carb; 0.3 g Fiber;
Ingredients
- 2 chicken thighs, boneless
- 1 tbsp unsalted butter
- 2 tsp minced garlic
- 2 tbsp chopped cilantro
- ½ of a lemon, juiced

Seasoning:
- 1 tbsp melted coconut oil
- 1/3 tsp salt
- ¼ tsp ground black pepper

How to Prepare:

1. Turn on the oven, then set it to 450 degrees F, and let it preheat.
2. Meanwhile, take a baking pan, grease it with butter, place chicken thighs in it, season with salt and black pepper, and then drizzle with oil and lemon juice.
3. Sprinkle cilantro and garlic on top of chicken pieces and bake for 20 to 30 minutes until the chicken has cooked and turned golden brown. Serve.

83 – Eggplant and Chicken Casserole

Serves: 2; Preparation: 5 minutes; Cook time: 30 minutes
Nutrition facts: 169 Calories; 9 g Fats; 18 g Protein; 2 g Net Carb; 2 g Fiber;
Ingredients
- 2 chicken thighs, boneless
- ¼ tsp garlic powder
- 1/3 of a large eggplant
- 2 tbsp grated parmesan cheese
- 1 tbsp tomato sauce

Seasoning:
- 1 ¼ tsp coconut oil
- 1/4 tsp salt
- 1/4 tsp ground black pepper
- ½ tsp dried oregano

How to Prepare:
1. Turn on the oven, then set it to 375 degrees F, and let it preheat.
2. Prepare chicken thighs and for this, butterfly each chicken thigh, then pound them by using a meat mallet, until 1/4-inch thick and then season one side of chicken with 1/8 tsp each of salt and black pepper on both side.
3. Take a skillet pan, place it over medium-high heat, add 2/3 tsp oil and when hot, add chicken in it, seasoned side down, and cook for 7 minutes per side until golden browned, set aside until required.
4. While chicken cooks, take the reserved eggplant from previous recipes and cut it into two slices.
5. Place eggplant slices onto a baking sheet lined with parchment paper, drizzle with ¼ tsp oil and season with ¼ tsp oregano, 1/8 tsp each of salt and black pepper on each slice.
6. When the chicken has cooked, top a piece of chicken over each slice of eggplant, then top with tomato sauce and cheese and bake for 15 minutes until cheese starts bubbling and the top is golden brown. Serve.

84 – Chicken Salad

Serves: 2; Preparation: 10 minutes; Cook time: 12 minutes
Nutrition facts: 192 Calories; 15 g Fats; 12 g Protein; 0.5 g Net Carb; 1.5 g Fiber;
Ingredients
- 2 chicken thighs, boneless
- 1 ½ cup water
- 2 tbsp mayonnaise
- 1 green onion, sliced
- 2 tbsp chopped cilantro

Seasoning:
- 1 tbsp coconut oil
- ½ tsp salt

How to Prepare:
1. Turn on the instant pot, press the sauté button, add oil and let heat until it melts.
2. Season chicken with salt, add it into the instant pot, and cook for 4 minutes per side.
3. Pour in water, shut with lid, and cook on manual setting for 3 minutes at high pressure.
4. When done, do natural pressure release, then transfer chicken to a cutting board and shred it by using two forks, reserve chicken broth for later use.
5. Prepare salad and for this, transfer chicken to a bowl, add remaining ingredients and toss until combined.
6. Taste the salad to adjust seasoning and Serve.

85 – Baked Sausage

Serves: 2; Preparation: 5 minutes; Cook time: 20 minutes
Nutrition facts: 137.5 Calories; 12.3 g Fats; 5.3 g Protein; 0.8 g Net Carb; 0.5 g Fiber;
Ingredients

- 3-ounce chicken sausage
- 2 tbsp tomato sauce
- 3 tbsp cheddar cheese
- 3 oz whipped topping

Seasoning:

- ¼ tsp salt
- 1/8 tsp ground black pepper

How to Prepare:

1. Turn on the oven, then set it to 400 degrees F and let it preheat.
2. Take a baking dish, grease it with oil, place chicken sausages in it, and then bake for 15 minutes.
3. Meanwhile, prepare the sauce and for this, place tomato sauce in a bowl, add whipped topping and stir until well mixed.
4. When chicken sausages have cooked, spread prepared sauce over them, sprinkle with cheese, and cook for 5 minutes until cheese has melted and golden brown.

86 – Sesame Chicken Thighs

Serves: 2; Preparation: 5 minutes; Cook time: 20 minutes
Nutrition facts: 130 Calories; 8.8 g Fats; 10.7 g Protein; 0.7 g Net Carb; 1.3 g Fiber;
Ingredients

- 2 chicken thighs, boneless
- 2 tsp soy sauce
- 4 tbsp sesame seeds

Seasoning:

- ½ tsp garlic powder
- 1 tbsp apple cider vinegar
- ½ tsp ginger powder

How to Prepare:

1. Turn on the oven, then set it to 375 degrees F and let it preheat.
2. Meanwhile, prepare the sauce and for this, place soy sauce and vinegar in a small bowl, add garlic powder and ginger powder and stir until combined.
3. Place chicken thighs in a plastic bag, pour in the sauce, seal the bag and turn the bag upside down until chicken has coated with the sauce.
4. Place sesame seeds in a shallow dish, dredge chicken thighs in it until covered, then place chicken into a baking dish greased with oil and bake for 15 to 20 minutes until thoroughly cooked. Serve.

87 – Lemon-Rosemary Chicken

Serves: 2; Preparation: 5 minutes; Cook time: 6 minutes
Nutrition facts: 97.5 Calories; 6.6 g Fats; 8.8 g Protein; 0.1 g Net Carb; 0.7 g Fiber;
Ingredients

- 2 chicken thighs, boneless
- ½ of a lemon, juiced, zested
- 1 tsp chopped rosemary
- ½ tsp minced garlic
- 1 tbsp avocado oil

Seasoning:

- 1/3 tsp salt
- 1/4 tsp ground black pepper

How to Prepare:

1. Take a grill pan, place it over medium-high heat, grease it with oil and let it preheat.
2. Meanwhile, place chicken thighs in a plastic bag, add remaining ingredients in it, seal the bag and turn it upside down until evenly coated.
3. Transfer chicken onto the grill pan, cook for 3 minutes per side until thoroughly cooked and then serve.

88 – BBQ Chicken Tender

Serves: 2; Preparation: 5 minutes; Cook time: 14 minutes
Nutrition facts: 196 Calories; 12.6 g Fats; 14.7 g Protein; 2.9 g Net Carb; 3 g Fiber;
Ingredients
- 2 chicken thighs, boneless
- 4 tbsp chopped almond
- 1/3 cup low-carb BBQ sauce
- 1 tbsp avocado oil

How to Prepare:
1. Turn on the oven, then set it to 375 degrees F and let it preheat.
2. Meanwhile, cut chicken into strips, then coat it with BBQ sauce and dredge with chopped almonds.
3. Take a baking sheet, line it with parchment paper, place prepared chicken tenders on it, then drizzle with oil and cook for 7 minutes.
4. Brush BBQ on both sides of chicken tender, continue cooking for 5 to 7 minutes, and then serve.

89 – Cheesy Chicken Stuffed Bell Pepper

Serves: 2; Preparation: 5 minutes; Cook time: 18 minutes
Nutrition facts: 114.3 Calories; 8.3 g Fats; 7 g Protein; 2.5 g Net Carb; 1 g Fiber;
Ingredients
- 4 oz ground turkey
- 2 medium red bell peppers, cored, destemmed
- 2 oz cream cheese, softened
- 2 oz grated cheddar cheese
- 2 tbsp tomato sauce

Seasoning:
- ¼ tsp salt
- 1/3 tsp paprika
- 1/8 tsp ground black pepper

How to Prepare:
1. Turn on the oven, then set it to 350 degrees F and let it preheat.
2. Then prepare bell peppers, place them on a baking sheet lined with parchment sheet, spray with avocado oil and bake for 6minutes.
3. Meanwhile, take a skillet pan and when hot, add turkey, season with salt, paprika, and black pepper and cook for 7 minutes until golden brown.
4. When done, distribute half of the turkey between bell peppers, then top with 1 tbsp cream cheese and tomato sauce, and cover with remaining turkey.
5. Top turkey evenly with cheddar cheese and broil for 3 minutes until cheese has melted and golden brown. Serve.

90 – Grilled Spiced Chicken Thighs

Serves: 2; Preparation: 5 minutes; Cook time: 10 minutes
Nutrition facts: 97.2 Calories; 8.2 g Fats; 5.8 g Protein; 0.2 g Net Carb; 0 g Fiber;
Ingredients
- 2 chicken thighs, boneless
- 1 tsp seafood seasoning
- 2 tbsp unsalted butter, melted
- 1 tbsp avocado oil

How to Prepare:
1. Take a shallow dish, place chicken thighs in it, add oil and ½ tsp seasoning and toss until well coated.
2. Then take a grill pan, place it over medium heat, spray it with oil and when hot, add chicken thighs and cook for 10 minutes until cooked.
3. Meanwhile, place butter in a separate dish bowl, add remaining seasoning, and stir until combined.
4. Add grilled chicken in it, toss until combined, and serve.

91 – Taco Lime Grilled Chicken

Serves: 2; Preparation: 5 minutes; Cook time: 12 minutes
Nutrition facts: 128.3 Calories; 9 g Fats; 11.6 g Protein; 0.3 g Net Carb; 0 g Fiber;
Ingredients
- 2 chicken thighs, boneless

- ½ of a lime, juiced
- 1 ½ tsp taco seasoning
- 1 tbsp avocado oil

How to Prepare:
1. Prepare the marinade and for this, take a small bowl, add lemon juice and taco seasoning and stir until mixed.
2. Brush chicken with prepared marinade and then marinate for 15 minutes.
3. Then take a grill pan, place it over medium-high heat, grease it with oil and when hot, add marinated chicken and cook for 5 minutes per side until thoroughly cooked.
4. When done, transfer chicken to a cutting board, let it cool for 5 minutes, then cut the chicken into slices and serve.

92 – Chicken with Cauliflower Rice

Serves: 2; Preparation: 5 minutes; Cook time: 15 minutes
Nutrition facts: 185 Calories; 14 g Fats; 12.5 g Protein; 1.9 g Net Carb; 0.4 g Fiber;
Ingredients
- 3 oz cauliflower florets, grated
- 1 chicken thigh, boneless, diced
- 1 tsp soy sauce
- 1 tsp apple cider vinegar
- 1 tbsp grated mozzarella cheese

Seasoning:
- 1/3 tsp salt
- 1/3 tsp ground black pepper
- ¼ tsp dried rosemary
- 2 tbsp avocado oil

How to Prepare:
1. Take a skillet pan, place it over medium heat, add 1 tbsp oil in it and when hot, add chicken pieces and cook for 3 minutes.
2. Then drizzle with soy sauce and vinegar, season with ¼ tsp salt and black pepper, toss until mixed and cook for 5 minutes until nicely golden and cooked through.
3. When done, transfer chicken to a plate, add remaining oil in the pan, and when hot, add cauliflower.
4. Season cauliflower with salt and black pepper, toss until mixed and cook for 4 minutes until cooked.
5. Return chicken into the pan, toss until mixed and then cook for 1 minute until hot. Sprinkle with cheese, cook for 1 minute until cheese melts, and then serve.

93 – Sausage and Vegetable Soup

Serves: 2; Preparation: 5 minutes; Cook time: 25 minutes
Nutrition facts: 222.5 Calories; 16.8 g Fats; 11.7 g Protein; 4.6 g Net Carb; 2.1 g Fiber;
Ingredients
- 4 oz chicken sausage, sliced, cooked
- 3 oz green beans, diced
- 2 oz chopped spinach
- 1 ounce chopped cauliflower florets
- 1 ounce chopped broccoli florets

Seasoning:
- 1/3 tsp salt
- ¼ tsp ground black pepper
- ¼ tsp paprika
- 1 ½ tbsp avocado oil
- 1 ½ cup water

How to Prepare:
1. Take a saucepan, place it over medium heat, pour in water and sausage, and bring the mixture to boil.
2. Then continue boiling for 3 minutes, then remaining ingredients, stir, and simmer the soup for 20 minutes until sausage and vegetables are cooked.
3. Ladle soup into bowls and serve.

94 – Garlic Chicken with Mozzarella

Serves: 2; Preparation: 5 minutes; Cook time: 10 minutes

Nutrition facts: 294 Calories; 19.6 g Fats; 28 g Protein; 1.4 g Net Carb; 0.1 g Fiber;
Ingredients
- 2 chicken thighs, boneless
- 4 basil leaves, chopped
- 2 cloves of garlic, peeled, sliced
- 2 tbsp avocado oil
- 1 tbsp grated mozzarella cheese

Seasoning:
- 1/3 tsp salt
- 1/3 tsp ground black pepper
- ½ tsp dried oregano

How to Prepare:
1. Prepare chicken thighs and for this, create a pocket into each chicken thigh and then place them in a baking dish.
2. Stuff chicken with basil and garlic, drizzle with oil, season with salt, black pepper, and oregano and bake for 8 minutes or until chicken is almost cooked.
3. Then sprinkle cheese on top of each chicken, continue baking for 2 minutes until cheese has melted and the top is browned, and serve.

95 – Basil Stuffed Chicken

Serves: 2; Preparation: 10 minutes; Cook time: 20 minutes
Nutrition facts: 263.5 Calories; 19.9 g Fats; 19.8 g Protein; 101.30 g Net Carb; 0 g Fiber;
Ingredients
- 2 chicken thighs, boneless
- ¼ tsp minced garlic
- 1 tsp dried basil
- 2 tbsp cream cheese
- 2 tbsp grated mozzarella cheese

Seasoning:
- ¼ tsp ground black pepper
- ¼ tsp salt
- 1 tbsp avocado oil

How to Prepare:
1. Turn on the oven, then set it to 375 degrees F and let it preheat.
2. Meanwhile, take a bowl, add garlic, basil, cream cheese, mozzarella, and black pepper and stir until mixed.
3. Make a pocket into each chicken with a knife, stuffed it evenly with prepared mixture, place chicken into a baking dish, drizzle with oil, season with salt, and bake for 15 to 20 minutes until chicken is thoroughly cooked. Serve.

96 – Paprika Chicken with Lime

Serves: 2; Preparation: 1 hour and 5 minutes; Cook time: 10 minutes;
Nutrition facts: 212.5 Calories; 7.3 g Fats; 35.6 g Protein; 0.6 g Net Carb; 0.5 g Fiber;
Ingredients
- 2 chicken thighs
- ½ of a lime, juiced, zested
- 1/3 tsp ground cumin
- ½ tsp paprika
- 1 cup of water

Seasoning:
- 1/3 tsp salt
- ¼ tsp ground black pepper

How to Prepare:
1. Take a small bowl, add lime juice, lime zest, paprika, salt, and black pepper and then stir until combined.
2. Brush this spice mixture thoroughly on all sides of chicken thighs, place chicken into a bowl, cover with a plastic wrap and then let it marinate for a minimum of 1 hour.
3. When ready to cook, plug in the instant pot, pour water into the inner pot, insert a steamer rack, and place chicken on it.
4. Shut with lid, press the "manual" button, then cook the chicken for 10 minutes, and when done, do quick pressure release.
5. Transfer chicken to a plate, reserve the broth for later use and serve chicken straight away.

97 – Cajun Chicken

Serves: 2; Preparation: 5 minutes; Cook time: 10 minutes;
Nutrition facts: 225 Calories; 16 g Fats; 20.1 g Protein; 0.6 g Net Carb; 0 g Fiber;
Ingredients
- 2 chicken thighs
- 1 tbsp Cajun seasoning
- 2 tbsp butter, unsalted, melted

How to Prepare:
1. Take a small bowl, add butter in it, stir in Cajun seasoning and then brush this mixture on all sides of chicken.
2. Take a griddle pan, place it over medium-high heat, grease it with oil and when hot, add prepared chicken thighs, and then grill for 5 minutes per side until thoroughly cooked. Serve.

98 – Chicken and Cabbage Plate

Serves: 2; Preparation: 10 minutes; Cook time: 10 minutes;
Nutrition facts: 261 Calories; 23 g Fats; 12 g Protein; 1.75 g Net Carb; 0.7 g Fiber;
Ingredients
- 2 chicken thighs
- 4 oz green cabbage, shredded
- 2 scallions, sliced
- 2 tbsp coconut oil
- 1/4 cup mayonnaise

Seasoning:
- 1/2 tsp salt
- 1/2 tsp ground black pepper

How to Prepare:
1. Take a frying pan, place it over medium heat, add 1 tbsp oil and wait until it melts.
2. Season chicken with ¼ tsp salt and black pepper, add to the frying pan, and cook for 5 minutes per side until thoroughly cooked.
3. When done, transfer chicken to a cutting board, let it cool for 5 minutes, and then shred by using two forks.
4. Distribute cabbage and scallion between two plates, top with shredded chicken and mayonnaise, drizzle with remaining oil and season with remaining salt and black pepper. Serve.

99 – Grilled Curry Chicken

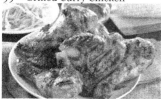

Serves: 2; Preparation: 35 minutes; Cook time: 10 minutes;
Nutrition facts: 221 Calories; 12.8 g Fats; 25 g Protein; 1.7 g Net Carb; 0 g Fiber;
Ingredients
- 2 chicken thighs
- 2/3 tbsp curry powder
- 1 tbsp coconut oil
- 6 tbsp Greek yogurt, full-fat

Seasoning:
- 1/4 tsp salt
- 1/4 tsp ground black pepper

How to Prepare:
1. Take a medium bowl, add yogurt in it, and then whisk in salt, black pepper, and curry powder.
2. Add chicken thighs, toss until well coated and let it marinate in the refrigerator for 30 minutes.
3. When ready to cook, take a griddle pan, place it over medium-high heat, grease it with oil and when hot, add marinated chicken and cook for 5 minutes per side until thoroughly cooked. Serve.

100 – Chicken Coconut Curry

Serves: 2; Preparation: 5 minutes; Cook time: 15 minutes;
Nutrition facts: 177 Calories; 15.5 g Fats; 13.2 g Protein; 0.4 g Net Carb; 0.1 g Fiber;
Ingredients
- 2 boneless chicken thighs, skinless
- 2/3 tsp garlic powder
- 1 tsp curry powder

- ½ tbsp avocado oil
- ½ cup coconut milk, unsweetened, full-fat

Seasoning:
- ½ tsp ginger powder
- 1/3 tsp salt
- ¼ tsp ground black pepper

How to Prepare:
1. Cut chicken into bite-size pieces and then season with salt and black pepper.
2. Take a medium saucepan, place it over medium heat, add oil and when hot, add chicken pieces and cook for 5 to 7 minutes until chicken is no longer pink and golden brown.
3. Take a medium bowl, pour coconut milk in it, and then stir in curry powder.
4. Pour this mixture over chicken, bring it to simmer, then switch heat to medium-low level and cook for 5 to 7 minutes or more until chicken has cooked through.
5. Serve chicken curry with cauliflower rice.

101 – Cheesy BBQ Chicken Thighs

Serves: 2; Preparation: 35 minutes; Cook time: 10 minutes;
Nutrition facts: 293 Calories; 17.8 g Fats; 29.5 g Protein; 5 g Net Carb; 4 g Fiber;
Ingredients
- 2 boneless chicken thighs, skinless
- 1/3 tsp salt
- ¼ tsp ground black pepper
- 4 tbsp hot BBQ sauce, keto
- 2 tbsp grated parmesan cheese

How to Prepare:
1. Take a medium bowl, place chicken thighs in it, season with salt and black pepper, and then add BBQ sauce.
2. Toss until well coated and let it marinate in the refrigerator for 30 minutes.
3. Then take a griddle pan, place it over medium-high heat, grease it with oil and when hot, place chicken thighs on it, and then grill for 5 minutes per side until almost cooked, brushing with reserved BBQ marinade frequently. Sprinkle with cheese, cook for 1 minute until cheese has melted and then serve.

102 – Spiced Chicken Drumsticks

Serves: 2; Preparation: 5 minutes; Cook time: 15 minutes;
Nutrition facts: 275 Calories; 14.1 g Fats; 35.2 g Protein; 0.6 g Net Carb; 0.1 g Fiber;
Ingredients
- 2 chicken drumsticks, drumsticks
- ½ tsp garlic powder
- ½ tsp onion powder
- ½ tsp smoked paprika
- 1 tbsp avocado oil

Seasoning:
- ¼ tsp salt
- ¼ tsp ground black pepper

How to Prepare:
1. Turn on the oven, then set it to 400 degrees F and let it preheat.
2. Meanwhile, take a plastic bag, place all the ingredients in it, seal the bag and turn it upside down to coat chicken with the spices.
3. Take a pan, place chicken on it, and then bake for 10 to 15 minutes until cooked through and browned, turning halfway. Serve.

103 – Chili Lime Baked Chicken Legs

Serves: 2; Preparation: 5 minutes; Cook time: 10 minutes;
Nutrition facts: 248 Calories; 19 g Fats; 14 g Protein; 0 g Net Carb; 0 g Fiber;
Ingredients
- 2 chicken drumsticks
- ½ tsp red chili powder
- ½ tsp smoked paprika
- ¼ of a lime, juiced
- 1 ½ tbsp avocado oil

Seasoning:
- 1/3 tsp salt

- ¼ tsp ground black pepper

How to Prepare:
1. Turn on the oven, then set it to 450 degrees F and let it preheat.
2. Prepare the marinade and for this, take a small bowl, place salt, black pepper, red chili powder, paprika, lime juice, and oil in it and then stir until well combined.
3. Brush the marinade generously on all sides of chicken and then let marinate for 20 minutes.
4. When the chicken has marinated, take a baking sheet, line it with aluminum foil, place a cookie rack on it, then place marinated chicken on it and bake for 15 to 20 minutes until thoroughly cooked and crisp, turning halfway. Serve.

104 – Garlicky Salt and Pepper Chicken

Serves: 2; Preparation: 5 minutes; Cook time: 12 minutes;
Nutrition facts: 320 Calories; 18.5 g Fats; 34 g Protein; 1.9 g Net Carb; 0.5 g Fiber;
Ingredients
- 2 chicken drumsticks
- 2 green onions, diced
- 1 ½ tsp garlic powder
- ½ tsp red pepper flakes
- 2 tsp sesame oil

Seasoning:
- ½ tsp salt
- 1/3 tsp ground black pepper
- 1 tbsp avocado oil

How to Prepare:
1. Turn on the oven, then set it to 400 degrees F and let it preheat.
2. Meanwhile, take a small bowl, place salt and black pepper in it, and then stir until mixed.
3. Take a small baking sheet, grease it with avocado oil, place chicken drumsticks on it, season with the salt-pepper mixture until coated completely and then bake for 10 to 12 minutes until cooked and crispy, turning halfway.
4. When chicken is almost cooked, take a small skillet pan, place it over medium-low heat, add sesame oil and when hot, add onion, sprinkle with garlic powder and cook for 3 to 4 minutes until golden brown. When the chicken has baked, transfer it to a medium bowl, drizzle with garlic-onion oil and toss until coated. Transfer chicken to a dish, top with garlic-onion mixture, and then serve.

105 – Smoked Paprika Drumsticks

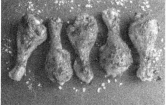

Serves: 2; Preparation: 5 minutes; Cook time: 20 minutes;
Nutrition facts: 200 Calories; 12 g Fats; 20 g Protein; 2 g Net Carb; 1 g Fiber;
Ingredients
- 2 chicken drumsticks
- ¼ tbsp smoked paprika
- ¼ tsp onion powder
- 2 tbsp butter, unsalted, melted
- 2/3 tbsp nutritional yeast

Seasoning:
- ¼ tsp salt
- 1/8 tsp ground black pepper
- 1/8 tsp cayenne pepper
- ¼ tsp garlic powder

How to Prepare:
1. Turn on the oven, then set it to 350 degrees F and let it preheat.
2. Take a plastic bag, add chicken in it, add remaining ingredients except for butter, seal the bag, and shake it well to coat chicken with the spice.
3. Take a baking sheet, line it with foil, place a cookie sheet on it, then place chicken on it and cook for 10 minutes.
4. Then brush chicken with melted butter and continue baking for 5 to 10 minutes until crispy. Serve.

106 – Herb Roasted Chicken Drumsticks

Serves: 2; Preparation: 5 minutes; Cook time: 12 minutes;
Nutrition facts: 377 Calories; 27 g Fats; 27 g Protein; 4 g Net Carb; 1 g Fiber;
Ingredients
- 2 chicken drumsticks
- ¼ of a lime, juiced

- ½ tsp Italian herb blend
- ½ tsp garlic powder
- 2 tbsp avocado oil

Seasoning:
- 1/3 tsp salt

How to Prepare:
1. Turn on the oven, then set it to 400 degrees F and let it preheat.
2. Meanwhile, place chicken into a bowl, add remaining ingredients except for oil and toss until well coated.
3. Transfer chicken drumsticks into a baking sheet greased with avocado oil and then bake for 10 to 12 minutes until cooked and slightly crispy, turning halfway.

107 – Chicken Wrap with Egg

Serves: 2; Preparation: 10 minutes; Cook time: 10 minutes;
Nutrition facts: 225 Calories; 19.6 g Fats; 11.2 g Protein; 0.5 g Net Carb; 0 g Fiber;
Ingredients
- 2 eggs
- 2 tbsp coconut oil
- 2 chicken thighs, boneless, diced

Seasoning:
- 1/2 tsp salt
- 1/3 tsp ground black pepper
- ¼ tsp Cajun pepper

How to Prepare:
1. Prepare chicken and for this, dice chicken into pieces and then season with ¼ tsp salt, 1/8 tsp black pepper, and Cajun pepper.
2. Take a medium skillet pan, add 1 tbsp oil and when hot, add chicken and cook for 5 to 7 minutes until cooked, set aside until required.
3. Prepare egg wraps and for this, take a medium bowl, crack eggs in it, add remaining salt and black pepper, and then whisk until blended.
4. Take a frying pan, place it over medium-low heat, add 1 tbsp coconut oil and when it melts, pour in half of the egg, spread it evenly into a thin layer by rotating the pan and cook for 2 minutes.
5. Then flip the pan, cook for 1 minute, and transfer to a plate.
6. Repeat with the remaining egg to make another wrap, divide chicken between wraps, then roll each egg wrap and serve.

108 – Jalapeño Popper Chicken

Serves: 2; Preparation: 5 minutes; Cook time: 10 minutes;
Nutrition facts: 227 Calories; 16 g Fats; 17 g Protein; 0 g Net Carb; 0 g Fiber;
Ingredients
- 2 strips of bacon, diced, cooked
- 2 chicken thighs
- 1 jalapeno pepper, deseeded, diced
- 2 tbsp cream cheese
- 2 tbsp grated parmesan cheese

Seasoning:
- 1/3 tsp garlic powder
- 1/3 tsp salt

How to Prepare:
1. Turn on the oven, then set it to 375 degrees F and let it preheat.
2. Meanwhile, take a baking dish, place chicken thighs in it, and then season with salt and garlic powder.
3. Spread with cream cheese, sprinkle with cheese, jalapeno pepper, and bacon and then bake for 15 minutes until the chicken has thoroughly cooked. Serve.

109 – Chicken Caprese

Serves: 2; Preparation: 10 minutes; Cook time: 25 minutes;
Nutrition facts: 273 Calories; 14.7 g Fats; 33.1 g Protein; 0.9 g Net Carb; 0.5 g Fiber;
Ingredients
- 2 chicken thighs, boneless
- ½ tbsp Italian seasoning
- 1 tbsp apple cider vinegar
- 2 oz mozzarella cheese, sliced
- 2 tbsp diced tomato

Seasoning:
- 1 tsp garlic powder
- 1/3 tsp salt
- 1/4 tsp ground black pepper
- 1 tsp dried basil
- 1 tsp avocado oil

How to Prepare:
1. Turn on the oven, then set it to 375 degrees F and let it preheat.
2. Meanwhile, take a medium skillet pan, place it over medium heat, add oil and when hot, add chicken, season with salt, black pepper, and Italian seasoning and cook for 2 to 3 minutes per side until browned.
3. Remove pan from heat, drizzle with vinegar, top with diced tomatoes, and then bake for 12 to 15 minutes until the chicken has cooked.
4. Top chicken with mozzarella cheese, continue baking for 4 to 5 minutes until cheese has melted, then sprinkle with basil and serve.

110 – Parmesan Chicken and Kale Sauté

Serves: 2; Preparation: 5 minutes; Cook time: 10 minutes;
Nutrition facts: 303.3 Calories; 15.7 g Fats; 31.6 g Protein; 5 g Net Carb; 3.9 g Fiber;
Ingredients
- 2 chicken thighs, boneless, cut into strips
- ½ bunch of kale
- 1 tsp garlic powder
- 1 tbsp avocado oil
- 4 tbsp grated parmesan cheese
- 1/3 tsp salt
- 1/4 tsp ground black pepper
- 1/3 tsp red pepper flakes

How to Prepare:
1. Take a medium skillet pan, place it over medium heat, add oil and when hot, add chicken in it, season with salt and black pepper and cook for 5 minutes until thoroughly cooked.
2. Transfer chicken to a plate, add kale into the pan, sprinkle with garlic and red pepper flakes and cook for 3 to 4 minutes until kale is just tender.
3. Return chicken into the pan, stir until mixed, sprinkle with parmesan cheese, stir until combined, and remove the pan from heat. Serve.

111 – Cauliflower Tortillas with Chicken

Serves: 2; Preparation: 5 minutes; Cook time: 10 minutes;
Nutrition facts: 201 Calories; 12 g Fats; 18.9 g Protein; 0.8 g Net Carb; 1.7 g Fiber;
Ingredients
- 5 oz grated cauliflower
- 2 chicken thighs, boneless
- 1 tbsp avocado oil
- 1 tbsp Cajun spice
- 1 egg
- 1/3 tsp salt
- ½ tsp dried oregano
- ½ tsp paprika

How to Prepare:
1. Turn on the oven, then set it to 375 degrees F and let it preheat.
2. Place grated cauliflower in a heatproof bowl, cover with a plastic wrap and microwave for 2 to 3 minutes until steamed.
3. Then drain cauliflower, wrap into cheesecloth and twist well to squeeze moisture as much as possible and place in a medium bowl.
4. Add eggs, stir in salt, oregano, and paprika until well combined and then shape the mixture into two balls.
5. Take a baking sheet, line it with parchment sheet, place balls on it, spread it to make tortilla circles, and then bake for 4 to 5 minutes side until golden brown and cooked. Meanwhile, prepare chicken and for this, brush chicken with oil, sprinkle with Cajun seasoning until coated, and let it marinate for 10 minutes.
6. Then take a griddle pan, place it over medium-high heat, add oil and when hot, place chicken on it and grill for 5 minutes per side or more until thoroughly cooked.
7. When tortilla has cooked, cut the chicken into slices or shred with a fork, top it over tortillas evenly and then serve.

112 – Cheesy Marinara Chicken with Mushroom

Serves: 2; Preparation: 5 minutes; Cook time: 15 minutes;

Nutrition facts: 215 Calories; 9.8 g Fats; 28.8 g Protein; 0.9 g Net Carb; 0.7 g Fiber;
Ingredients
- 2 chicken thighs, boneless
- 2 oz marinara sauce
- 1-ounce sliced mushroom
- 2 tbsp grated mozzarella cheese
- ½ tbsp Italian seasoning
- 1/3 tsp salt

How to Prepare:
1. Turn on the oven, then set it to 375 degrees F and let it preheat.
2. Take a casserole dish, place chickens in it, sprinkle with salt and Italian seasoning and then top with sliced mushrooms.
3. Cover with marinara sauce, then sprinkle with mozzarella cheese and bake for 12 to 15 minutes until thoroughly cooked. Serve.

113 – Chicken Cheese Wrap

Serves: 2; Preparation: 15 minutes; Cook time: 10 minutes;
Nutrition facts: 380 Calories; 24.7 g Fats; 31.1 g Protein; 7.5 g Net Carb; 0 g Fiber;
Ingredients
- 4 oz of grated parmesan cheese
- 1 tbsp avocado oil
- 1 chicken thighs, boneless
- ¼ tsp salt
- 1/8 tsp ground black pepper
- ¼ tsp paprika
- ¼ tsp cayenne pepper

How to Prepare:
1. Take a heatproof bowl, place cheese in it, microwave for 15 seconds, stir and microwave for another 10 seconds.
2. Shape the cheese into two balls, place a cheese ball on a parchment sheet, and then cover it with another parchment sheet.
3. Let the cheese cool for 10 seconds, use hands to spread cheese into a circle, and then roll into a thin circle by using a rolling pin.
4. Cut extra parchment sheet around the circle, keep cheese tortilla into the refrigerator and repeat with the other cheese ball.
5. Then prepare chicken and for this, brush it with oil and season with salt, black pepper, paprika, and cayenne pepper.
6. Take a griddle pan, place it over medium-high heat and when hot, place chicken on it and cook for 4 to 5 minutes per side until through cooked.
7. When done, shred chicken or slice it, top chicken evenly on prepared cheese tortilla, roll gently, and then serve.

114 – Creamy Chicken with Mushroom

Serves: 2; Preparation: 5 minutes; Cook time: 25 minutes;
Nutrition facts: 375 Calories; 28.7 g Fats; 28.1 g Protein; 1.5 g Net Carb; 0.4 g Fiber;
Ingredients
- 2 chicken thighs, boneless
- 2 oz sliced mushroom
- 1 green onion, sliced
- ¼ of lime, zested, juiced
- 2 oz whipping cream
- 1/3 tsp salt
- ¼ tsp ground black pepper
- 1 ½ tbsp avocado oil
- ¼ cup wine

How to Prepare:
1. Turn on the oven, then set heat to 350 degrees F and let it preheat.
2. Take a medium skillet pan, place it over medium-high heat, add oil and when hot, place chicken thighs in it and cook for 2 to 3 minutes per side or more until nicely golden brown.
3. Transfer chicken to a plate, set aside until required, add mushrooms in the pan, cook for 2 minutes per side until nicely browned and then to the plate containing chicken. Add green onions into the pan, cook for 1 to 2 minutes until tender and then remove the pan from heat.
4. Add lemon juice and wine into the pan, return it over medium heat, stir well and simmer the mixture until reduced by half.
5. Add lime zest and cream, season with salt and black pepper, stir until mixed and bring it to a simmer.
6. Return chicken thighs into the pan, place mushrooms in the empty space of the pan and then bake for 10 to 15 minutes until the chicken has thoroughly cooked.

115 – Ranch Yogurt Marinated Chicken

Serves: 2; Preparation: 30 minutes; Cook time: 10 minutes;
Nutrition facts: 240 Calories; 13.1 g Fats; 27.6 g Protein; 1.8 g Net Carb; 0 g Fiber;
Ingredients

- 2 chicken thighs, boneless
- 1/3 tbsp chopped dill
- 1/3 tbsp chopped parsley
- 1/3 tbsp garlic powder
- 4 tbsp yogurt
- 1/3 tsp salt
- 1 tbsp avocado oil

How to Prepare:
1. Take a medium bowl, place yogurt in it, and then whisk in dill, parsley, garlic, and salt until combined.
2. Add chicken, toss until well coated, and then let it marinate for 30 minutes.
3. When the chicken has marinated, take a skillet pan, place it over medium heat, add oil, and when hot, add marinated chicken in it along with yogurt mixture and cook for 7 to 10 minutes until the chicken has thoroughly cooked. Serve.

116 – Italian Chicken

Serves: 2; Preparation: 10 minutes; Cook time: 12 minutes;
Nutrition facts: 276 Calories; 14 g Fats; 33 g Protein; 2 g Net Carb; 0 g Fiber;
Ingredients
- 2 chicken thighs, boneless cubed
- 1 tbsp chopped parsley
- ¼ of lime, juiced
- 2 tbsp avocado oil
- 2 oz almond milk, unsweetened
  Seasoning:
- ¼ tsp garlic powder
- 1/3 tsp salt
- ¼ tsp ground black pepper
- 1 tbsp Italian seasoning mix

How to Prepare:
1. Take a medium bowl, place milk in it, add remaining ingredients except for chicken and whisk until well combined.
2. Cut chicken into bite-size cubes, add to the milk mixture, toss until well coated and let it marinate for 15 minutes.
3. When ready to cook, take a grill pan, place it over medium-high heat, grease it with avocado oil and let it preheat.
4. Place marinated chicken on the grill pan and then cook for 3 to 4 minutes per side until thoroughly cooked. Serve.

117 – Asian Chicken

Serves: 2; Preparation: 5 minutes; Cook time: 8 minutes;
Nutrition facts: 235 Calories; 12.3 g Fats; 27.6 g Protein; 1.8 g Net Carb; 0.5 g Fiber;
Ingredients
- 2 chicken thighs, boneless
- 4 green onions, sliced
- ¼ tsp ginger powder
- 1 tbsp soy sauce
- 1 tbsp fish sauce
- ¼ tsp salt; ¼ tsp red pepper flakes
- ¼ tsp garlic powder
- 1 tbsp avocado oil

How to Prepare:
1. Prepare the sauce and for this, take a small bowl, add ginger powder, soy sauce, fish sauce, red pepper flakes, and garlic powder and stir until combined.
2. Take a medium skillet pan, add ½ tbsp oil and when hot, add green onions and cook for 1 to 2 minutes until beginning to golden.
3. Transfer green onions to a plate, add chicken, sprinkle with salt and then cook for 3 to 4 minutes per side until thoroughly cooked.
4. Transfer chicken to a plate, switch heat to medium-low level, pour in the sauce and bring it to a gentle boil.
5. Then add chicken and green onion, toss until well coated, and cook for 1 minute until glazed. Serve.

118 – Stuffed Chicken with Cheese and Greens

Serves: 2; Preparation: 5 minutes; Cook time: 15 minutes;
Nutrition facts: 483 Calories; 33.5 g Fats; 38.3 g Protein; 3.2 g Net Carb; 2.8 g Fiber;
Ingredients
- ¼ bunch of chards, chopped

- 4 oz spinach, chopped
- 2 chicken thighs, boneless
- 2 oz cheddar cheese
- 2 tbsp avocado oil

Seasoning:
- ½ tsp salt
- 1/3 tsp ground black pepper

How to Prepare:
1. Make a pocket into each chicken thigh by making a cut in the thickest part of chicken thighs, fill the pocket with cheese and then season chicken with 1/3 tsp salt and ¼ black pepper.
2. Take a medium skillet pan, place it over medium-high heat, add oil and when hot, add chicken and cook for 4 to 5 minutes per until thoroughly cooked and golden brown.
3. Distribute chicken to a plate, return pan over medium heat, add remaining oil and when hot, add chards and spinach, season with remaining salt and black pepper, and cook for 3 minutes until leaves have wilted and tender. Add chard and spinach evenly to the chicken and then serve.

119 – Lime Butter Chicken with Green Beans

Serves: 2; Preparation: 10 minutes; Cook time: 15 minutes;
Nutrition facts: 495 Calories; 38.2 g Fats; 29.1 g Protein; 4.7 g Net Carb; 2.6 g Fiber;
Ingredients
- 2 chicken thighs, boneless
- 6 oz green beans
- ¼ of lime, juiced
- 4 tbsp butter, unsalted, softened
- 2 oz whipping cream

Seasoning:
- 1/3 tsp salt
- ¼ tsp ground black pepper
- ½ tsp garlic powder
- 1/3 tsp paprika

How to Prepare:
1. Turn on the oven, then set it to 392 degrees F and let it preheat.
2. Meanwhile, take a casserole dish, spread green beans in the bottom, and then top with chicken thighs.
3. Prepare the sauce and for this, take a small bowl, place butter in it, add remaining ingredients and stir until well combined.
4. Pour the sauce over chicken thighs and then bake for 12 to 15 minutes until thoroughly cooked, basting the chicken with sauce halfway. Serve.

120 – Chicken with Lime and Olives

Serves: 2; Preparation: 5 minutes; Cook time: 10 minutes;
Nutrition facts: 290 Calories; 18.4 g Fats; 27.3 g Protein; 0.3 g Net Carb; 1.2 g Fiber;
Ingredients
- 2 chicken thighs, boneless
- ¼ of lime, sliced
- 3 oz green olives
- 1 tbsp avocado oil
- ¼ tsp salt; 1/8 tsp ground black pepper

How to Prepare:
1. Turn on the oven, then set it to 400 degrees F and let it preheat.
2. Meanwhile, prepare the chicken and for this, sprinkle salt and black pepper evenly on chicken thighs.
3. Take a medium skillet pan, place it over medium-high heat, add oil and when hot, place chicken thighs in it and cook for 2 to 3 minutes per side until golden brown.
4. Transfer chicken to a casserole dish and then bake for 10 minutes until thoroughly cooked.
5. When done, add lime slices into the pan, add oil, cook for 30 seconds per side until golden, add olives, stir until mixed and cook for 30 seconds until hot.
6. Top olives and lime slices over chicken and then serve.

121 – Egg Curry

Serves: 2; Preparation: 5 minutes; Cook time: 8 minutes;
Nutrition facts: 245 Calories; 16.9 g Fats; 13.3 g Protein; 5.4 g Net Carb; 3.7 g Fiber;
Ingredients
- 2 eggs, boiled
- 2 oz grape tomatoes, chopped
- ½ tsp garlic powder
- 1 ½ tbsp avocado oil

- ¼ cup yogurt
- ½ tsp salt
- ½ tsp turmeric powder
- ½ tsp cumin powder
- ½ tsp red chili powder
- ¼ cup of water

How to Prepare:
1. Take a medium saucepan, place it over low level, add oil and when hot, add tomatoes, stir in all the spices, sprinkle with garlic powder and cook for 1 minute.
2. Then add yogurt, stir until mixed, switch heat to medium-low level, and cook for 2 minutes.
3. Peel the eggs, add them to the curry, pour in water, stir until mixed and continue cooking for 3 minutes, covering the pan. Serve.

122 – Creamy Balsamic Chicken with Green Beans

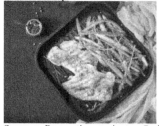

Serves: 2; Preparation: 5 minutes; Cook time: 15 minutes;
Nutrition facts: 362 Calories; 22.8 g Fats; 28.8 g Protein; 9.8 g Net Carb; 1 g Fiber;
Ingredients
- 2 chicken thighs, boneless
- 4 oz green beans
- 1 tbsp mustard paste
- ¼ cup balsamic vinegar
- ¼ cup yogurt

Seasoning:
- ¼ tsp salt
- 1/8 tsp ground black pepper
- 1 tbsp stevia
- 2 tbsp and 1 tsp avocado oil

How to Prepare:
1. Prepare the sauce and for this, take a medium bowl, add yogurt in it and then whisk in salt, stevia, mustard, 2 tbsp oil, and vinegar until combined.
2. Take a medium skillet pan, place it over medium heat, add remaining oil and when hot, add chicken and then cook for 2 to 3 minutes per side until nicely browned on all sides. Pour in the prepared sauce, add green beans, stir until coated, and then cook for 7 to 10 minutes until beans have turned tender and chicken have thoroughly cooked. Sprinkle with black pepper and then serve.

123 – Chicken and Broccoli Foil Pack

Serves: 2; Preparation: 5 minutes; Cook time: 15 minutes;
Nutrition facts: 336 Calories; 22.4 g Fats; 28.6 g Protein; 3 g Net Carb; 2 g Fiber;
Ingredients
- 2 chicken thighs, boneless
- 6 oz broccoli florets
- 1 tsp minced garlic
- ¼ tsp dried thyme
- 2 tbsp melted butter, unsalted

Seasoning:
- ¼ tsp salt
- 1/8 tsp ground black pepper
- ¼ tsp dried basil

How to Prepare:
1. Turn on the oven, then set it to 400 degrees F and let it preheat.
2. Meanwhile, cut chicken into cubes, add broccoli florets along with remaining ingredients and toss until well coated.
3. Take two large pieces of aluminum foil, distribute chicken and broccoli between them, wrap and seal the edges and bake for 15 minutes until thoroughly cooked.

124 – Creamy Chicken Soup

Serves: 2; Preparation: 5 minutes; Cook time: 20 minutes;
Nutrition facts: 307 Calories; 25 g Fats; 18 g Protein; 2 g Net Carb; 0 g Fiber;
Ingredients
- 2 chicken thighs, boneless

- 1.5 oz cream cheese, cubed
- 1 tbsp butter, unsalted
- 2 tbsp whipping cream
- 2 oz of chicken bone broth
- ¼ tsp garlic powder
- 1/3 tsp salt; ¼ tsp ground black pepper
- 1 tsp Italian seasoning
- 2/3 cup water

How to Prepare:
1. Take a small saucepan, place it over medium heat, pour in water, add chicken, and cook for 10 to 12 minutes until the chicken has through cooked.
2. When done, transfer chicken to cutting and then shred it by using two forks; reserve the broth.
3. Take a medium saucepan, place it over medium heat, add butter, and when it melts, add shredded chicken, stir until coated, and cook for 2 minutes until warm.
4. Add cream cheese, sprinkle with all the spice and then cook for 2 minutes until cheese has melted.
5. Pour in the reserved broth along with chicken broth, add cream, stir until combined, and then bring to a boil.
6. Then switch heat to the low level and simmer the soup for 3 minutes until slightly thick. Ladle soup into two bowls and then serve.

Pork

125 – Bacon and Egg Fat Bombs

Serves: 2; Preparation: 25 minutes; Cook time: 10 minutes;
Nutrition facts: 92.5 Calories; 9.2 g Fats; 2.5 g Protein; 0.1 g Net Carb; 0.6 g Fiber;
Ingredients
- 2 slices of turkey bacon
- 1 large egg, hard-boiled
- 2 tbsp unsalted butter, softened
- 1 tbsp whipped topping
- ¾ tsp grated cheddar cheese
- ¼ tsp salt; ¼ tsp ground black pepper

How to Prepare:
1. Turn on the oven, then set it to 375 degrees F, and let preheat.
2. Then take a baking sheet, line it with parchment paper, place bacon slices on it and cook for 10 minutes until nicely golden brown.
3. Meanwhile, boil the egg and for this, place a medium pot half-full with water over medium heat and bring to boil.
4. Then add egg and cook for 10 minutes until hard-boiled.
5. Transfer the egg in a bowl containing chilled water, let it rest for 5 minutes, and then peel it.
6. Chop the egg, then place it in a bowl, season with salt and black pepper, add whipped topping and cheese, stir until well combined, and refrigerate for 15 minutes until solid. Crumble the roasted bacon into small pieces and then place it in a shallow dish.
7. Remove the solid egg mixture from the refrigerator and shape the mixture into two large balls.
8. Roll the egg balls into crumbled bacon until evenly coated, then place the ball on a plate and store the balls for up to 5 days in the refrigerator.
9. When ready to serve, let the balls rest for some time at room temperature until slightly softened and then serve.

126 – Bacon and Egg Breakfast Muffin

Serves: 2; Preparation: 5 minutes; Cook time: 20 minutes;
Nutrition facts: 78 Calories; 5.3 g Fats; 6.1 g Protein; 0.1 g Net Carb; 0.4 g Fiber;
Ingredients
- 2 slices of turkey bacon
- 2 large eggs
- ½ tbsp chopped parsley
- ½ tbsp chopped green onion
- 1 tbsp whipped topping

How to Prepare:
1. Turn on the oven, then set it to 375 degrees F, and let preheat.
2. Take a skillet pan, place it over medium heat and when hot, add bacon and cook for 3 to 5 minutes until crispy.
3. Transfer bacon to a cutting board and then chop it, reserving the grease in the pan.
4. Crack the eggs in a bowl, whisk until blended, then add chopped bacon, green onion and whipped topping and stir until well combined.
5. Take two silicone muffin cups, coat them with bacon grease, then evenly fill with the prepared mixture and bake for 15 to 20 minutes or until the edges of muffins are golden brown. When done, take out muffin from silicone cups, let cool for 5 minutes and serve.

127 – Garlic Parmesan Bacon Knots

Serves: 2; Preparation: 5 minutes; Cook time: 15 minutes;
Nutrition facts: 27 Calories; 2 g Fats; 2 g Protein; 0.5 g Net Carb; 0.5 g Fiber;
Ingredients
- 4 slices of turkey bacon
- ¼ tsp garlic powder
- ¼ tsp red pepper flakes
- ¼ tsp Italian seasoning
- 2 tbsp grated parmesan cheese

How to Prepare:
1. Turn on the oven, then set it to 425 degrees F, and let preheat.
2. Working on a slice of bacon at a time, tie it into a double knot and then place it on a baking sheet.
3. Prepare remaining bacon knots in the same manner, season evenly with garlic powder, red pepper, and Italian seasoning and then bake for 7 to 10 minutes until almost crisp.
4. Then sprinkle cheese over bacon knots and continue baking for 3 to 4 minutes until cheese has melted. Serve.

128 – Bacon and Eggs Cups

Serves: 2; Preparation: 10 minutes; Cook time: 18 minutes
Nutrition facts: 67 Calories; 4 g Fats; 5 g Protein; 0 g Net Carb; 0 g Fiber;
Ingredients
- 2 eggs
- 2 slices of bacon
- 1/4 tsp salt
- 1/4 tsp ground black pepper

How to Prepare:
1. Turn on the oven, then set it to 400 degrees F and let it preheat.
2. Then place bacon on a baking sheet, bake for 5 to 8 minutes until tender-crisp, and when done, cool bacon for 5 minutes and pat dry with paper towels.
3. Take two silicone muffin cups, grease them with oil, place a slice of bacon into each cup, wrapping it around the sides and then crack an egg into each cup.
4. Season egg with salt and black pepper and cook for 8 to 10 minutes until bacon has crispy and eggs have set. Serve.

129 – Bacon butter

Serves: 2; Preparation: 5 minutes; Cook time: 5 minutes
Nutrition facts: 150 Calories; 16 g Fats; 1 g Protein; 0.5 g Net Carb; 1 g Fiber;
Ingredients
- 2 oz unsalted butter, softened
- 3 slices of bacon, chopped
- ½ tsp minced garlic
- ½ tsp dried basil
- ½ tsp tomato paste

For Seasoning:
- ¼ tsp salt
- ¼ tsp ground black pepper

How to Prepare:
1. Take a skillet pan, place it over medium heat, add 1 tbsp butter and when it starts to melts, add chopped bacon and cook for 5 minutes.
2. Then remove the pan from heat, add remaining butter, along with basil and tomato paste, season with salt and black pepper and stir until well mixed.
3. Transfer bacon butter into an airtight container, cover with the lid, and refrigerate for 1 hour until solid. Serve.

130 – Sausage and Fried Eggs

Serves: 2; Preparation: 5 minutes; Cook time: 18 minutes
Nutrition facts: 263 Calories; 19 g Fats; 20.4 g Protein; 2.6 g Net Carb; 0 g Fiber;
Ingredients
- 2 sausage links
- 2 eggs
- 1 tbsp avocado oil
- ¼ tsp salt; ¼ tsp ground black pepper

How to Prepare:
1. Take a skillet pan, place it over medium heat, add oil and when hot, add sausage and cook for 5 to 8 minutes until golden brown on all sides.
2. Push sausage to a side, then crack eggs in it and cook for 3 to 5 minutes per side until cooked to the desired level.
3. Transfer sausage and eggs to two serving plates, season with salt and black pepper, and then serve.

131 – Bacon Sandwich

Serves: 2; Preparation: 5 minutes; Cook time: 20 minutes
Nutrition facts: 251.3 Calories; 22.1 g Fats; 12 g Protein; 0.4 g Net Carb; 1 g Fiber;
Ingredients
- 4 slices of bacon

- 2 eggs, fried
- ½ of a medium avocado, sliced
- 2 tbsp tomato sauce

How to Prepare:
1. Turn on the oven, then set it to 375 degrees F and let it preheat.
2. Meanwhile, cut each bacon slice into six strips, then weave three horizontal bacon strips with three vertical bacon strips to create one slice of the sandwich; create three more sandwich slices in the same manner.
3. Place the bacon slices onto a baking sheet lined with parchment paper and bake for 15 to 20 minutes until bacon has thoroughly cooked.
4. When done, pat dry bacon slices with a paper towel, let them rest for 5 minutes until crispy, and then prepare the sandwich.
5. For this, top two slices of bacon with a fried egg, then layer with avocado slices and add 1 tbsp tomato sauce. Cover the top with remaining bacon slices and serve.

132 – Bacon and Cheese Roll-ups

Serves: 2; Preparation: 10 minutes; Cook time: 10 minutes;
Nutrition facts: 165 Calories; 12.5 g Fats; 12.4 g Protein; 0.8 g Net Carb; 0 g Fiber;
Ingredients
- 2 oz mozzarella cheese, sliced, full-fat
- 4 slices of bacon

How to Prepare:
1. Take a skillet pan, place it over medium heat and when hot, add bacon slices and cook for 3 minutes per side until crisp.
2. When done, transfer bacon to the cutting board, cool for 5 minutes, and then chop. Cut cheese into thin slices, top with chopped bacon, and then roll the cheese.

133 – Egg Wrap with Bacon

Serves: 2; Preparation: 10 minutes; Cook time: 10 minutes;
Nutrition facts: 160 Calories; 10.7 g Fats; 12.8 g Protein; 1.9 g Net Carb; 0 g Fiber;
Ingredients
- 2 slices of turkey bacon
- 2 eggs
- 2 tbsp grated parmesan cheese
- 1/8 tsp salt; 1/8 tsp ground black pepper

How to Prepare:
1. Take a medium bowl, crack eggs in it, add salt and black pepper, and then whisk until blended.
2. Take a medium skillet pan, place it over medium heat and when hot, add bacon and cook for 3 to 5 minutes until crispy.
3. Transfer bacon to a cutting board, cool it for 3 minutes, chop it, and then set aside until required.
4. Pour half of the blended egg into the pan and then cook for 2 minutes or more until the egg has almost cooked.
5. Sprinkle 1 tbsp of cheese on all over the egg, place half of the chopped bacon in the center of the roll, and then fold it on thirds.
6. Transfer egg roll to a plate and repeat with the remaining blended egg, bacon, and cheese. Serve.

134 – Sausage and Tomato Muffin

Serves: 2; Preparation: 5 minutes; Cook time: 10 minutes;
Nutrition facts: 160 Calories; 12.7 g Fats; 10.3 g Protein; 0.5 g Net Carb; 0.1 g Fiber;
Ingredients
- 2 oz ground sausage
- 1 tbsp chopped spinach
- 1 ounce diced tomato
- 2 tsp shredded parmesan cheese
- 1 egg
- ½ tsp salt; ¼ tsp ground black pepper
- ¼ tsp garlic powder
- ¼ tsp paprika
- ¼ tsp dried parsley

How to Prepare:
1. Turn on the oven, then set it to 350 degrees F and let it preheat.
2. Meanwhile, take a medium bowl, crack the egg in it, add ¼ tsp salt and 1/8 tsp black pepper and stir until combined.
3. Take another bowl, place sausage in it, add remaining in garlic powder, salt, black pepper, paprika, and parsley and stir until combined.
4. Divide sausage mixture between two ramekins or muffin cups, pour in egg batter, top with cheese, spinach, and tomato and then bake for 15 to 20 minutes until done.

135 – Green Eggs and Ham Omelet

Serves: 2; Preparation: 5 minutes; Cook time: 10 minutes;
Nutrition facts: 215 Calories; 18.4 g Fats; 9.6 g Protein; 1.5 g Net Carb; 0.6 g Fiber;
Ingredients
- 2 tbsp diced ham
- 2 oz chopped spinach
- 2 eggs
- 1 tbsp avocado oil
- 1 tbsp butter, unsalted
- ¼ tsp salt; 1/8 tsp ground black pepper

How to Prepare:
1. Take a medium bowl, place ham and spinach in it, add eggs, season with salt and black pepper and then whisk until combined.
2. Take a medium skillet pan, place it over medium heat, add oil and butter and when butter melts, pour in egg mixture, spread evenly and cook for 2 to 3 minutes per side until thoroughly cooked. Transfer omelet to a plate, cut it in half and then serve.

136 – Chorizo, Egg, and Avocado Breakfast skillet

Serves: 2; Preparation: 5 minutes; Cook time: 12 minutes;
Nutrition facts: 440 Calories; 37.1 g Fats; 18.7 g Protein; 4.4 g Net Carb; 3.3 g Fiber;
Ingredients
- ¼ of avocado, pitted, diced
- ¼ of yellow onion, sliced
- 1.5 oz green olives
- 4 oz chorizo, crumbled
- 2 eggs
- ¼ tsp salt
- ¼ tsp paprika
- 1/8 tsp ground black pepper
- 1 tbsp avocado oil

How to Prepare:
1. Take a medium skillet pan, place it over medium-high heat, add ½ tbsp oil and when hot, add onion, season with half of the salt and black pepper and cook for 2 minutes.
2. Add chorizo, sprinkle with paprika and continue cooking for 5 minutes until cooked.
3. Transfer chorizo to a plate, add remaining oil into the pan, and wait until it gets hot.
4. Crack eggs into a bowl, add remaining salt and black pepper, whisk until blended, then add the egg into the pan and cook for 3 to 4 minutes until scrambled to the desired level. Return chorizo into the pan, add olives and avocado, stir until mixed and cook for 30 seconds until hot.
5. Distribute meat, eggs, and avocado between two plates and then serve.

137 – Cheese and Bacon Balls

Serves: 2; Preparation: 10 minutes; Cook time: 8 minutes;
Nutrition facts: 137 Calories; 13 g Fats; 5.5 g Protein; 1 g Net Carb; 0 g Fiber;
Ingredients
- 2 slices of bacon
- 1 ¼ tbsp butter, unsalted
- 1 ¼ oz cream cheese, full-fat
- 1 ¼ oz shredded mozzarella cheese, full-fat
- 1/8 tsp red chili flakes

How to Prepare:
1. Take a frying pan, place it over medium heat and when hot, add bacon slices and cook for 3 minutes per side until crisp.
2. Transfer bacon slices to a cutting board, let them cool for 5 minutes, chop them, then transfer chopped bacon into a medium bowl and set aside until required.
3. Take a shallow dish, add bacon grease from the pan, then add remaining ingredients and mix by using an electric hand mixer until combined.
4. Shape the mixture into balls, roll each ball into chopped bacon until coated, and then serve.

138 – Omelet Sandwich

Serves: 2; Preparation: 10 minutes; Cook time: 10 minutes;
Nutrition facts: 345 Calories; 29.2 g Fats; 12.8 g Protein; 3.1 g Net Carb; 3.8 g Fiber;
Ingredients
- 2 2/3 tbsp coconut flour

- 1 tsp baking powder
- 3 eggs
- 2 tsp grated mozzarella cheese
- 2 sliced of bacon, cooked
- 2 tbsp avocado oil
- 1/4 tsp salt; 1/4 tsp ground black pepper
- 1 tbsp butter, unsalted

How to Prepare:
1. Turn on the oven, then set it to 375 degrees F and let it preheat.
2. Meanwhile, prepare the batter for this, add all the ingredients in a bowl, reserving cheese, 1 egg, and 1/8 tsp salt, and then whisk until well combined.
3. Take a 4 by 4 inches heatproof baking pan, grease it with oil, pour in the prepared batter and bake 10 minutes until bread is firm.
4. Meanwhile, crack the remaining egg in a bowl, add black pepper and remaining salt and whisk until combined.
5. Take a medium skillet pan, add butter and when it melts, pour in eggs and cook for 3 minutes until almost cooked.
6. Then sprinkle cheese on one half of the egg, fold over and transfer the egg to a plate.
7. When done, let the bread cool in the pan for 5 minutes, then transfer it to a wire rack and cool for 20 minutes.
8. Slice the bread, place prepared omelet between slices, top with bacon and then serve as a sandwich.

139 – Sausage Wrap

Serves: 2; Preparation: 5 minutes; Cook time: 15 minutes;
Nutrition facts: 350 Calories; 31.7 g Fats; 13.1 g Protein; 2.6 g Net Carb; 0 g Fiber;
Ingredients
- 2 eggs
- 2 tbsp avocado oil
- 3 oz ground sausage, crumbled
- 1/2 tsp salt; 1/3 tsp ground black pepper
- ¼ tsp paprika
- ¼ tsp cayenne pepper

How to Prepare:
1. Prepare sausage
2. and for this, take a medium skillet pan, add 1 tbsp oil and when hot, add ground sausage, season with ¼ tsp salt, 1/8 tsp ground black pepper, paprika, and cayenne pepper and cook then for 5 to 7 minutes until done, set aside until required.
3. Prepare egg wraps and for this, take a medium bowl, crack eggs in it, add remaining salt and black pepper, and then whisk until blended.
4. Take a frying pan, place it over medium-low heat, add 1 tbsp oil and when it melts, pour in half of the egg, spread it evenly into a thin layer by rotating the pan and cook for 2 minutes. Then flip the pan, cook for 1 minute, and transfer to a plate.
5. Repeat with the remaining egg to make another wrap, divide sausage between wraps, then roll each egg wrap and serve.

140 – Ham and Cheese Deviled Eggs

Serves: 2; Preparation: 10 minutes; Cook time: 0 minutes;
Nutrition facts: 114 Calories; 9 g Fats; 6 g Protein; 1 g Net Carb; 0 g Fiber;
Ingredients
- 1 tbsp chopped ham
- 2 eggs, boiled
- 2 tbsp mayonnaise
- ¼ tsp mustard paste
- 1 tsp grated parmesan cheese
- 1/8 tsp dried tarragon; 1/8 tsp ground black pepper

How to Prepare:
1. Peel the boiled eggs, then slice in half lengthwise and transfer egg yolks to a medium bowl by using a spoon.
2. Mash the egg yolk, add remaining ingredients and mash until smooth and well combined.
3. Spoon the egg yolk mixture into egg whites, sprinkle with some black pepper and then serve.

141 – Ham and Cream Cheese Jalapeño Poppers

Serves: 2; Preparation: 10 minutes; Cook time: 7 minutes;
Nutrition facts: 104 Calories; 7.5 g Fats; 5 g Protein; 2.2 g Net Carb; 0.8 g Fiber;
Ingredients
- 4 jalapeno pepper
- 2 tbsp chopped ham
- 1 ounce cream cheese
- 1 tbsp grated parmesan cheese
- 1 tbsp grated mozzarella cheese
- 1/4 tsp ground black pepper
- 1/8 tsp paprika

How to Prepare:
1. Turn on the oven, then set it to 400 degrees F and let it preheat.
2. Prepare the peppers and for this, cut each pepper in half lengthwise and remove seeds and stem.
3. Take a small bowl, place ham in it, add remaining ingredients, and then stir until combined.
4. Spoon ham mixture into peppers and then bake for 5 to 7 minutes until peppers have turned soft. Serve.

142 – Sausage and Egg Cup

Serves: 2; Preparation: 10 minutes; Cook time: 15 minutes;
Nutrition facts: 390 Calories; 33.5 g Fats; 19.1 g Protein; 0.9 g Net Carb; 0.1 g Fiber;
Ingredients

- 4 oz ground sausage, crumbled
- 2 tbsp chopped spinach
- 1/2 tsp salt
- 2 eggs
- 2 tbsp grated cheddar cheese; 1/4 tsp ground black pepper

How to Prepare:
1. Turn on the oven, then set it to 350 degrees F and let it preheat.
2. Take a medium skillet pan, place it over medium heat and when hot, add the sausage in it and then cook for 3 until beginning to brown.
3. Add spinach, stir until mixed and cook for 2 to 3 minutes until the spinach has wilted and sausage has thoroughly cooked.
4. When the sausage has cooked, transfer it to a bowl, add cheese, 1/3 tsp salt and 1/8 tsp black pepper, stir until mixed, and then transfer the mixture evenly between two ramekins or silicone muffin cups.
5. Crack an egg into each cup, season with remaining salt and black pepper and then bake for 10 to 15 minutes until the egg has cooked to the desired level. Serve.

143 – Chorizo Jalapeno Poppers

Serves: 2; Preparation: 10 minutes; Cook time: 15 minutes;
Nutrition facts: 273 Calories; 22 g Fats; 12.9 g Protein; 1.9 g Net Carb; 0.4 g Fiber;
Ingredients

- 4 jalapeno peppers
- 2 oz chorizo
- 2 tbsp grated cheddar cheese
- 4 slices of bacon
- 1/3 tsp salt; 1/8 tsp ground black pepper

How to Prepare:
1. Turn on the oven, then set it to 350 degrees F and let it preheat.
2. Meanwhile, cut each jalapeno in half lengthwise and then remove its seeds and ribs.
3. Take a medium bowl, place chorizo in it, add cheese, salt, and black pepper and stir until mixed.
4. Fill chorizo mixture evenly into peppers, bring together halves, wrap each pepper with a bacon slice and then secure with a toothpick.
5. Place wrapped jalapeno onto a baking tray lined with parchment and then bake for 10 to 15 minutes until peppers have turned tender and bacon has crisp. Serve.

144 – Chorizo and Avocado Cheese Wrap

Serves: 2; Preparation: 10 minutes; Cook time: 10 minutes;
Nutrition facts: 405 Calories; 34.4 g Fats; 18.1 g Protein; 3.9 g Net Carb; 1.2 g Fiber;
Ingredients

- 4 oz grated cheddar cheese
- 2.5 oz chorizo, crumbled; 2 tsp avocado oil
- ¼ of avocado, sliced
- ¼ tsp paprika
- 1/3 tsp salt; 1/8 tsp ground black pepper

How to Prepare:
1. Take a heatproof bowl, place cheese in it, microwave for 15 seconds, stir and microwave for another 10 seconds.
2. Shape the cheese into two balls, place a cheese ball on a parchment sheet, and then cover it with another parchment sheet.
3. Let the cheese cool for 10 seconds, use hands to spread cheese into a circle, and then roll into a thin circle by using a rolling pin.
4. Cut extra parchment sheet around the circle, keep cheese tortilla into the refrigerator and repeat with the other cheese ball.
5. Then prepare chorizo and for this, take a medium skillet pan, place it over medium heat, add oil and when hot, add chorizo, crumble it and cook for 2 minutes until meat begins to brown.
6. Then season it with salt, black pepper, and paprika, stir until mixed and continue cooking for 3 to 4 minutes until cooked.
7. Distribute chorizo evenly on prepared cheese tortilla, top with avocado slices, roll gently, and then serve.

145 – Cheesy Kale and Sausage Patties

Serves: 2; Preparation: 5 minutes; Cook time: 8 minutes;
Nutrition facts: 410 Calories; 35 g Fats; 19.2 g Protein; 1.8 g Net Carb; 1.3 g Fiber;

Ingredients
- 4 oz ground sausage
- ½ bunch of kale, chopped
- ½ tsp garlic powder
- 1 1/2 tbsp avocado oil
- 2 tbsp grated parmesan cheese

Seasoning:
- ¼ tsp salt
- 1/8 tsp ground black pepper

How to Prepare:
1. Take a large skillet pan, place it over medium heat, add ½ tbsp oil and when hot, add kale, sprinkle with garlic powder and cook for 2 minutes until wilted.
2. Transfer kale to a medium bowl, add sausage and cheese, sprinkle with salt and black pepper, mix well and then shape the mixture into four patties.
3. Return skillet pan over medium heat, add oil and when hot, place patties in it, and then cook for 2 to 3 minutes per side until golden brown and cooked.
4. Serve.

146 – Bacon and Cheeseburger Breakfast Quiche

Serves: 2; Preparation: 10 minutes; Cook time: 25 minutes;
Nutrition facts: 470 Calories; 39.7 g Fats; 22 g Protein; 4 g Net Carb; 0.7 g Fiber;
Ingredients
- 2 slices of bacon, chopped
- 4 oz ground sausage, crumbled
- 2 eggs
- 2 tbsp whipping cream
- 2 tbsp grated parmesan cheese

Seasoning:
- 1 green onion, chopped
- ¼ tsp salt
- 1/8 tsp ground black pepper

How to Prepare:
1. Turn on the oven, then set it to 350 degrees F and let it preheat.
2. Meanwhile, take a medium skillet pan, place it over medium heat and when hot, add bacon and cook for 2 to 3 minutes until crisp.
3. Transfer bacon to a plate, add sausage, season with salt and black pepper, stir in green onion and cook for 5 to 7 minutes until cooked.
4. Then take a pie pan, spread three-fourth of the bacon in the bottom of the pan, top with sausage and then sprinkle cheese on top.
5. Take a medium bowl, crack eggs in it, add cream and whisk until blended.
6. Pour egg over meat in the pie pan, sprinkle with remaining bacon and then bake for 15 to 20 minutes until cooked through and the top is nicely golden brown.
7. When done, let quiche cool for 5 minutes, then cut it into slices and serve.

147 – Spiced Bacon Deviled Eggs

Serves: 2; Preparation: 5 minutes; Cook time: 0 minutes;
Nutrition facts: 155.5 Calories; 12.8 g Fats; 8.9 g Protein; 1.1 g Net Carb; 0.1 g Fiber;
Ingredients
- 2 eggs, boiled
- 1 slice of bacon, chopped, cooked
- ¼ tsp cayenne pepper
- ¼ tsp dried rosemary
- 1 tbsp mayonnaise

Seasoning:
- ½ tsp mustard paste

How to Prepare:
1. Peel the boiled eggs, then slice in half lengthwise and transfer egg yolks to a medium bowl by using a spoon.
2. Mash the egg yolk, add remaining ingredients and stir until well combined. Spoon the egg yolk mixture into egg whites, and then serve.

148 – Pork Chops with Thyme

Serves: 2; Preparation: 5 minutes; Cook time: 10 minutes;
Nutrition facts: 363 Calories; 23 g Fats; 34 g Protein; 3 g Net Carb; 2 g Fiber;
Ingredients
- 2 pork chops
- ½ of a lemon, cut into wedges
- 1 tsp dried thyme
- ¾ tbsp unsalted butter, diced

Seasoning:

- 2 ½ tsp coconut oil, divided
- 1 tsp salt
- 1 tsp ground black pepper

How to Prepare:
1. Turn on the oven, then set it to 350 degrees F, and let preheat.
2. Meanwhile, place pork chops on clean working space, brush the exposed side with ¾ tsp oil, then sprinkle with ½ tsp salt, black pepper, and thyme and gently massage into the meat.
3. Take a small skillet pan, place it over high heat, add ½ tbsp oil and when hot, add a pork chop in it, seasoned side down, then drizzle with ¼ tsp olive, sprinkle with 1/8 tsp each of salt, black pepper and thyme and cook for 2 minutes per side until seared.
4. Take a sheet pan, grease it with oil, place seared pork chops on it, add lemon wedges, top with diced butter and bake for 25 minutes or until a meat thermometer inserted into the thickest part of the chop reads 145 degrees F. Serve pork chops with roasted lemon.

149 – Brussels Sprouts with Sausage

Serves: 2; Preparation: 5 minutes; Cook time: 18 minutes
Nutrition facts: 130.5 Calories; 10 g Fats; 6 g Protein; 2.3 g Net Carb; 1.6 g Fiber;
Ingredients
- 2 oz sausage, diced
- 3 oz Brussel sprouts, halved
- 1 tbsp avocado oil
- ¼ cup of water

Seasoning:
- 1/3 tsp salt
- 1/4 tsp ground black pepper

How to Prepare:
1. Take a skillet pan, place it over medium heat, add oil and when hot, add diced sausage and cook for 3 minutes until golden brown.
2. Add sprouts, pour in water, season with salt and black pepper, and cook for 7 to 10 minutes until sprouts are just tender, covering the pan.
3. Then uncover the pan, switch heat to medium-high level and continue cooking for 2 to 3 minutes or until all the liquid in the pan has evaporated and Brussel sprouts are golden brown. Serve.

150 – Pork and Cabbage Stew

Serves: 2; Preparation: 5 minutes; Cook time: 45 minutes;
Nutrition facts: 222 Calories; 16.7 g Fats; 15.4 g Protein; 1.4 g Net Carb; 0.8 g Fiber;
Ingredients
- 4 oz ground pork
- 2 green onions, sliced
- ¾ cup shredded cabbage
- ½ tbsp apple cider vinegar
- 1 1/2 cups water, cold

Seasoning:
- ¼ tsp salt
- 2 tsp avocado oil

How to Prepare:
1. Take a medium pot, place it over medium-high heat, add oil and when hot, add pork and cook for 3 to 4 minutes until golden brown.
2. Switch heat to the low level, add remaining ingredients into the pot, stir until mixed and cook for 30 to 45 minutes until pork and cabbage have cooked; add more water if cooking liquid starts to run out. When done, taste to adjust seasoning and then serve.

151 – Ground Pork Cutlets with Parmesan

Serves: 2; Preparation: 35 minutes; Cook time: 12 minutes;
Nutrition facts: 297 Calories; 22.1 g Fats; 18.5 g Protein; 3.4 g Net Carb; 2.5 g Fiber;
Ingredients
- 3 oz ground pork
- 1 egg
- 2 tbsp coconut flour
- 1/3 tsp salt
- 3 tbsp grated parmesan cheese

Seasoning:
- 1/4 tsp ground black pepper
- 1 tbsp avocado oil

How to Prepare:

1. Take a medium bowl, add pork in it along with salt, black pepper, cheese, and egg and stir until well combined.
2. Shape the mixture into two patties, place them on a plate and refrigerate for 30 minutes.
3. Then take a skillet pan, add oil in it and let it preheat. Dredge patties into coconut flour, add into pan and fry for 3 minutes per side until golden brown and cooked.

152 – Tuscan Meatballs

Serves: 2; Preparation: 5 minutes; Cook time: 10 minutes;
Nutrition facts: 268 Calories; 20 g Fats; 21.5 g Protein; 0.6 g Net Carb; 0.1 g Fiber;
Ingredients
- 2 strips of bacon, chopped
- 4 oz ground pork
- 1 green onion, sliced
- 1 tbsp dried Italian herbs
- 1 egg
Seasoning:
- ½ tsp garlic powder
- 1/3 tsp salt
- 1/8 tsp ground black pepper
- 1 tsp avocado oil
How to Prepare:
1. Take a large bowl, place all the ingredients in it except for oil, stir until combined, and then shape the mixture into balls.
2. Take a large frying pan, place it over medium heat, add oil and when hot, add meatballs and then cook for 3 to 4 minutes per side until golden brown.
3. Serve straight away or with keto marinara sauce and zucchini noodles.

153 – Meat Stuffed Jalapeno Peppers

Serves: 2; Preparation: 5 minutes; Cook time: 15 minutes;
Nutrition facts: 154 Calories; 12 g Fats; 9 g Protein; 1 g Net Carb; 1 g Fiber;
Ingredients
- 2-ounce ground pork
- 2 jalapeno peppers, large
- 1/3 tbsp avocado oil
- 2 tsp cream cheese
Seasoning:
- ¼ tsp salt
- 1/8 tsp ground black pepper
How to Prepare:
1. Turn on the oven, then set it to 350 degrees F and let it preheat.
2. Meanwhile, take a medium skillet pan, place it over medium heat, add oil and when hot, add meat, season with salt and black pepper and then cook for 5 to 7 minutes until cooked.
3. Meanwhile, prepare the peppers and for this, slice peppers into lengthwise and then remove the seeds.
4. When the meat has cooked, spoon it into the pepper, top with cream cheese, and then bake for 5 minutes until thoroughly cooked and the top is golden brown.

154 – Caprese Meatballs

Serves: 2; Preparation: 5 minutes; Cook time: 10 minutes;
Nutrition facts: 220.5 Calories; 17.4 g Fats; 15 g Protein; 0.6 g Net Carb; 0.5 g Fiber;
Ingredients
- 1 tbsp almond flour
- 3 oz ground turkey
- 2 tsp diced tomato
- 1 egg white
- 2 tsp grated mozzarella cheese
Seasoning:
- ¼ tsp garlic powder
- ¼ tsp salt
- ¼ tsp dried basil
- 1 tbsp avocado oil

How to Prepare:
1. Take a medium bowl, place all the ingredients in it except for oil, stir until combined, and then shape the mixture into meatballs.
2. Take a frying pan, place it over medium heat, add oil and when hot, add meatballs and cook for 2 minutes per side until browned and cooked. Serve.

155 – Mushroom and Sausage Patties

Serves: 2; Preparation: 5 minutes; Cook time: 10 minutes;
Nutrition facts: 210 Calories; 18.7 g Fats; 6.5 g Protein; 0.8 g Net Carb; 0.8 g Fiber;
Ingredients
- 4 oz ground sausage, crumbled
- 3 oz mushrooms, chopped
- ½ bunch of kale, chopped
- ¼ tsp fennel seeds
- 1 tbsp coconut oil
Seasoning:
- ¼ tsp salt
- ¼ tsp garlic powder
How to Prepare:
1. Take a medium skillet pan, place it over medium heat, add oil and when it melts, add kale and mushroom, sprinkle with garlic powder and cook for 3 to 5 minutes until done.
2. Transfer kale and mushroom mixture into a bowl, add meat, season with salt, add fennel seeds and stir until well combined.
3. Shape the mixture into patties, then place them into the skillet pan and cook for 3 minutes per side until cooked through and golden. Serve.

156 – Pork Rubbed with Cocoa

Serves: 2; Preparation: 5 minutes; Cook time: 10 minutes;
Nutrition facts: 355 Calories; 27.4 g Fats; 25.5 g Protein; 0.9 g Net Carb; 0 g Fiber;
Ingredients
- 2 pork chops
- ½ tsp ground coriander
- ½ tsp ground nutmeg
- 2 tbsp cocoa powder, unsweetened
- 2 tbsp avocado oil
Seasoning:
- 2/3 tsp salt
- 1/2 tsp ground black pepper
How to Prepare:
1. Turn on the oven, then set it to 400 degrees F and let it preheat.
2. Take a small bowl, add cocoa and all the spices, stir until mixed, and then sprinkle on all sides of pork chops until coated.
3. Take a medium skillet pan, place it over medium heat, add oil and when hot, add pork chops and cook for 2 minutes per side until seared.
4. Transfer the pan containing pork chops into the oven and then bake for 10 minutes until thoroughly cooked. Serve.

157 – Butter Mushroom Pork Chops

Serves: 2; Preparation: 5 minutes; Cook time: 10 minutes;
Nutrition facts: 570 Calories; 45 g Fats; 36 g Protein; 3 g Net Carb; 1 g Fiber;
Ingredients
- 2 pork chops
- 2 oz sliced mushrooms
- 1 tbsp avocado oil
- 3 tbsp butter, unsalted
- ¼ cup of water
Seasoning:
- 3/4 tsp salt
- 1/2 tsp ground black pepper
- ¼ tsp paprika
How to Prepare:
1. Take a medium skillet pan, place it over medium heat, add oil and wait until it gets hot.

2. Season pork chops with ½ tsp salt and ¼ tsp black pepper, add them to the pan and cook for 3 minutes per side until brown.
3. Transfer pork chops to a plate, set aside until required, then add 2 tbsp butter into the pan and when it melts, add mushrooms, season with paprika and remaining salt and black pepper.
4. Cook for 3 minutes until sauté, pour in water, stir well, then add remaining butter and when it melts, return pork chops into the pan and simmer for 3 minutes until cooked. Serve.

158 – Pesto Smothered Pork Chops

Serves: 2; Preparation: 5 minutes; Cook time: 12 minutes;
Nutrition facts: 329 Calories; 23.3 g Fats; 26.2 g Protein; 2 g Net Carb; 1.3 g Fiber;
Ingredients
- 2 pork chops
- 1 tbsp almond flour
- 1 tbsp avocado oil
- 2 tbsp basil pesto
Seasoning:
- 1/3 tsp salt
- 1/4 tsp ground black pepper
How to Prepare:
1. Take a shallow dish, place flour in it stir in salt and black pepper, and then dredge pork chops in the mixture until coated.
2. Take a medium skillet pan, place it over medium heat, add oil and when hot, place pork chops in it and cook for 3 minutes per side until golden brown.
3. Then spread pesto on top of each pork chop, shut with lid, and cook for 4 minutes until pork chops have thoroughly cooked. Serve.

159 – Garlic and Lime Marinated Pork Chops

Serves: 2; Preparation: 20 minutes; Cook time: 10 minutes;
Nutrition facts: 180 Calories; 8 g Fats; 24.3 g Protein; 1.3 g Net Carb; 0.5 g Fiber;
Ingredients
- 2 pork chops
- 1 tsp minced garlic
- ¼ tsp cumin
- 1/3 tsp paprika
- ½ of lime, juiced, zested
Seasoning:
- ¼ tsp salt
- 1/8 tsp ground black pepper
- 1/3 tsp red chili powder
How to Prepare:
1. Take a shallow dish, place all the ingredients in it except for pork and then stir until combined.
2. Add pork chops, toss until coated and marinate for 15 minutes in the refrigerator.
3. Then take a griddle pan, place it over medium-high heat, spray with oil and when hot, place marinated pork chops in it and grill for 4 to 5 minutes per side until thoroughly cooked. Serve.

160 – Sausage Tortilla Wrap

Serves: 2; Preparation: 10 minutes; Cook time: 15 minutes;
Nutrition facts: 240 Calories; 21.3 g Fats; 9.5 g Protein; 0.5 g Net Carb; 1.3 g Fiber;
Ingredients
- 3 oz grated cauliflower
- 1 egg
- 2 oz sausage, crumbled
- 1 tbsp avocado oil
Seasoning:
- ¼ tsp dried oregano
- ½ tsp paprika
- ½ tsp salt
- 1/4 tsp ground black pepper
How to Prepare:
1. Turn on the oven, then set it to 375 degrees F and let it preheat.
2. Prepare sausage and spinach and for this, take a medium skillet pan, add oil in it and when hot, add sausage and cook for 2 minutes until it begins to golden brown.
3. Season with ¼ tsp paprika, ¼ tsp salt and 1/8 tsp black pepper, and continue cooking for 3 to 4 minutes until sausage has cooked through, set aside until required.

4. Prepare the wraps and for this, place grated cauliflower in a heatproof bowl, cover with plastic wrap, and then microwave for 2 to 3 minutes until tender.
5. Drain the cauliflower, squeeze moisture as much as possible by wrapping cauliflower in a cheesecloth, then place it in a bowl, add oregano, remaining paprika, salt, and black pepper, and egg and stir until well combined.
6. Divide the mixture into two portions, shape each portion into a ball, place it on a baking sheet lined with parchment and spread into a circle.
7. Bake cauliflower circles for 4 minutes per side until cooked and then remove from oven.
8. Top each cauliflower tortilla with sausage mixture and then serve.

161 – Ham and Cheese Rolls

Serves: 2; Preparation: 5 minutes; Cook time: 10 minutes;
Nutrition facts: 198 Calories; 13 g Fats; 17 g Protein; 3 g Net Carb; 0 g Fiber;
Ingredients
- 3 oz shredded mozzarella cheese
- 3 oz shredded parmesan cheese
- 2 oz diced ham
- 1 egg
Seasoning:
- ¼ tsp salt
- 1/8 tsp ground black pepper
How to Prepare:
1. Turn on the oven, then set it to 375 degrees F and let it preheat.
2. Meanwhile, take a medium bowl, place all the ingredients in it and stir until well combined.
3. Take a baking sheet, line it with parchment sheet, scoop the mixture onto the baking sheet, spread evenly into circles and then bake for 7 to 10 minutes until cheese has melted and crust has turned slightly golden brown. Serve.

162 – Ham and Cheese Burrito

Serves: 2; Preparation: 10 minutes; Cook time: 12 minutes;
Nutrition facts: 407 Calories; 31 g Fats; 26 g Protein; 2 g Net Carb; 0 g Fiber;
Ingredients
- 2 slices of ham
- 1 green onion, sliced
- 1 tbsp butter, unsalted
- 4 eggs
- 2 tbsp shredded parmesan cheese
- 3 oz shredded mozzarella cheese
Seasoning:
- ¼ tsp salt
How to Prepare:
1. Prepare burrito wrap and for this, crack eggs in a medium bowl, add parmesan cheese and salt and whisk until well combined.
2. Take a medium skillet pan, place it over medium-high heat, add ½ tbsp butter and when it melts, pour in half of the egg mixture and cook for 2 minutes until egg begin to set.
3. Place one ham slice in the center of egg, top with half of green onion and mozzarella cheese, cover with lid and cook for 2 to 3 minutes until cheese has melted and egg wrap has thoroughly cooked.
4. When done, slide wrap to a plate, let it cool for 3 minutes and then roll it like a burrito.
5. Make another burrito in the same manner and then serve.

163 – Cauliflower Tortilla with Sausage and Vegetables

Serves: 2; Preparation: 10 minutes; Cook time: 15 minutes;
Nutrition facts: 212 Calories; 17.5 g Fats; 10.5 g Protein; 1 g Net Carb; 1.6 g Fiber;
Ingredients
- 3 oz grated cauliflower
- 1 egg
- 2 oz sausage, crumbled
- 2 oz spinach
- 1 tbsp avocado oil
Seasoning:
- 1/8 tsp dried oregano
- ¼ tsp paprika
- 1/2 tsp salt

- 1/4 tsp ground black pepper

How to Prepare:
1. Turn on the oven, then set it to 375 degrees F and let it preheat.
2. Prepare the wraps and for this, place grated cauliflower in a heatproof bowl, cover with plastic wrap, and then microwave for 2 to 3 minutes until tender.
3. Drain the cauliflower, squeeze moisture as much as possible by wrapping cauliflower in a cheesecloth, then place it in a bowl, add oregano, 1/8 tsp paprika, ¼ tsp salt, and 1/8 tsp black pepper, and egg and stir until well combined.
4. Divide the mixture into two portions, shape each portion into a ball, place it on a baking sheet lined with parchment and spread into a circle.
5. Bake cauliflower circles for 4 minutes per side until cooked and then remove from oven.
6. While tortilla baked, prepare the sausage and for this, take a medium skillet pan, add oil and when hot, add sausage and cook for 3 minutes until nicely golden brown.
7. Add spinach and remaining ingredients, stir until mixed, and then cook for 3 to 5 minutes until spinach leaves have wilted and sausage have thoroughly cooked.
8. Top each cauliflower tortilla with the sausage-spinach mixture and then serve.

164 – Sausage with Zucchini Noodles

Serves: 2; Preparation: 5 minutes; Cook time: 12 minutes;
Nutrition facts: 320 Calories; 27.6 g Fats; 8.6 g Protein; 5.2 g Net Carb; 2.7 g Fiber;
Ingredients
- 1 large zucchini, spiralized into noodles
- 3 oz sausage
- ½ tsp garlic powder
- 4 oz marinara sauce
- 2 tsp grated parmesan cheese

Seasoning:
- 1/3 tsp salt
- 1/8 tsp dried basil
- ¼ tsp Italian seasoning
- 1 tbsp avocado oil

How to Prepare:
1. Take a skillet pan, place it over medium heat and when hot, add sausage, crumble it and cook for 5 minutes until nicely browned.
2. When done, transfer sausage to a bowl, drain the grease, add oil and when hot, add zucchini noodles, sprinkle with garlic, toss until mixed and cook for 3 minutes until zucchini begins to tender.
3. Add marinara sauce, return sausage into the pan, toss until mixed, add salt, basil and Italian seasoning, stir until mixed and cook for 2 to 3 minutes until hot.
4. When done, distribute marinara noodles between two plates, sprinkle with cheese and then serve.

165 – Scotch Eggs

Serves: 2; Preparation: 10 minutes; Cook time: 15 minutes;
Nutrition facts: 296 Calories; 24.8 g Fats; 15.2 g Protein; 1.5 g Net Carb; 0 g Fiber;
Ingredients
- 3 oz sausage, crumbled
- 2 eggs, boiled
- 1/3 tsp salt
- ½ tsp ground mustard
- 2 tbsp grated parmesan cheese

Seasoning:
- ¼ tsp ground black pepper

How to Prepare:
1. Turn on the oven, then set it to 370 degrees F and let it preheat.
2. Meanwhile, take a medium bowl, place sausage in it, add salt, black pepper, and mustard, stir until mixed, make two balls of the sausage mixture and then flatten it slightly into a patty.
3. Working on one egg at a time, peel an egg, place it in the center of a patty and spread sausage around it in even thickness until the egg is covered completely.
4. Repeat with the remaining egg and then roll eggs in the grated parmesan until well coated.
5. Place eggs in a baking sheet and then bake for 10 to 15 minutes until sausage has cooked and cheese has turned nicely browned, turning halfway.
6. Serve.

166 – Jalapeno Stuffed Meatballs with Bacon

Serves: 2; Preparation: 10 minutes; Cook time: 15 minutes;
Nutrition facts: 401 Calories; 34.5 g Fats; 15.7 g Protein; 3.7 g Net Carb; 1.3 g Fiber;

Ingredients
- 2 jalapeno pepper
- 2 slices of bacon
- 4 oz sausage, crumbled
- 1 tbsp grated parmesan cheese
- 3 tbsp cream cheese, softened

Seasoning:
- ¼ tsp garlic powder
- 1/8 tsp ground black pepper
- ¼ tsp salt

How to Prepare:
1. Turn on the oven, then set it to 350 degrees F and let it preheat.
2. Take a medium bowl, add the sausage in it along with cheese, garlic powder, salt, and black pepper, stir until well combined, shape the mixture into two balls and then press lightly to flatten each ball.
3. Prepare the peppers and for this, cut each jalapeno pepper in half, remove the seeds, then stuff with cream cheese and press the pepper halves back together.
4. Working on one pepper at a time, place it in the center of a patty, spread sausage around it in even thickness until pepper is covered completely, and then cover with a slice of bacon.
5. Repeat with the remaining pepper, place them in a baking sheet and then bake for 10 to 15 minutes until sausage has cooked and nicely browned, turning halfway.

167 – Sausage and Cheese Wrap

Serves: 2; Preparation: 10 minutes; Cook time: 10 minutes;
Nutrition facts: 461 Calories; 38.9 g Fats; 22 g Protein; 5.8 g Net Carb; 0 g Fiber;
Ingredients
- 2.5 oz grated parmesan cheese
- 1.5 oz grated cheddar cheese
- 2.5 oz sausage, crumbled
- 2 tsp avocado oil

Seasoning:
- 1/3 tsp salt
- 1/8 tsp ground black pepper
- ¼ tsp paprika

How to Prepare:
1. Take a heatproof bowl, place cheese in it, microwave for 15 seconds, stir and microwave for another 10 seconds.
2. Shape the cheese into two balls, place a cheese ball on a parchment sheet, and then cover it with another parchment sheet.
3. Let the cheese cool for 10 seconds, use hands to spread cheese into a circle, and then roll into a thin circle by using a rolling pin.
4. Cut extra parchment sheet around the circle, keep cheese tortilla into the refrigerator and repeat with the other cheese ball.
5. Then prepare sausage and for this, take a medium skillet pan, place it over medium heat, add oil and when hot, add sausage, crumble it and cook for 2 minutes until meat begin to brown. Then season it with salt, black pepper and paprika, stir until mixed and continue cooking for 3 to 4 minutes until cooked.
6. Distribute sausage evenly on prepared cheese tortilla, roll gently and then serve.

168 – Cauliflower Tortilla with Sausage

Serves: 2; Preparation: 10 minutes; Cook time: 15 minutes;
Nutrition facts: 255 Calories; 22 g Fats; 10.5 g Protein; 1.1 g Net Carb; 1.4 g Fiber;
Ingredients
- 4 oz grated cauliflower
- 1 egg
- 2.5 oz sausage, crumbled
- ¼ tsp dried oregano
- 2 tsp avocado oil

Seasoning:
- 2/3 tsp salt
- ¼ tsp ground black pepper
- ¾ tsp paprika

How to Prepare:
1. Turn on the oven, then set it to 375 degrees F and let it preheat.
2. Meanwhile, place grated cauliflower in a heatproof bowl, cover with a plastic wrap and then microwave for 2 to 3 minutes until steamed.
3. Drain the cauliflower, squeeze out moisture as much as possible by wrapping it in a cheesecloth and then place in a bowl.
4. Add egg, oregano, half of each salt, black pepper and paprika, stir until well mixed and then shape the mixture into two balls.
5. Take a baking sheet, line it with parchment sheet, place cauliflower balls in it and then spread each ball into tortilla shaped circle.
6. Place baking sheet into the oven and then bake the cauliflower tortilla for 7 minutes per side until thoroughly cooked.
7. Meanwhile, prepare sausage and for this, take a medium skillet pan, place it over medium heat, add oil and when hot, add sausage, crumble it and cook for 2 minutes until meat begin to brown. Then season it with remaining salt, black pepper and paprika, stir until mixed and continue cooking for 3 to 4 minutes until cooked.
8. Distribute sausage evenly on prepared cauliflower tortilla, roll gently and then serve.

169 – Sesame and Chorizo Cauliflower Rice

Serves: 2; Preparation: 5 minutes; Cook time: 12 minutes;
Nutrition facts: 229 Calories; 20.5 g Fats; 6.2 g Protein; 1.4 g Net Carb; 2 g Fiber;
Ingredients
- 8 oz grated cauliflower
- 2 oz chorizo
- 1/3 tsp ginger powder
- 1/3 tsp garlic powder
- 1 tbsp sesame oil

Seasoning:
- 1/3 tsp salt
- ¼ tsp ground black pepper
- 1 tbsp avocado oil

How to Prepare:
1. Take a medium skillet pan, place it over medium heat, add avocado oil and when hot, add chorizo and cook for 3 to 5 minutes until thoroughly cooked.
2. Transfer chorizo to a plate, wipe clean the pan, return it over medium heat, add sesame oil and when hot, add grated cauliflower and cook 3 minutes until almost cooked. Return chorizo into the pan, season with salt and black pepper, toss until mixed, and then continue cooking for 2 to 3 minutes until thoroughly cooked.
3. Distribute chorizo cauliflower rice between two plates, top with sesame seeds, and then serve.

170 – Chorizo with Herbs

Serves: 2; Preparation: 5 minutes; Cook time: 8 minutes;
Nutrition facts: 233 Calories; 18.3 g Fats; 13.2 g Protein; 2.7 g Net Carb; 0.2 g Fiber;
Ingredients
- 4.5 oz chorizo
- 1 tsp chopped basil
- 1 tsp chopped cilantro
- 2 tsp cream cheese
- 2 oz sour cream

Seasoning:
- 1 tbsp butter, unsalted
- ¼ tsp salt
- 1/8 tsp ground black pepper
- 1/3 tbsp Worcestershire sauce
- 1 tbsp chicken broth

How to Prepare:
1. Take a medium skillet pan, place it over medium heat, add butter and when it melts, add chorizo and cook for 4 to 5 minutes until thoroughly cooked.
2. Add remaining ingredients, stir until well mixed and then cook for 2 minutes until cooked. Serve.

171 – Spinach Meatloaf

Serves: 2; Preparation: 10 minutes; Cook time: 15 minutes;
Nutrition facts: 430 Calories; 30 g Fats; 30 g Protein; 4 g Net Carb; 3 g Fiber;
Ingredients
- 4 oz sausage
- 5 oz spinach, chopped
- 1 tsp garlic powder
- 2 eggs
- 3 tbsp coconut milk, unsweetened

Seasoning:
- 1/3 tsp salt
- ¼ tsp ground black pepper
- 1 tbsp Italian seasoning
- 2 tsp avocado oil

How to Prepare:

1. Turn on the oven, then set it to 400 degrees F and let it preheat.
2. Meanwhile, take a skillet pan, place it over medium heat, add oil and when hot, add sausage, sprinkle with garlic powder and cook for 4 to 5 minutes until thoroughly cooked.
3. Add spinach, stir well and then continue cooking for 2 minutes until sauté.
4. Meanwhile, crack eggs in a medium bowl, add salt, black pepper, Italian seasoning, and milk, whisk until blended, add sausage mixture and then stir until incorporated.
5. Take two ramekins, divide sausage mixture between them and then bake for 10 minutes until thoroughly cooked and firm.
6. When done, let meatloaf cool for 5 minutes, then cut it into slices and serve.

172 – Creamy Taco Soup

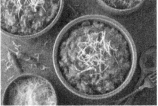

Serves: 2; Preparation: 5 minutes; Cook time: 12 minutes;
Nutrition facts: 375 Calories; 34.6 g Fats; 11.1 g Protein; 2.4 g Net Carb; 1.4 g Fiber;
Ingredients
- 4 oz sausage
- 1 green onion, sliced
- 1 tbsp chopped tomato
- 2 tbsp whipping cream
- 2 tbsp sour cream

Seasoning:
- ¼ tsp salt
- ½ tsp garlic powder
- ½ tsp red chili powder
- 4 oz of chicken bone broth
- ¼ of avocado, sliced

How to Prepare:
1. Take a medium saucepan, place it over medium heat and when hot, add sausage and onion, sprinkle with garlic powder and cook for 3 to 5 minutes until nicely browned.
2. Then season with all the spices, cook for another minute, add tomato, whipping cream and sour cream, and stir until well mixed.
3. Pour in broth, add water if needed, stir well and simmer the soup for 5 to 7 minutes until thoroughly cooked.
4. Ladle soup into two bowls, top with avocado and then serve.

173 – Chorizo Meatballs with Cauliflower Tortilla

Serves: 2; Preparation: 10 minutes; Cook time: 15 minutes;
Nutrition facts: 293 Calories; 23 g Fats; 13.8 g Protein; 4.5 g Net Carb; 2.8 g Fiber;
Ingredients
- 6 oz grated cauliflower
- 4 oz chorizo, crumbled
- 1 egg
- 3 oz marinara sauce
- 2 tsp avocado oil

Seasoning:
- 2/3 tsp salt
- ½ tsp ground black pepper
- ½ tsp paprika
- ½ tsp dried oregano

How to Prepare:
1. Turn on the oven, then set it to 375 degrees F and let it preheat.
2. Place grated cauliflower in a heatproof bowl, cover with a plastic wrap and microwave for 2 to 3 minutes until steamed.
3. Then drain cauliflower, wrap into cheesecloth and twist well to squeeze moisture as much as possible and place in a medium bowl.
4. Add eggs, stir in 1/3 tsp salt, ¼ tsp black pepper, oregano, and paprika until well combined and then shape the mixture into two balls.
5. Take a baking sheet, line it with parchment sheet, place balls on it, spread it to make tortilla circles, and then bake for 4 to 5 minutes side until golden brown and cooked.
6. Meanwhile, prepare the meatballs and for this, take a medium bowl, place chorizo in it, add remaining salt and black pepper, stir until mixed, and then shape the mixture into mini meatballs.
7. Take a medium skillet pan, place it over medium heat, add oil and when hot, add meatballs and cook for 3 to 4 minutes per side until cooked and nicely browned.
8. Transfer meatballs to a plate, add the marinara sauce into the pan, and then cook for 2 minutes until hot.
9. Add meatballs, toss until coated, cook for 1 minute and then remove the pan from heat. Divide meatballs between tortillas, then spoon with marinara sauce and serve.

174 – Bacon, Burger and Cabbage Stir Fry

Serves: 2; Preparation: 5 minutes; Cook time: 10 minutes;
Nutrition facts: 357 Calories; 22 g Fats; 32 g Protein; 4.5 g Net Carb; 2.4 g Fiber;
Ingredients
- 4 oz of chopped cabbage
- 2 slices of bacon, chopped
- 6 oz sausage, crumbled
- 1 green onion, chopped
- 1/3 tsp garlic powder

Seasoning:
- ¼ tsp salt
- 1/8 tsp ground black pepper
- 1 tbsp avocado oil

How to Prepare:
1. Take a medium skillet pan, add oil and when hot, add sausage and bacon and cook for 5 to 7 minutes until browned.
2. Transfer meat and bacon to a bowl, add green onion, sprinkle with garlic powder and cook for 2 minutes until sauté.
3. Add cabbage, fry for 2 minutes until tender-crisp, return sausage and bacon into the pan and then stir until combined.
4. Season cabbage with salt and black pepper, remove the pan from heat and then serve

175 – Cheesy Cabbage and Sausage Skillet

Serves: 2; Preparation: 5 minutes; Cook time: 15 minutes;
Nutrition facts: 377 Calories; 28.7 g Fats; 21.7 g Protein; 7.3 g Net Carb; 2.3 g Fiber;
Ingredients
- 1 cup chopped cabbage
- 4 oz sausage
- 1-ounce grape tomato, diced
- 1.5-ounce grated cheddar cheese
- 1.5-ounce grated parmesan cheese

Seasoning:
- 1 green onion, chopped
- ½ tsp garlic powder
- ¼ tsp salt
- 2 tbsp butter, unsalted

How to Prepare:
1. Turn on the oven, then set it to 400 degrees F and let it preheat.
2. Meanwhile, take a medium skillet pan, place it over medium heat, add butter and when it melts, add sausage, stir until mixed and cook for 3 to 4 minutes until nicely browned. Add onion and cabbage, sprinkle with garlic and salt, stir until mixed and cook for 5 minutes until the cabbage has turned soft.
3. Add tomatoes, stir until mixed, sprinkle cheeses on top, and then bake for 5 minutes until cheese bubbles and slightly brown. Serve.

176 – Sausage and Cream Cheese Balls

Serves: 2; Preparation: 10 minutes; Cook time: 10 minutes;
Nutrition facts: 320 Calories; 26 g Fats; 11.9 g Protein; 4.5 g Net Carb; 4.2 g Fiber;
Ingredients
- 3 oz sausage
- 3 tbsp coconut flour
- 5 tbsp grated cheddar cheese
- 1-ounce cream cheese
- 3 tbsp marinara sauce

Seasoning:
- 1/3 tsp garlic powder
- 1/3 tsp baking powder
- ¼ tsp salt
- 1/8 tsp ground black pepper
- 1/3 tsp Italian seasoning

How to Prepare:
1. Turn on the oven, then set it to 350 degrees F and let it preheat.
2. Meanwhile, take a shallow dish, place flour in it, add cheese, baking powder, and Italian seasoning and stir until mixed.
3. Add sausage, garlic powder, salt, and black pepper and cream cheese and stir until combined; don't overmix.

4. Shape the mixture into 1-inch balls, then place them on a baking sheet lined with parchment paper, spray with avocado oil and bake for 10 minutes until thoroughly cooked, turning halfway. When done, transfer balls to a dish, drizzle with marinara sauce, and then serve.

177 – Cheese, Olives and Sausage Casserole

Serves: 2; Preparation: 10 minutes; Cook time: 15 minutes;
Nutrition facts: 351 Calories; 30.6 g Fats; 15.7 g Protein; 1.7 g Net Carb; 0.9 g Fiber;
Ingredients
- 3 oz sausage
- 1.5 oz green olives, sliced
- 2 eggs
- 4 oz coconut milk, unsweetened
- 3 tbsp grated cheddar cheese

Seasoning:
- ¼ tsp ground black pepper
- 1/3 tsp salt
- 1/3 tsp mustard powder

How to Prepare:
1. Take a medium skillet pan, place it over medium heat and when hot, add sausage, crumble it and cook for 5 minutes until cooked.
2. Meanwhile, crack eggs in a medium bowl, add milk, salt, black pepper, and mustard and whisk until blended.
3. When sausage had cooked, add sausage mixture into the eggs, add onion and olives, 2 tbsp cheese, and then stir until mixed.
4. Then spoon the mixture into a casserole dish, cover with a lid and let it refrigerate for 1 hour until chilled.
5. When ready to bake, Turn on the oven, then set it to 350 degrees F and let it preheat.
6. Sprinkle cheese on the top casserole and then bake it for 10 minutes until cheese has melted. Serve.

178 – Curried Ground Sausage

Serves: 2; Preparation: 5 minutes; Cook time: 15 minutes;
Nutrition facts: 435 Calories; 42 g Fats; 12 g Protein; 1.4 g Net Carb; 0.8 g Fiber;
Ingredients
- 5 oz sausage, crumbled
- 1 green onion, sliced
- 2 oz spinach
- 1-ounce chicken bone broth
- 1-ounce whipping cream

Seasoning:
- 1 tbsp avocado oil
- ½ tsp garlic powder
- 1 tbsp curry powder
- ¼ cup of water

How to Prepare:
1. Take a medium saucepan, place it over medium heat, add ½ tbsp oil and when hot, add ground sausage and cook for 4 to 5 minutes until cooked.
2. When done, transfer sausage to a bowl, add remaining oil and when hot, add green onion, sprinkle with garlic powder and cook for 2 minutes until sauté.
3. Sprinkle with curry powder, continue cooking for 30 seconds until fragrant, pour in chicken broth and water, add sausage and spinach, stir until mixed and simmer for 5 minutes until thickened slightly. Taste to adjust seasoning, stir in cream and then remove the pan from heat. Serve.

179 – Portobello Mushrooms with Sausage and Cheese

Serves: 2; Preparation: 10 minutes; Cook time: 20 minutes;
Nutrition facts: 310 Calories; 26 g Fats; 10.7 g Protein; 6.6 g Net Carb; 1.1 g Fiber;
Ingredients
- 2 Portobello mushroom caps
- 2 oz sausage
- 1 tbsp melted butter, unsalted
- 2 tbsp grated parmesan cheese

Seasoning:
- 1/8 tsp garlic powder
- 1/8 tsp red chili powder
- ¼ tsp salt

- 2 tsp avocado oil

How to Prepare:
1. Turn on the oven, then set it to 425 degrees F and let it preheat.
2. Meanwhile, remove the stems from mushroom caps, chop them and then brush the caps with butter inside-out.
3. Take a frying pan, place it over medium heat, add oil and when hot, add sausage, crumble it, sprinkle with garlic powder and then cook for 5 minutes until cooked.
4. Stir in mushroom stems, season with salt and black pepper, continue cooking for 3 minutes until cooked and then remove the pan from heat.
5. Distribute sausage-mushroom mixture into mushroom caps, sprinkle cheese, and red chili powder on top and then bake for 10 to 12 minutes until mushroom caps have turned tender and cooked. Serve.

180 – Sausage and Cauliflower Rice

Serves: 2; Preparation: 5 minutes; Cook time: 15 minutes;
Nutrition facts: 333 Calories; 31.3 g Fats; 9.1 g Protein; 0.8 g Net Carb; 2.5 g Fiber;
Ingredients
- 7 oz grated cauliflower
- 3 oz sausage
- 1 green onion, sliced
- ½ tsp garlic powder
- 2 tbsp avocado oil

Seasoning:
- 1/3 tsp salt
- ¼ tsp ground black pepper
- 6 tbsp water

How to Prepare:
1. Take a medium skillet pan, place it over medium heat, add 1 tbsp oil and when hot, add sausage and cook for 4 to 5 minutes until nicely browned.
2. Switch heat to medium-low level, pour in 4 tbsp water and then simmer for 5 to 7 minutes until sausage has thoroughly cooked.
3. Transfer sausage to a bowl, wipe clean the pan, then return it over medium heat, add oil and when hot, add cauliflower rice and green onion, sprinkle with garlic powder, salt, and black pepper.
4. Stir until mixed, drizzle with 2 tbsp water, and cook for 5 minutes until softened. Add sausage, stir until mixed, cook for 1 minute until hot and then serve.

181 – Cheesy Sausage and Egg Bake

Serves: 2; Preparation: 5 minutes; Cook time: 18 minutes;
Nutrition facts: 439 Calories; 38.9 g Fats; 19.7 g Protein; 2.2 g Net Carb; 0 g Fiber;
Ingredients
- 4 oz sausage
- 1 egg
- 2 tbsp grated cheddar cheese
- 1 ½ tbsp grated mozzarella cheese
- 1 ½ tbsp grated parmesan cheese

Seasoning:
- ¼ tsp salt
- 1/8 tsp ground black pepper
- 2 tsp avocado oil

How to Prepare:
1. Turn on the oven, then set it to 375 degrees F and let it preheat.
2. Meanwhile, take a medium skillet pan, place it over medium heat, add oil and when hot, add sausage and cook for 5 minutes until cooked.
3. Meanwhile, crack the egg in a medium bowl, add salt, black pepper, and cheeses, reserving 1 tbsp cheddar cheese and whisk until mixed.
4. When the sausage has cooked, transfer it to the bowl containing egg batter and stir until combined.
5. Take a baking pan, grease it with oil, pour in sausage mixture, sprinkle remaining cheddar cheese in the top, and then bake for 10 to 12 minutes until cooked.
6. When done, let sausage cool for 5 minutes, then cut it into squares and then serve.

182 – Sausage and Marinara Casserole

Serves: 2; Preparation: 5 minutes; Cook time: 12 minutes;

Nutrition facts: 485 Calories; 44.4 g Fats; 15.6 g Protein; 3.7 g Net Carb; 1.1 g Fiber;
Ingredients
- 2 oz chorizo
- 4 oz sausage
- 1 tbsp avocado oil
- 4 oz marinara sauce
- 2 tbsp grated cheddar cheese

Seasoning:
- ¼ tsp salt
- 1/8 tsp ground black pepper
- ¼ tsp dried thyme

How to Prepare:
1. Take a medium skillet pan, place it over medium heat, add oil and when hot, add chorizo and sausage and cook for 4 to 5 minutes until meat is no longer pink.
2. Add the marinara sauce into the pan, stir in salt, black pepper, and thyme, cook for 1 minute until hot and then transfer meat mixture into a casserole dish.
3. Sprinkle cheese over the top of casserole and then bake for 7 minutes until thoroughly cooked. Serve.

183 – Double Cheese Meatloaf

Serves: 2; Preparation: 10 minutes; Cook time: 20 minutes;
Nutrition facts: 578 Calories; 50.6 g Fats; 27.4 g Protein; 2.6 g Net Carb; 0.3 g Fiber;
Ingredients
- 2 slices of bacon, chopped, cooked
- 6 oz of sausage
- 2 tbsp grated mozzarella cheese
- 2 tbsp grated cheddar cheese

Seasoning:
- 1/3 tsp salt
- 1/4 tsp ground black pepper
- 1 tsp dried parsley
- 2 tbsp marinara sauce
- 1 egg

How to Prepare:
1. Turn on the oven, then set it to 375 degrees F and let it preheat.
2. Meanwhile, take a medium bowl, place all the ingredients in it except for marinara and stir until well combined.
3. Spoon the mixture into a mini loaf pan, top with marinara, and then bake for 20 to 25 minutes until cooked through and done.
4. When done, let meatloaf cool for 5 minutes, then cut it into slices and then serve.

184 – Spinach Sausage Ball Pasta

Serves: 2; Preparation: 10 minutes; Cook time: 12 minutes;
Nutrition facts: 505 Calories; 41.6 g Fats; 18.7 g Protein; 6.5 g Net Carb; 6 g Fiber;
Ingredients
- 1 pound cabbage, shredded
- 4 oz sausage
- 2 oz spinach, chopped
- 2 tbsp grated parmesan cheese
- 2 tbsp marinara sauce

Seasoning:
- 1/3 tsp salt
- ¼ tsp ground black pepper
- 2 tbsp avocado oil

How to Prepare:
1. Take a medium bowl, place sausage in it, add spinach and cheese in it, season with 1/3 tsp salt and black pepper, stir until well combined, and then shape the mixture into balls.
2. Take a medium skillet pan, place it over medium heat, add 1 tbsp oil and when hot, add meatballs and cook for 3 to 4 minutes per side until cooked and nicely golden brown.
3. When transfer meatballs to a plate, add remaining oil into the pan and, when hot, add cabbage and then cook for 3 minutes until tender-crisp.
4. Return meatballs into the pan, add marinara sauce, toss until well mixed and cook for 1 minute until hot. Serve.

Beef

185 – Beef with Cabbage Noodles

Serves: 2; Preparation: 5 minutes; Cook time: 18 minutes
Nutrition facts: 188.5 Calories; 12.5 g Fats; 15.5 g Protein; 2.5 g Net Carb; 1 g Fiber;
Ingredients
- 4 oz ground beef
- 1 cup chopped cabbage
- 4 oz tomato sauce
- ½ tsp minced garlic
- ½ cup of water

Seasoning:
- ½ tbsp coconut oil
- ½ tsp salt
- ¼ tsp Italian seasoning
- 1/8 tsp dried basil

How to Prepare:
1. Take a skillet pan, place it over medium heat, add oil and when hot, add beef and cook for 5 minutes until nicely browned.
2. Meanwhile, prepare the cabbage and for it, slice the cabbage into thin shred.
3. When the beef has cooked, add garlic, season with salt, basil, and Italian seasoning, stir well and continue cooking for 3 minutes until beef has thoroughly cooked.
4. Pour in tomato sauce and water, stir well and bring the mixture to boil.
5. Then reduce heat to medium-low level, add cabbage, stir well until well mixed and simmer for 3 to 5 minutes until cabbage is softened, covering the pan.
6. Uncover the pan and continue simmering the beef until most of the cooking liquid has evaporated. Serve.

186 – Roast Beef and Mozzarella Plate

Serves: 2; Preparation: 5 minutes; Cook time: 0 minutes;
Nutrition facts: 267.7 Calories; 24.5 g Fats; 9.5 g Protein; 1.5 g Net Carb; 2 g Fiber;
Ingredients
- 4 slices of roast beef
- ½ ounce chopped lettuce
- 1 avocado, pitted
- 2 oz mozzarella cheese, cubed
- ½ cup mayonnaise

Seasoning:
- ¼ tsp salt
- 1/8 tsp ground black pepper
- 2 tbsp avocado oil

How to Prepare:
1. Scoop out flesh from avocado and divide it evenly between two plates.
2. Add slices of roast beef, lettuce, and cheese and then sprinkle with salt and black pepper.
3. Serve with avocado oil and mayonnaise.

187 – Beef and Broccoli

Serves: 2; Preparation: 5 minutes; Cook time: 10 minutes;
Nutrition facts: 245 Calories; 15.7 g Fats; 21.6 g Protein; 1.7 g Net Carb; 1.3 g Fiber;
Ingredients
- 6 slices of beef roast, cut into strips
- 1 scallion, chopped
- 3 oz broccoli florets, chopped
- 1 tbsp avocado oil
- 1 tbsp butter, unsalted

Seasoning:
- ¼ tsp salt
- 1/8 tsp ground black pepper
- 1 ½ tbsp soy sauce
- 3 tbsp chicken broth

How to Prepare:

1. Take a medium skillet pan, place it over medium heat, add oil and when hot, add beef strips and cook for 2 minutes until hot.
2. Transfer beef to a plate, add scallion to the pan, then add butter and cook for 3 minutes until tender.
3. Add remaining ingredients, stir until mixed, switch heat to the low level and simmer for 3 to 4 minutes until broccoli is tender.
4. Return beef to the pan, stir until well combined and cook for 1 minute. Serve.

188 – Garlic Herb Beef Roast

Serves: 2; Preparation: 5 minutes; Cook time: 10 minutes;
Nutrition facts: 140 Calories; 12.7 g Fats; 5.5 g Protein; 0.1 g Net Carb; 0.2 g Fiber;
Ingredients
- 6 slices of beef roast
- ½ tsp garlic powder
- 1/3 tsp dried thyme
- ¼ tsp dried rosemary
- 2 tbsp butter, unsalted

Seasoning:
- 1/3 tsp salt
- 1/4 tsp ground black pepper

How to Prepare:
1. Prepare the spice mix and for this, take a small bowl, place garlic powder, thyme, rosemary, salt, and black pepper and then stir until mixed.
2. Sprinkle spice mix on the beef roast.
3. Take a medium skillet pan, place it over medium heat, add butter and when it melts, add beef roast and then cook for 5 to 8 minutes until golden brown and cooked.

189 – Sprouts Stir-fry with Kale, Broccoli, and Beef

Serves: 2; Preparation: 5 minutes; Cook time: 8 minutes;
Nutrition facts: 125 Calories; 9.4 g Fats; 4.8 g Protein; 1.7 g Net Carb; 2.6 g Fiber;
Ingredients
- 3 slices of beef roast, chopped
- 2 oz Brussels sprouts, halved
- 4 oz broccoli florets
- 3 oz kale
- 1 ½ tbsp butter, unsalted
- 1/8 tsp red pepper flakes

Seasoning:
- ¼ tsp garlic powder
- ¼ tsp salt
- 1/8 tsp ground black pepper

How to Prepare:
1. Take a medium skillet pan, place it over medium heat, add ¾ tbsp butter and when it melts, add broccoli florets and sprouts, sprinkle with garlic powder, and cook for 2 minutes.
2. Season vegetables with salt and red pepper flakes, add chopped beef, stir until mixed and continue cooking for 3 minutes until browned on one side.
3. Then add kale along with remaining butter, flip the vegetables and cook for 2 minutes until kale leaves wilts. Serve.

190 – Beef and Vegetable Skillet

Serves: 2; Preparation: 5 minutes; Cook time: 15 minutes
Nutrition facts: 332.5 Calories; 26 g Fats; 23.5 g Protein; 1.5 g Net Carb; 1 g Fiber;
Ingredients
- 3 oz spinach, chopped
- ½ pound ground beef
- 2 slices of bacon, diced
- 2 oz chopped asparagus

Seasoning:
- 3 tbsp coconut oil
- 2 tsp dried thyme
- 2/3 tsp salt
- ½ tsp ground black pepper

How to Prepare:
1. Take a skillet pan, place it over medium heat, add oil and when hot, add beef and bacon and cook for 5 to 7 minutes until slightly browned.

2. Then add asparagus and spinach, sprinkle with thyme, stir well and cook for 7 to 10 minutes until thoroughly cooked.
3. Season skillet with salt and black pepper and serve.

191 – Beef, Pepper and Green Beans Stir-fry

Serves: 2; Preparation: 5 minutes; Cook time: 18 minutes
Nutrition facts: 282.5 Calories; 17.6 g Fats; 26.1 g Protein; 2.9 g Net Carb; 2.1 g Fiber;
Ingredients
- 6 oz ground beef
- 2 oz chopped green bell pepper
- 4 oz green beans
- 3 tbsp grated cheddar cheese

Seasoning:
- ½ tsp salt
- ¼ tsp ground black pepper
- ¼ tsp paprika

How to Prepare:
1. Take a skillet pan, place it over medium heat, add ground beef and cook for 4 minutes until slightly browned.
2. Then add bell pepper and green beans, season with salt, paprika, and black pepper, stir well and continue cooking for 7 to 10 minutes until beef and vegetables have cooked through.
3. Sprinkle cheddar cheese on top, then transfer pan under the broiler and cook for 2 minutes until cheese has melted and the top is golden brown. Serve.

192 – Cheesy Meatloaf

Serves: 2; Preparation: 5 minutes; Cook time: 4 minutes
Nutrition facts: 196.5 Calories; 13.5 g Fats; 18.7 g Protein; 18.7 g Net Carb; 0 g Fiber;
Ingredients
- 4 oz ground turkey
- 1 egg
- 1 tbsp grated mozzarella cheese
- ¼ tsp Italian seasoning
- ½ tbsp soy sauce

Seasoning:
- ¼ tsp salt
- 1/8 tsp ground black pepper

How to Prepare:
1. Take a bowl, place all the ingredients in it, and stir until mixed.
2. Take a heatproof mug, spoon in prepared mixture and microwave for 3 minutes at high heat setting until cooked.
3. When done, let meatloaf rest in the mug for 1 minute, then take it out, cut it into two slices and serve.

193 – Roast Beef and Vegetable Plate

Serves: 2; Preparation: 10 minutes; Cook time: 10 minutes;
Nutrition facts: 313 Calories; 26 g Fats; 15.6 g Protein; 2.8 g Net Carb; 1.9 g Fiber;
Ingredients
- 2 scallions, chopped in large pieces
- 1 ½ tbsp coconut oil
- 4 thin slices of roast beef
- 4 oz cauliflower and broccoli mix
- 1 tbsp butter, unsalted

Seasoning:
- 1/2 tsp salt
- 1/3 tsp ground black pepper
- 1 tsp dried parsley

How to Prepare:
1. Turn on the oven, then set it to 400 degrees F, and let it preheat.
2. Take a baking sheet, grease it with oil, place slices of roast beef on one side, and top with butter.
3. Take a separate bowl, add cauliflower and broccoli mix, add scallions, drizzle with oil, season with remaining salt and black pepper, toss until coated and then spread vegetables on the empty side of the baking sheet. Bake for 5 to 7 minutes until beef is nicely browned and vegetables are tender-crisp, tossing halfway.
4. Distribute beef and vegetables between two plates and then serve.

194– Steak and Cheese Plate

Serves: 2; Preparation: 5 minutes; Cook time: 10 minutes;
Nutrition facts: 714 Calories; 65.3 g Fats; 25.3 g Protein; 4 g Net Carb; 5.3 g Fiber;
Ingredients
- 1 green onion, chopped
- 2 oz chopped lettuce
- 2 beef steaks
- 2 oz of cheddar cheese, sliced
- ½ cup mayonnaise

Seasoning:
- ¼ tsp salt
- 1/8 tsp ground black pepper
- 3 tbsp avocado oil

How to Prepare:
1. Prepare the steak, and for this, season it with salt and black pepper.
2. Take a medium skillet pan, place it over medium heat, add oil and when hot, add seasoned steaks, and cook for 7 to 10 minutes until cooked to the desired level.
3. When done, distribute steaks between two plates, add scallion, lettuce, and cheese slices. Drizzle with remaining oil and then serve with mayonnaise.

195 – Garlicky Steaks with Rosemary

Serves: 2; Preparation: 25 minutes; Cook time: 12 minutes;
Nutrition facts: 213 Calories; 13 g Fats; 22 g Protein; 1 g Net Carb; 0 g Fiber;
Ingredients
- 2 beef steaks
- 1/4 of a lime, juiced
- 1 ½ tsp garlic powder
- ¾ tsp dried rosemary
- 2 ½ tbsp avocado oil

Seasoning:
- ½ tsp salt
- ¼ tsp ground black pepper

How to Prepare:
1. Prepare steaks, and for this, sprinkle garlic powder on all sides of steak.
2. Take a shallow dish, place 1 ½ tbsp oil and lime juice in it, whisk until combined, add steaks, turn to coat and let it marinate for 20 minutes at room temperature.
3. Then take a griddle pan, place it over medium-high heat and grease it with remaining oil.
4. Season marinated steaks with salt and black pepper, add to the griddle pan and cook for 7 to 12 minutes until cooked to the desired level.
5. When done, wrap steaks in foil for 5 minutes, then cut into slices across the grain. Sprinkle rosemary over steaks slices and then serve. .

Turkey

196 – Breakfast Patties

Serves: 2; Preparation: 5 minutes; Cook time: 10 minutes;
Nutrition facts: 154.5 Calories; 8.5 g Fats; 15.5 g Protein; 4 g Net Carb; 4 g Fiber;
Ingredients
- ½ pound ground turkey
- ½ tsp garlic powder
- 1/2 tsp smoked paprika
- 1 tbsp coconut oil
- 2 leaves of iceberg lettuce

Seasoning:
- 1/2 tsp dried thyme
- ½ tsp salt
- 1/4 tsp ground black pepper

How to Prepare:
1. Take a medium bowl, place ground turkey in it, and then add remaining ingredients except for oil.
2. Stir well until combined and then shape the mixture into two patties.
3. Take a skillet pan, place it over medium heat, add oil and when hot, add patties and cook for 4 to 5 minutes per side until nicely browned and thoroughly cooked.
4. Wrap each patty in a lettuce leaf and serve.

197 – Open Breakfast Sandwich

Serves: 2; Preparation: 10 minutes; Cook time: 13 minutes
Nutrition facts: 150.8 Calories; 13.5 g Fats; 5.5 g Protein; 1 g Net Carb; 0.8 g Fiber;
Ingredients
- 1 egg
- 4 oz ground turkey
- 1 tbsp whipped topping
- 2 oz cheddar cheese, grated
- 1 tsp sriracha sauce

Seasoning:
- 1 tsp coconut oil
- ¾ tsp salt
- ½ tsp ground black pepper

How to Prepare:
1. Place ground turkey and beef in a bowl, season with ½ tsp salt and ¼ tsp black pepper, stir until well mixed, and shape the mixture into two patties.
2. Take a skillet pan, place it over medium heat, and when hot, add sausage patties and cook for 3 to 5 minutes per side until browned and thoroughly cooked, transfer patties to a plate and reserve the pan.
3. Place grated cheese in a small heatproof bowl, add whipped topping, stir well, and microwave for 30 seconds until melted.
4. Stir the cheese mixture, add sriracha sauce, stir well, and set aside until required.
5. Crack the egg in a bowl, season with remaining salt and black pepper and whisk until combined.
6. Return pan over medium-low heat, add oil and when hot, pour in the egg and cook for 3 minutes until omelet has cooked to the desired level.
7. Assemble sandwich and for it, cut the omelet into half, then stuff with cheese mixture, place omelet on top of the patty and serve.

198– Meat and Eggs

Serves: 2; Preparation: 10 minutes; Cook time: 8 minutes
Nutrition facts: 325.5 Calories; 26.4 g Fats; 21.2 g Protein; 0.8 g Net Carb; 0 g Fiber;
Ingredients
- 4 oz ground turkey
- 2 tbsp unsalted butter
- 1 egg, beaten

Seasoning:
- ½ tsp salt
- 1/4 tsp ground black pepper

How to Prepare:

1. Take a skillet pan, place it over medium heat, add butter and when it melts, pour in eggs, season with 1/8 tsp salt, and 1/8 tsp black pepper and cook eggs for 3 minutes until scrambled to desire level.
2. Add ground turkey into the pan, season with remaining salt and black pepper and cook for 5 minutes until cooked. Serve.

199 – Breakfast Cups

Serves: 2; Preparation: 10 minutes; Cook time: 15 minutes
Nutrition facts: 241 Calories; 16.3 g Fats; 22.3 g Protein; 0.7 g Net Carb; 1.2 g Fiber;
Ingredients
- 4 oz ground turkey
- 2 tbsp chopped spinach
- ¼ tsp garlic powder
- 2 eggs
- 1 tbsp grated parmesan cheese
Seasoning:
- ½ tsp salt
- 1/3 tsp ground black pepper
- ½ tsp dried thyme
- 1/8 tsp paprika
How to Prepare:
1. Turn on the oven, then set it to 400 degrees F, and let preheat.
2. Meanwhile, place ground turkey in a bowl, season with 1/3 tsp salt, ¼ tsp black pepper, garlic, thyme and paprika, and stir well until combined.
3. Take two silicone muffin cups, divide the turkey mixture between the cups, and then spread it evenly in the bottom and sides of the cup to create a muffin tin.
4. Add 1 tbsp chopped spinach and ½ tbsp parmesan cheese into each cup, then crack an egg on top, season with remaining salt and black pepper, and bake for 15 to 20 minutes until meat is thoroughly cooked and eggs has cooked to the desired level. Serve.

200 – Meat Bagels

Serves: 2; Preparation: 5 minutes; Cook time: 20 minutes
Nutrition facts: 268 Calories; 20.1 g Fats; 19.9 g Protein; 1.1 g Net Carb; 0.3 g Fiber;
Ingredients
- 4 oz ground turkey
- 1 slice of bacon, chopped
- 1 egg
- 2 tbsp tomato sauce
- 2 oz coleslaw
Seasoning:
- ½ tsp paprika
- ½ tsp salt
- ¼ tsp ground black pepper
- 1 tbsp unsalted butter, softened
How to Prepare:
1. Turn on the oven, then set it to 400 degrees F and let it preheat.
2. Meanwhile, take a bowl, place all the ingredients in it, mix well, and then shape the mixture into two bagels.
3. Place bagels into a baking dish, bake for 20 minutes until cooked through, and when done, let them cool for 10 minutes.
4. Slice the bagel, fill with coleslaw, and serve.

201 – Ground Turkey Stuffed Zucchini Boats

Serves: 2; Preparation: 10 minutes; Cook time: 20 minutes;
Nutrition facts: 291 Calories; 22 g Fats; 14.5 g Protein; 5.5 g Net Carb; 1.5 g Fiber;
Ingredients
- 1 medium zucchini
- 0.25-pounds ground turkey
- ½ cup tomato sauce
- ½ cup grated cheddar cheese
- 1 tbsp coconut oil, melted

Seasoning:
- ½ tsp of sea salt
- ½ tsp garlic power
- ½ tsp Italian seasoning

How to Prepare:
1. Turn on the oven, then set it to 400 degrees F and let it preheat.
2. Meanwhile, cut the zucchini in half lengthwise and then create a well by scooping out some center with a spoon.
3. Take a medium baking sheet, line it with aluminum foil, place zucchini halved on it, drizzle with ½ tbsp oil, season with ¼ tsp salt, and roast for 15 to 20 minutes until softened.
4. Meanwhile, take a skillet pan, place it over medium heat, add remaining oil and when hot, add ground turkey and cook for 7 to 10 minutes or until nicely browned.
5. Sprinkle garlic and salt over turkey and continue cooking for 1 minute until fragrant, remove the pan from heat.
6. Pour in tomato sauce, season with Italian seasoning, add 1/3 cup cheese and stir well.
7. When zucchini halves have roasted, pat them dry with paper towels and stuff the wells with prepared meat mixture.
8. Sprinkle remaining cheese on top and continue baking for 5 minutes until cheese has melted and turned golden-brown. Serve hot.

202 – Turkey Lettuce Wraps

Serves: 2; Preparation: 5 minutes; Cook time: 15 minutes;
Nutrition facts: 210 Calories; 17 g Fats; 10 g Protein; 2.5 g Net Carb; 0.5 g Fiber;
Ingredients
- ¼ pound ground turkey
- 2 leaves of iceberg lettuce
- 1 tbsp sesame oil
- 2 tbsp soy sauce
- 1 tbsp grated cheddar cheese

Seasoning:
- 1 tsp garlic powder
- 1 tsp coconut oil
- ¼ tsp salt
- ¼ tsp cracked black pepper

How to Prepare:
1. Take a skillet pan, place it over medium heat, add coconut oil and when hot, add turkey and cook for 7 to 10 minutes until nicely browned.
2. Meanwhile, rinse the leaves of lettuce and pat dry with a paper towel, set aside until required.
3. Prepare the sauce, and for this, whisk together sesame oil, soy sauce, garlic powder, salt, and black pepper.
4. Pour the sauce into the cooked turkey and continue cooking for 3 minutes or until the sauce has evaporated.
5. Evenly divide the meat between two lettuce leaves, top with cheddar cheese, wrap it and serve.

203 – Taco Stuffed Avocados

Serves: 2; Preparation: 10 minutes; Cook time: 10 minutes;
Nutrition facts: 210 Calories; 16 g Fats; 13 g Protein; 2 g Net Carb; 1.5 g Fiber;
Ingredients
- ¼ pound ground turkey
- 2-ounce tomato sauce
- 1 medium avocado, pitted, halved
- ½ cup shredded cheddar cheese
- 2 tbsp shredded lettuce

Seasoning:
- 1/8 tsp garlic powder
- ¼ tsp salt
- ½ tbsp red chili powder

How to Prepare:
1. Take a skillet pan, place it over medium heat, add ground turkey and cook for 5 minutes until nicely golden brown.
2. Reserve the grease for later use, then season the turkey with garlic powder, salt, and red chili powder, stir in tomato sauce and cook for 3 minutes until meat has thoroughly cooked.
3. Cut avocado into half, remove its pit and then stuff the crater with prepared meat.
4. Top meat with cheddar cheese and lettuce and serve.

204 – Cheeseburger

Serves: 2; Preparation: 5 minutes; Cook time: 15 minutes;
Nutrition facts: 203 Calories; 17.5 g Fats; 8.8 g Protein; 1.3 g Net Carb; 1 g Fiber;
Ingredients
- ½ pound ground turkey

- 2 slices of turkey bacon, cooked, crumbled
- 2-ounce shredded parmesan cheese, divided
- 2 tbsp basil pesto
- 2 leaf of iceberg lettuce

Seasoning:
- 1 tsp dried oregano
- 1 tbsp mustard
- ½ tsp salt
- 1 tsp garlic powder
- 1 tsp paprika powder

How to Prepare:
1. Take a bowl, place ground turkey in it, add oregano, mustard, salt, garlic powder, paprika, mustard, and half of the cheese, stir until well mixed, and shape the mixture into two patties.
2. Place a medium skillet pan over medium heat, add bacon and cook for 5 minutes until crispy, set aside until required.
3. Add patties into the pan, cook for 4 to 5 minutes until the bottom has turned brown, then flip the patties, top each patty with remaining cheese and continue cooking for 4 minutes until done. Serve each patty on a lettuce leaf, top it with bacon and 1 tbsp pesto, wrap it and serve.

205 – Turkey with Pesto and Vegetables

Serves: 2; Preparation: 5 minutes; Cook time: 15 minutes;
Nutrition facts: 312 Calories; 25 g Fats; 17.1 g Protein; 2.5 g Net Carb; 2.2 g Fiber;
Ingredients
- 3 oz ground turkey
- ½ of zucchini, sliced in rounds
- 2 tbsp chopped parsley
- 2 green onions, sliced
- 2 tbsp Italian basil pesto

Seasoning:
- 1 tbsp avocado oil
- ¼ tsp salt
- 1 tsp grated parmesan cheese

How to Prepare:
1. Take a medium skillet pan, place it over medium heat and when hot, add turkey and cook for 3 to 5 minutes until golden brown.
2. Transfer turkey to a plate, then add oil and green onion into the pan and cook for 2 minutes until softened.
3. Add zucchini, cook for 3 to 4 minutes until tender, return ground turkey into the pan, and then season with salt.
4. Stir in pesto sauce and parsley, switch heat to the low level and then cook for 2 to 3 minutes until done, covering the pan.
5. When done, sprinkle with parmesan cheese and then Serve.

206 – Slow Cooked Stuffed Tomatoes with Meat

Serves: 2; Preparation: 10 minutes; Cook time: 4 hours
Nutrition facts: 191.5 Calories; 12.6 g Fats; 16.3 g Protein; 2.3 g Net Carb; 1.1 g Fiber;
Ingredients
- 2 tomatoes
- 4 oz ground turkey
- 1 tbsp Italian seasoning
- 2 tbsp grated cheddar cheese
- ¼ tsp salt
- 1/8 tsp ground black pepper

How to Prepare:
1. Cut a thin slice from the top and end of tomatoes and then use a spoon to remove seeds of each tomato.
2. Mix together sausage, Italian seasoning, and salt and ground black pepper to taste, then fill this mixture evenly into tomatoes and sprinkle with cheese.
3. Grease a 4-quart slow cooker with a non-stick cooking spray and spread tomatoes with basil in the bottom and mix in 3/4 cup water.
4. Arrange stuffed tomatoes into the slow cooker, then cover and seal the slow cooker with its lid.
5. Plugin the slow cooker and adjust the cooking timer for 4 hours and let cook at high heat setting or until cooked. Serve warm.

207 – Bacon Burger

Serves: 2; Preparation: 5 minutes; Cook time: 15 minutes
Nutrition facts: 262.5 Calories; 22.5 g Fats; 11 g Protein; 1.5 g Net Carb; 2 g Fiber;

Ingredients
- 2 oz diced bacon
- 4 oz ground turkey
- 2 tbsp mustard paste

Seasoning:
- ¼ tsp salt
- ¼ tsp ground black pepper

How to Prepare:
1. Take a skillet pan, place it over medium heat, add bacon slices, and cook for 5 minutes until crispy.
2. Then transfer bacon to a cutting board, let it cool for 5 minutes, then chop them and transfer into a bowl.
3. Add remaining ingredients, except for mustard, stir well and shape the mixture into two patties.
4. Return pan over medium heat, add patties in it and then cook for 4 minutes per side. Then smear patties with mustard and continue cooking for 1 minute until seared.

208 – Ground Turkey Chili

Serves: 2; Preparation: 10 minutes; Cook time: 27 minutes
Nutrition facts: 314 Calories; 20.1 g Fats; 24.1 g Protein; 6.8 g Net Carb; 4.1 g Fiber;
Ingredients
- 4 oz ground turkey
- 1 jalapeno pepper, cored, cut into small cubes
- ½ tsp minced garlic
- 6 oz tomato sauce
- ¾ cup of water

Seasoning:
- ½ tbsp coconut oil
- ¾ tsp salt
- ¼ tsp red chili powder
- ½ tsp cumin
- ¼ tsp ground black pepper

How to Prepare:
1. Take a skillet pan, place it over medium heat, add oil and when it melts, add turkey and cook for 3 to 4 minutes until turkey is slightly brown.
2. Then add garlic and jalapeno pepper, season with salt, red chili powder, cumin, and black pepper, stir well, and continue cooking for 3 minutes.
3. Add tomato sauce, water, stir well and simmer the chili for 20 to 25 minutes until the sauce has reduced and thickened to the desired level.
4. Taste the chili to adjust seasoning and serve with sliced avocado.

209 – Egg Roll Bowl

Serves: 2; Preparation: 5 minutes; Cook time: 8 minutes
Nutrition facts: 144.8 Calories; 9.7 g Fats; 11.2 g Protein; 2 g Net Carb; 1 g Fiber;
Ingredients
- ¼ pound ground turkey
- ½ tsp minced garlic
- 6-ounce coleslaw mix
- 2/3 tbsp apple cider vinegar
- 1 tsp avocado oil

Seasoning:
- ½ tsp salt
- ½ tbsp soy sauce
- 1 tbsp water
- 1 tsp sesame oil

How to Prepare:
1. Take a skillet pan, place it over medium heat, add avocado oil and when hot, add ground turkey and cook for 5 minutes until browned.
2. Add garlic, stir, and cook for 30 seconds until fragrant, add coleslaw mix and water, toss until well mixed and cook for 2 minutes until coleslaw has softened.
3. Place soy sauce and vinegar in a small bowl, add sesame oil and salt and then stir until well mixed.
4. Drizzle the soy sauce mixture on coleslaw mixture, toss until combined and remove the pan from heat. Serve.

210 – Turkey and Broccoli Bowl

Serves: 2; Preparation: 5 minutes; Cook time: 15 minutes
Nutrition facts: 120.3 Calories; 8.3 g Fats; 8.4 g Protein; 2 g Net Carb; 1 g Fiber;
Ingredients

- 4 oz ground turkey
- 4 oz broccoli florets
- 4 oz cauliflower florets, riced
- 1 tsp soy sauce
- ¼ tsp red pepper flakes

Seasoning:
- 1/3 tsp salt
- ¼ tsp ground black pepper
- 1 tbsp avocado oil

How to Prepare:
1. Take a skillet pan, place it over medium heat, add avocado oil and when hot, add beef, crumble it and cook for 8 minutes until no longer pink.
2. Then add broccoli florets and riced cauliflower, stir well, drizzle with soy sauce and sesame oil, season with salt, black pepper, and red pepper flakes and continue cooking for 5 minutes until vegetables have thoroughly cooked.
3. Serve.

211 – Burger Plate

Serves: 2; Preparation: 10 minutes; Cook time: 10 minutes;
Nutrition facts: 283 Calories; 24.6 g Fats; 12 g Protein; 2 g Net Carb; 2.6 g Fiber;
Ingredients
- 3 oz ground turkey
- 1 tbsp tex-mex seasoning
- 2 tbsp avocado oil
- 2 oz chopped lettuce
- 1/3 cup mayonnaise

Seasoning:
- ¼ tsp salt
- ¼ tsp ground black pepper

How to Prepare:
1. Take a medium bowl, place ground turkey in it, add tex-mex seasoning, salt, and black pepper, stir until well combined, and shape the mixture into two patties.
2. Take a medium skillet pan, place it over medium heat, add oil and when hot, add prepared patties and cook for 4 minutes per side until golden brown and thoroughly cooked.
3. When done, distribute patties between two plates, add lettuce, and serve with mayonnaise.

212 – Meatballs Lettuce Wrap

Serves: 2; Preparation: 5 minutes; Cook time: 10 minutes;
Nutrition facts: 412 Calories; 38 g Fats; 14.4 g Protein; 1.7 g Net Carb; 0.4 g Fiber;
Ingredients
- 3 oz ground turkey
- ¼ tsp garlic powder
- 1/3 tsp ground cumin
- ¾ tsp Greek seasoning
- 2 lettuce leaves

Seasoning:
- 1/4 cup mayonnaise
- 1 tbsp avocado oil

How to Prepare:
5. Take a medium bowl, place ground turkey in it, add garlic powder, cumin, and Greek seasoning, stir until well mixed and then shape the mixture into meatballs.
6. Take a medium skillet pan, place it over medium heat, add oil and when hot, add meatballs and cook for 2 to 3 minutes per side until golden brown and cooked.
7. Distribute meatballs between lettuce leaves, drizzle with mayonnaise, and then serve.

213 – Turkey Burger Plate

Serves: 2; Preparation: 10 minutes; Cook time: 10 minutes;
Nutrition facts: 312 Calories; 26.2 g Fats; 17.1 g Protein; 1.5 g Net Carb; 0.1 g Fiber;
Ingredients
- 3 oz ground turkey
- 2 tbsp mayonnaise
- 1 tsp avocado oil
- 2 eggs

Seasoning:

- 1/8 tsp garlic powder
- ¼ tsp salt
- 1/8 tsp ground black pepper
- ¾ tsp Sriracha sauce

How to Prepare:
1. Prepare the burgers and for this, take a medium bowl, place meat in it, add garlic powder, some salt, and black pepper, stir until combined, and then shape the mixture into two patties.
2. Take a medium pan, place it over medium heat, add oil and when hot, add patties in it, and then cook for 3 to 4 minutes per side until browned and cooked.
3. Meanwhile, prepare the mayonnaise and for this, take a small bowl, place mayonnaise in it, add Sriracha sauce and some salt and black pepper and stir until combined. When patties are done, divide them between two plates and then add mayonnaise on the side.
4. Return pan over medium heat, crack an egg in it, and cook for 2 to 3 minutes until fried to the desired level. Top patties with fried eggs and then serve.

214 – Meaty Zucchini Noodles

Serves: 2; Preparation: 5 minutes; Cook time: 15 minutes;
Nutrition facts: 229 Calories; 17 g Fats; 15 g Protein; 2 g Net Carb; 0.5 g Fiber;
Ingredients
- 1 medium zucchini
- 1/2 pound ground turkey
- ¼ tsp dried oregano
- ¼ tsp garlic powder
- ½ tsp curry powder
- ½ tsp salt
- ½ tsp ground black pepper

How to Prepare:
1. Prepare zucchini noodles, and for this, cut off the bottom and top of zucchini and then use a spiralizer to convert into noodles, set aside until required.
2. Return the skillet pan with bacon grease over medium-high heat, add ground beef, stir well and cook for 5 minutes until meat is no longer pink.
3. Season with oregano, garlic powder, curry powder, salt, and black pepper and cook for 5 to 7 minutes until turkey has cooked through.
4. Then add zucchini noodles, toss until well mixed, and continue cooking 5 minutes until noodles have cooked to desired doneness.
5. Divide zucchini noodles evenly between two plates and serve.

215 – Stir-Fried Zucchini and Turkey

Serves: 2; Preparation: 5 minutes; Cook time: 8 minutes;
Nutrition facts: 82 Calories; 5.6 g Fats; 5.2 g Protein; 2.4 g Net Carb; 1.3 g Fiber;
Ingredients
- 1 large zucchini, sliced
- ¼ pound ground turkey
- 3 tbsp shredded cheddar cheese
- 1 tsp soy sauce

Seasoning:
- 2/3 tsp salt, divided
- ¼ tsp red chili pepper
- ½ tsp ground black pepper

How to Prepare:
1. Take a skillet pan, place it over high heat and when hot, add ¾ tsp oil and turkey, season with 1/3 tsp salt and black pepper and cook for 3 to 5 minutes until stir-fried.
2. Transfer turkey to a plate, add zucchini slices into the pan, drizzle with soy sauce and sesame oil, and salt, stir well, and cook for 2 minutes until zucchini has almost cooked. Return turkey into the pan, toss well until mixed, and then remove the pan from heat.
3. Evenly divide turkey and zucchini between two plates, top evenly with cheese and serve.

216 – Casserole with Turkey and Broccoli

Serves: 2; Preparation: 5 minutes; Cook time: 15 minutes;
Nutrition facts: 323 Calories; 27.5 g Fats; 16.5 g Protein; 2.5 g Net Carb; 1.5 g Fiber;
Ingredients
- 4-ounce broccoli florets
- ½ pound ground turkey
- 2-ounce unsalted butter
- ¼ cup shredded cheddar cheese

Seasoning:
- 1/3 tsp salt
- 1/8 tsp cracked black pepper

How to Prepare:
1. Take a medium skillet pan, place it over medium-high heat, add butter and when it melted, add turkey and broccoli and cook for 5 to 7 minutes until beef has thoroughly cooked.
2. Season beef and broccoli with salt and black pepper, then reduce heat to a low level and continue cooking for 3 to 5 minutes or until broccoli has fried.
3. Remove pan from heat, transfer beef and broccoli to a casserole, sprinkle cheese on top and broil for 3 minutes, or until cheese melts. Serve.

217 – Ground Turkey and Veggie Stir-Fry

Serves: 2; Preparation: 5 minutes; Cook time: 25 minutes;
Nutrition facts: 183 Calories; 11 g Fats; 15 g Protein; 4 g Net Carb; 2 g Fiber;
Ingredients
- 0.25-ounce ground turkey
- ¼ cup spinach
- ½ of a large zucchini, diced
- 2 green onion, sliced
- 2 slices of bacon, cooked, crumbled

Seasoning:
- ¾ tsp garlic powder
- ¾ tsp cayenne pepper
- ½ tsp salt
- 1 tbsp soy sauce

How to Prepare:
1. Take a skillet pan, place it over medium-high heat, add bacon slices and cook for 5 minutes until crispy.
2. When done, transfer bacon to a cutting board and set aside until required.
3. Add zucchini and green onions into the pan, cook for 5 minutes until stir-fry, then transfer vegetables to a plate and set aside.
4. Add ground turkey into the pan, season with ¼ tsp of salt, cook for 7 to 10 minutes until nicely browned, and then transfer to a bowl, set aside until required.
5. Add spinach into the pan, cook for 3 minutes, or until leaves have wilted and then drain well into the colander.
6. Return turkey, zucchini, and green onion into the pan, season with garlic powder, cayenne pepper, remaining salt, stir well, and cook for 1 minute until fragrant.
7. Drizzle with soy sauce, toss until well coated, add spinach and bacon, stir well combined and cook for 1 minute until thoroughly heated. Serve.

218 – Meatloaf with Basil Pesto

Serves: 2; Preparation: 5 minutes; Cook time: 5 minutes;
Nutrition facts: 185 Calories; 12 g Fats; 17.1 g Protein; 1.3 g Net Carb; 1 g Fiber;
Ingredients
- 3 oz ground turkey
- ¼ tsp onion powder
- 2 tbsp grated parmesan cheese
- 2 tbsp Italian basil pesto

Seasoning:
- ¼ tsp salt

How to Prepare:
4. Take a bowl, place all the ingredients in it, and stir until mixed.
5. Take a heatproof mug, spoon in prepared mixture and microwave for 3 minutes at high heat setting until cooked.
6. When done, let meatloaf rest in the mug for 1 minute, then take it out, cut it into two slices, and serve.

219 – Burgers with Tomato Butter

Serves: 2; Preparation: 10 minutes; Cook time: 13 minutes
Nutrition facts: 192.8 Calories; 16.7 g Fats; 8.5 g Protein; 2.5 g Net Carb; 1.25 g Fiber;
Ingredients
- 4 oz ground turkey
- 4 oz unsalted butter
- 4 ounce shredded cabbage
- ½ tsp tomato sauce

Seasoning:

- 1 ¼ tsp salt
- ¾ tsp ground black pepper
- ½ tsp thyme

How to Prepare:
1. Turn on the oven, then set it to 220 degrees F, and let it preheat.
2. Meanwhile, prepare patties and for this, place ground turkey in a bowl, add ½ tsp salt, ¼ tsp black pepper, thyme, stir well and then shape the mixture into two patties.
3. Take a frying pan, add 1-ounce butter in it, and when it melted, add chicken patties and cook for 3 to 4 minutes per side until nicely browned and cooked.
4. When done, transfer patties to a plate and set aside, then add 1-ounce butter in the pan and when it melts, add cabbage.
5. Switch heat to medium-high level, season with ½ tsp salt, ¼ tsp ground black pepper, and cook for 3 to 5 minutes until the cabbage has fried, and when done, transfer the cabbage to a plate.
6. Prepare tomato butter and for this, place remaining butter in a small bowl, add tomato sauce, add remaining salt and black pepper and stir well by using an electric mixer until mixed. Serve patties with fried cabbage and tomato butter.

220 – Taco Minced

Serves: 2; Preparation: 5 minutes; Cook time: 12 minutes
Nutrition facts: 164 Calories; 8 g Fats; 11 g Protein; 4 g Net Carb; 3 g Fiber;
Ingredients
- 4 oz ground turkey
- 1/8 tsp garlic powder
- 1/8 tsp onion powder
- 2 tbsp water
- 3 oz tomato sauce

Seasoning:
- 1 tbsp avocado oil
- ¼ tsp salt
- ¾ tsp red chili powder
- 1/3 tsp cumin

How to Prepare:
1. Take a skillet pan, place it over medium heat and when hot, add turkey and cook for 5 to 8 minutes until nicely browned.
2. Drain the grease, add remaining ingredients and simmer for 2 to 3 minutes until thick and done. Serve.

221 – Turkey Sesame Coleslaw

Serves: 2; Preparation: 5 minutes; Cook time: 13 minutes
Nutrition facts: 117.5 Calories; 8.4 g Fats; 8 g Protein; 1.8 g Net Carb; 1 g Fiber;
Ingredients
- 4 oz ground turkey
- 6 oz coleslaw
- 1 tbsp sesame oil
- 1 tbsp fish sauce

How to Prepare:
1. Take a skillet pan, place it over medium heat, add turkey, drizzle with sesame oil and fish sauce and cook for 5 to 8 minutes until turkey has thoroughly cooked.
2. Add coleslaw, toss until mixed, and then cook for 3 minutes until softened. Serve.

222 – Turkey Spinach Sliders

Serves: 2; Preparation: 5 minutes; Cook time: 10 minutes
Nutrition facts: 240 Calories; 20 g Fats; 14.4 g Protein; 0.3 g Net Carb; 0.4 g Fiber;
Ingredients
- 2 tbsp chopped spinach
- ½ tsp minced garlic
- 3 oz ground turkey
- 1 ½ tbsp avocado oil
- 2 oz chopped lettuce

Seasoning:
- 1/3 tsp salt
- 1/3 tsp ground black pepper
- ¼ tsp ground cumin

How to Prepare:
1. Take a bowl, place all the ingredients in it, except for oil and lettuce, stir until combined, and then shape the mixture into two patties.

2. Take a skillet pan, place it over medium heat, add oil and when hot, add patties and cook for 5 minutes per side until cooked. Serve patties with chopped lettuce.

223 – Buttery Turkey and Broccoli

Serves: 2; Preparation: 5 minutes; Cook time: 8 minutes
Nutrition facts: 315 Calories; 27 g Fats; 15.8 g Protein; 1.9 g Net Carb; 1.4 g Fiber;
Ingredients
- 3 oz broccoli florets
- 4 oz ground turkey
- 3 tbsp unsalted butter
- ½ tsp dried rosemary
- 2 tbsp water

Seasoning:
- ¼ tsp salt
- 1/8 tsp ground black pepper

How to Prepare:
1. Take a heatproof bowl, place broccoli florets in it, cover it with plastic wrap, poke some holes in it with a fork and microwave for 2 minutes until steamed.
2. Meanwhile, take a skillet pan, place it over medium heat, add turkey and butter and cook for 3 minutes.
3. Then season the turkey with salt, black pepper, and rosemary and continue cooking for 5 minutes until cooked and browned.
4. Serve turkey with steamed broccoli florets.

224 – Ground Turkey, Spinach and Eggs

Serves: 2; Preparation: 5 minutes; Cook time: 12 minutes;
Nutrition facts: 317 Calories; 21.5 g Fats; 27.5 g Protein; 1.5 g Net Carb; 1 g Fiber;
Ingredients
- 3 oz ground turkey
- 2 oz spinach
- 1 1/3 tbsp butter, unsalted
- 2 eggs
- 1 tbsp grated parmesan cheese

Seasoning:
- 2/3 tsp garlic powder
- 1 ½ tsp chipotle seasoning
- ½ tsp salt
- ¼ tsp ground black pepper

How to Prepare:
1. Take a medium skillet pan, place it over medium heat, add butter and when it melts, add turkey, sprinkle with garlic and cook for 3 to 5 minutes until nicely browned.
2. Add spinach, stir until mixed, and then cook for 2 to 3 minutes until spinach leaves wilts.
3. Crack eggs in a small bowl, whisk until frothy, add to the skillet pan, season with chipotle seasoning, salt, and black pepper and cook for 3 to 4 minutes until the egg has cooked. Sprinkle with cheese, cook for 1 minute until cheese has melted and then serve.

225 – Teriyaki Turkey Rice Bowl

Serves: 2; Preparation: 5 minutes; Cook time: 15 minutes;
Nutrition facts: 210 Calories; 13.3 g Fats; 15 g Protein; 4.6 g Net Carb; 1.3 g Fiber;
Ingredients
- 3 oz ground turkey
- 1 cup of broccoli rice
- ½ tsp sesame seeds
- 2 tbsp avocado oil
- 3 tbsp soy sauce

Seasoning:
- 1 tsp garlic powder
- 2/3 tsp salt
- ½ tsp red pepper flakes

How to Prepare:
1. Take a medium skillet pan, place it over medium heat, add 1 tbsp oil and when hot, add broccoli rice and cook for 5 to 7 minutes until thoroughly cooked.
2. Remove pan from heat and then distribute broccoli rice between two bowls.
3. Add remaining oil into the pan and when hot, add ground turkey and cook for 3 to 4 minutes until golden brown.
4. Sprinkle with garlic, salt, and red pepper flakes, drizzle with soy sauce, stir until mixed and cook for 4 to 5 minutes until thoroughly cooked.
5. Top ground turkey over broccoli, sprinkle with sesame seeds, and some red chili flakes and then serve.

226 – Ground Turkey with Cauliflower Skillet

Serves: 2; Preparation: 5 minutes; Cook time: 15 minutes;
Nutrition facts: 275 Calories; 21 g Fats; 12.6 g Protein; 5.4 g Net Carb; 1.2 g Fiber;
Ingredients
- 3 oz ground turkey
- 4 oz cauliflower florets, chopped
- ¼ of a lime, juiced
- 2 tbsp avocado oil
- 3 tbsp water

Seasoning:
- 2/3 tsp salt
- 1/2 tsp ground black pepper
- 1 ½ tbsp soy sauce
- 1 tbsp hot sauce

How to Prepare:
1. Take a medium skillet pan, place it over medium heat, add 1 tbsp oil and when hot, add cauliflower florets and cook for 3 to 5 minutes until golden brown.
2. Drizzle lime juice over cauliflower florets, season with 1/3 tsp salt, ¼ tsp ground black pepper, stir until mixed and transfer cauliflower to a plate.
3. Return skillet pan over medium heat, add remaining oil and when hot, add turkey, crumble it and cook for 3 to 5 minutes until no longer pink.
4. Season with remaining salt and black pepper, drizzle with soy sauce and hot sauce, stir until mixed and cook for 3 minutes.
5. Push turkey to one side of the pan, add cauliflower florets to the empty side of the skillet, and cook for 2 minutes until florets are hot. Serve.

227 – Herby Meatloaf

Serves: 2; Preparation: 5 minutes; Cook time: 8 minutes;
Nutrition facts: 320 Calories; 21 g Fats; 30.4 g Protein; 2.6 g Net Carb; 1.1 g Fiber;
Ingredients
- 3-ounce ground turkey
- ½ tsp dried thyme
- ½ tsp dried rosemary
- ¼ cup shredded parmesan cheese
- 3 tbsp tomato ketchup

Seasoning:
- ¼ tsp onion powder
- ½ tbsp dried parsley
- ½ tsp Worcestershire sauce
- ¼ tsp salt

How to Prepare:
1. Place all the ingredients in a bowl except for ketchup, stir until well-mixed and then shape the mixture into a loaf.
2. Transfer prepared meatloaf into a grease heatproof sage mug or bowl, smear ketchup on top and microwave for 6 to 8 minutes at 250 watts until meat is no longer pink and golden brown; don't overcook otherwise the meat will be too dry.
3. When done, let meatloaf rest in the mug for 5 minutes, then take it out, cut the meatloaf in half and serve.

228 – Sloppy Joes

Serves: 2; Preparation: 5 minutes; Cook time: 20 minutes;
Nutrition facts: 235 Calories; 16 g Fats; 15.3 g Protein; 7.4 g Net Carb; 0.3 g Fiber;
Ingredients
- 3 oz ground turkey
- 2 green onions, chopped
- ½ tsp mustard paste
- 1/3 cup tomato ketchup
- 1 tbsp avocado oil

Seasoning:
- 1/3 tsp salt
- ¼ tsp chipotle pepper

How to Prepare:
1. Take a medium skillet pan, place it over medium heat and when hot, add beef and green onion and cook for 4 to 5 minutes until golden brown.
2. Drain the fat, switch heat to medium-low level, add remaining ingredients, stir until mixed, and then simmer for 10 to 15 minutes until done.
3. Serve.

229 – Jalapeno Stuffed Meatloaf

Serves: 2; Preparation: 5 minutes; Cook time: 20 minutes;
Nutrition facts: 201 Calories; 13.5 g Fats; 15.4 g Protein; 3 g Net Carb; 1 g Fiber;
Ingredients
- 2 oz ground turkey
- ½ jalapeno pepper, chopped
- ¼ tsp minced garlic
- 1 egg
- 1 tbsp cream cheese, softened

Seasoning:
- ¼ tsp salt
- 1/8 tsp ground black pepper
- ½ tbsp Italian seasoning
- ½ tbsp soy sauce
- 2 tbsp tomato ketchup

How to Prepare:
1. Turn on the oven, then set it to 400 degrees F and let it preheat.
2. Take a medium bowl, add beef, add remaining ingredients except for jalapeno, cream cheese, and ketchup and stir until well combined.
3. Take a mini loaf pan, place half of the meatloaf mixture in it, spread cream cheese on top, sprinkle with jalapeno, and cover with remaining meatloaf mixture.
4. Spread tomato ketchup on top and then bake for 20 minutes until done. Cut meatloaf into slices and then Serve.

230 – Spinach and Meat Curry Bowl

Serves: 2; Preparation: 5 minutes; Cook time: 12 minutes;
Nutrition facts: 230 Calories; 16.5 g Fats; 16.1 g Protein; 1.1 g Net Carb; 1.2 g Fiber;
Ingredients
- 2 oz ground turkey
- 2 oz ground pork
- 2 green onions, sliced
- 3 oz spinach, chopped
- 2 tbsp whipped topping

Seasoning:
- 1 tbsp curry powder
- 1 tbsp avocado oil

How to Prepare:
1. Take a medium skillet pan, place it over medium heat, add oil and when hot, add onion and cook for 2 minutes.
2. Season with curry powder, cook for 30 seconds until fragrant, then add turkey and pork, stir well and cook for 5 to 7 minutes until thoroughly cooked.
3. Stir in whipped topping and spinach, cook for 3 minutes until spinach leaves wilts, and then remove the pan from heat.
4. Serve.

Fish & Seafood

231 – Tuna Egg Boats

Serves: 2; Preparation: 5 minutes; Cook time: 12 minutes;
Nutrition facts: 224 Calories; 15.4 g Fats; 15.7 g Protein; 1 g Net Carb; 9.2 g Fiber;
Ingredients
- 2 oz tuna, packed in water
- 1 avocado, pitted
- 2 eggs
- ¼ tsp salt
- 1/8 tsp ground black pepper

How to Prepare:
1. Turn on the oven, then set it to 425 degrees F and let it preheat.
2. Meanwhile, prepare the avocado and for this, cut the avocado into half, remove the pit and then scoop out some of the flesh to make the hollow bigger.
3. Distribute tuna evenly between avocado halves, crack the egg into each hollow and bake the egg boats for 10 to 12 minutes until the egg has cooked to the desired level.
4. When done, season egg boats with salt and black pepper and serve.

232 – Breakfast Tuna Egg Wrap

Serves: 2; Preparation: 10 minutes; Cook time: 6 minutes;
Nutrition facts: 321.5 Calories; 28.6 g Fats; 15.3 g Protein; 0.8 g Net Carb; 0.1 g Fiber;
Ingredients
- 2 eggs
- 1 tbsp avocado oil
- 2 oz tuna, packed in water
- 3 tbsp mayonnaise
- 1/4 tsp salt
- 1/8 tsp ground black pepper
- ¼ tsp cayenne pepper

How to Prepare:
1. Prepare tuna and for this, place tuna in a medium bowl, add cayenne pepper and mayonnaise and stir until combined.
2. Prepare egg wraps and for this, take a medium bowl, crack eggs in it, add salt and black pepper, and then whisk until blended.
3. Take a frying pan, place it over medium-low heat, add oil and when it melts, pour in half of the egg, spread it evenly into a thin layer by rotating the pan and cook for 2 minutes. Then flip the pan, cook for 1 minute, and transfer to a plate.
4. Repeat with the remaining egg to make another wrap, divide tuna between wraps, then roll each egg wrap and serve.

233 – Smoked Salmon Deviled Eggs

Serves: 2; Preparation: 5 minutes; Cook time: 0 minutes;
Nutrition facts: 202 Calories; 16 g Fats; 12.4 g Protein; 1.4 g Net Carb; 0.1 g Fiber;
Ingredients
- 1 green onion, green part chopped only
- 1 ½ ounce smoked salmon, minced
- 2 eggs, boiled
- 1-ounce cream cheese, softened
- 1 tbsp mayonnaise
- ¼ tsp salt
- 1/8 tsp ground black pepper

How to Prepare:
1. Peel the boiled eggs, then slice in half lengthwise and transfer egg yolks to a medium bowl by using a spoon.
2. Mash the egg yolk, add remaining ingredients and mash until smooth and well combined.
3. Spoon the egg yolk mixture into egg whites, sprinkle with some more black pepper and then serve.

234 – Egg Avocado Boats with Smoked Salmon

Serves: 2; Preparation: 10 minutes; Cook time: 6 minutes;
Nutrition facts: 207.5 Calories; 15.7 g Fats; 10.9 g Protein; 1.1 g Net Carb; 4.6 g Fiber;

Ingredients
- 1 avocado, halved, pitted
- 2 eggs
- 1 ounce smoked salmon

Seasoning:
- ¼ tsp salt
- ¼ tsp ground black pepper

How to Prepare:
1. Turn on the oven, then set it to 392 degrees F and let it preheat.
2. Meanwhile, cut avocado in half, remove the pit, scoop out some avocado from the center and then press salmon in it.
3. Crack the egg into each avocado and then bake for 5 to 6 minutes until eggs have cooked to desired doneness.
4. When done, sprinkle salt and black pepper over eggs and then serve.

235 – Shrimp Omelet

Serves: 2; Preparation: 5 minutes; Cook time: 8 minutes;
Nutrition facts: 245 Calories; 19.5 g Fats; 15.7 g Protein; 0.6 g Net Carb; 0 g Fiber;
Ingredients
- 2 oz shrimps
- 1 tbsp butter, unsalted
- 2 tbsp grated parmesan cheese
- 2 eggs
- 2 tsp avocado oil

Seasoning:
- ¼ tsp salt
- 1/8 tsp ground black pepper
- 1 tbsp water

How to Prepare:
1. Take a small bowl, crack eggs in it, add water and whisk until combined.
2. Take a medium skillet pan, place it over medium heat, add oil and when hot, add shrimps and cook for 2 to 3 minutes per side until pink and cooked.
3. Add butter into the pan and when it melts, pour in the egg and let it cook for 2 minutes until omelet begins to firm.
4. Sprinkle omelet on one half of the omelet, sprinkle cheese on top, then fold by covering shrimps with the other half of egg and let it cook for 2 minutes until cheese melts. Transfer omelet to a cutting board, cut it in half, and then serve.

236 – Tuna Cakes

Serves: 2; Preparation: 5 minutes; Cook time: 8 minutes;
Nutrition facts: 111.5 Calories; 7.5 g Fats; 9.5 g Protein; 0.4 g Net Carb; 0.1 g Fiber;
Ingredients
- 5-ounce tuna, packed in water
- 1 tbsp mustard
- 1 tsp garlic powder
- 1 tbsp coconut oil

Seasoning:
- ¼ tsp salt
- 1/8 tsp ground black pepper

How to Prepare:
1. Drain the tuna, add it in a medium bowl and break it well with a fork.
2. Then add remaining ingredients, stir until well mixed and then shape the mixture into four patties.
3. Take a medium skillet pan, place it over medium heat, add oil and when hot, add tuna patties and cook for 3 minutes per side until golden brown.
4. Serve patties straight away or serve as a wrap with iceberg lettuce.

237 – Avocado and Salmon

Serves: 2; Preparation: 10 minutes; Cook time: 0 minutes
Nutrition facts: 525 Calories; 48 g Fats; 19 g Protein; 3 g Net Carb; 1 g Fiber;
Ingredients
- 1 avocado, halved, pitted
- 2 oz flaked salmon, packed in water
- 1 tbsp mayonnaise

- 1 tbsp grated cheddar cheese

Seasoning:
- 1/8 tsp salt
- 2 tbsp coconut oil

How to Prepare:
1. Prepare the avocado and for this, cut avocado in half and then remove its seed.
2. Drain the salmon, add it in a bowl along with remaining ingredients, stir well and then scoop into the hollow on an avocado half. Serve.

238 – Salmon Patties

Serves: 2; Preparation: 5 minutes; Cook time: 6 minutes
Nutrition facts: 276 Calories; 15.6 g Fats; 33.1 g Protein; 0.6 g Net Carb; 0.1 g Fiber;
Ingredients
- 4 oz flaked salmon, packed in water
- 1 egg
- 2 tbsp mayonnaise
- 1/8 tsp garlic powder
- 1 tbsp chopped cilantro

Seasoning:
- 1 tsp coconut oil
- 1/8 tsp salt
- 1/16 tsp ground black pepper

How to Prepare:
1. Prepare the patties and for this, place all the ingredients in a bowl, stir well, and then shape the mixture into two patties.
2. Take a skillet pan, place it over medium heat, add oil and when hot, add salmon patties and cook for 3 minutes per side until golden brown. Serve.

239 – Bacon and Salmon Bites

Serves: 2; Preparation: 10 minutes; Cook time: 15 minutes
Nutrition facts: 120 Calories; 9 g Fats; 10 g Protein; 1 g Net Carb; 0.2 g Fiber;
Ingredients
- 1 salmon fillets
- 4 bacon slices, halved
- 2 tbsp chopped cilantro

Seasoning:
- ¼ tsp salt
- 1/8 tsp ground black pepper

How to Prepare:
1. Turn on the oven, then set it to 350 degrees F, and let it preheat.
2. Meanwhile, cut salmon into bite-size pieces, then wrap each piece with a half slice of bacon, secure with a toothpick and season with salt and black pepper.
3. Take a baking sheet, place prepared salmon pieces on it and bake for 13 to 15 minutes until nicely browned and thoroughly cooked.
4. When done, sprinkle cilantro over salmon and serve.

240 – Panini Styled Mayo Salmon

Serves: 2; Preparation: 5 minutes; Cook time: 10 minutes
Nutrition facts: 132.7 Calories; 11.1 g Fats; 8 g Protein; 0.3 g Net Carb; 0 g Fiber;
Ingredients
- 2 salmon fillets
- 4 tbsp mayonnaise

How to Prepare:
1. Turn on the Panini press, spray it with oil and let it preheat.
2. Then spread 1 tbsp of mayonnaise on each side of salmon, place them on Panini press pan, shut with lid, and cook for 7 to 10 minutes until salmon has cooked to the desired level.
3. Serve.

241 – Tuna and Spinach Salad

Serves: 2; Preparation: 5 minutes; Cook time: 0 minutes
Nutrition facts: 191 Calories; 16.6 g Fats; 9.6 g Protein; 0.8 g Net Carb; 0.2 g Fiber;
Ingredients
- 4 oz tuna, packed in water
- 2 oz chopped spinach
- 1 tbsp grated mozzarella cheese
- 1/3 cup mayonnaise

Seasoning:
- ¼ tsp salt
- 1/8 tsp ground black pepper

How to Prepare:
1. Take a bowl, add mayonnaise in it along with cheese, season with salt and black pepper and whisk until combined.
2. Then add tuna and spinach, toss until mixed and serve.

242 – Tuna and Spinach Salad

Serves: 2; Preparation: 5 minutes; Cook time: 10 minutes;
Nutrition facts: 398.5 Calories; 15.5 g Fats; 62.8 g Protein; 0.7 g Net Carb; 1.3 g Fiber;
Ingredients
- 2 oz of spinach leaves
- 2 oz tuna, packed in water
- ¼ tsp ground black pepper
- 1/4 tsp sea salt
- 2 tbsp coconut oil, melted

How to Prepare:
1. Take a salad bowl, place spinach leaves in it, drizzle with 1 tbsp oil, sprinkle with 1/8 tsp of salt and black pepper, and then toss until mixed.
2. Top with tuna, sprinkle with remaining salt and black pepper, drizzle with oil and then serve.

243 – Italian Keto Plate

Serves: 2
Preparation: 5 minutes; Cook time: 0 minutes;
Nutrition facts: 412 Calories; 35 g Fats; 20 g Protein; 4 g Net Carb; 1.5 g Fiber;
Ingredients
- 2 oz fresh mozzarella cheese, sliced
- 2 oz tuna, packed in water
- 1 Roma tomato, halved
- 1/4 cup avocado oil
- 8 green olives
- ¼ tsp salt
- 1/8 tsp ground black pepper

How to Prepare:
1. Take two serving plates and then distribute tomato, cheese, and tuna evenly between them.
2. Season with salt and black pepper and then serve with avocado oil.

244 – Chicken with Green Beans and Spinach

Serves: 2; Preparation: 5 minutes; Cook time: 18 minutes;
Nutrition facts: 444 Calories; 37.5 g Fats; 22.2 g Protein; 2.6 g Net Carb; 1.8 g Fiber;
Ingredients
- 2 oz spinach leaves
- 3 oz green beans
- 2 chicken thighs

- 2 tbsp butter, unsalted
- 4 tbsp mayonnaise, full-fat

Seasoning:
- 1/3 tsp salt
- 1/8 tsp ground black pepper

How to Prepare:
1. Take a frying pan, place it over medium heat, add 1 tbsp butter and wait until it melts.
2. Season chicken with salt and black pepper, add to the frying pan and then cook for 4 to 5 minutes per side until golden brown and thoroughly cooked.
3. Add remaining butter, then green beans and fry them for 3 to 4 minutes until tender-crisp.
4. Add spinach, toss until mixed, and continue frying for 2 minutes until spinach leaves wilts.
5. Distribute chicken and vegetables between two plates and then serve with mayonnaise.

245 – Red Curry Glazed Mahi-Mahi

Serves: 2; Preparation: 5 minutes; Cook time: 7 minutes;
Nutrition facts: 272 Calories; 14 g Fats; 32 g Protein; 2 g Net Carb; 0 g Fiber;
Ingredients
- 2 Mahi-Mahi fillets
- 1/2 tbsp Thai red curry paste
- 1/2 tsp coconut sugar
- 1 tbsp coconut oil

Seasoning:
- ¼ tsp salt
- ¼ tsp ground black pepper

How to Prepare:
1. Turn on the broiler and let it preheat.
2. Take a baking sheet, line it with aluminum foil, and then place salmon on it.
3. Take a small bowl, add salt, black pepper, sugar, red curry paste and oil and stir until well combined.
4. Brush the paste on all sides of fish and then broil for 7 minutes until cooked through and glazed. Serve.

246 – Fish and Egg Plate

Serves: 2
Preparation: 5 minutes; Cook time: 10 minutes;
Nutrition facts: 547 Calories; 44.4 g Fats; 19.1 g Protein; 11.8 g Net Carb; 12 g Fiber;
Ingredients
- 2 eggs
- 1 tbsp butter, unsalted
- 2 pacific whitening fillets
- ½ oz chopped lettuce
- 1 scallion, chopped

Seasoning:
- 3 tbsp avocado oil
- 1/3 tsp salt
- 1/3 tsp ground black pepper

How to Prepare:
1. Cook the eggs and for this, take a frying pan, place it over medium heat, add butter and when it melts, crack the egg in the pan and cook for 2 to 3 minutes until fried to desired liking.
2. Transfer fried egg to a plate and then cook the remaining egg in the same manner.
3. Meanwhile, season fish fillets with ¼ tsp each of salt and black pepper.
4. When eggs have fried, sprinkle salt and black pepper on them, then add 1 tbsp oil into the frying pan, add fillets and cook for 4 minutes per side until thoroughly cooked. When done, distribute fillets to the plate, add lettuce and scallion, drizzle with remaining oil, and then serve.

247 – Sesame Tuna Salad

Serves: 2
Preparation: 35 minutes; Cook time: 0 minutes;
Nutrition facts: 322 Calories; 25.4 g Fats; 17.7 g Protein; 2.6 g Net Carb; 3 g Fiber;
Ingredients
- 6 oz of tuna in water
- ½ tbsp chili-garlic paste

- ½ tbsp black sesame seeds, toasted
- 2 tbsp mayonnaise
- 1 tbsp sesame oil

Seasoning:
- 1/8 tsp red pepper flakes

How to Prepare:
1. Take a medium bowl, all the ingredients for the salad in it except for tuna, and then stir until well combined.
2. Fold in tuna until mixed and then refrigerator for 30 minutes. Serve.

248 – Keto Tuna Sandwich

Serves: 2; Preparation: 10 minutes; Cook time: 10 minutes;
Nutrition facts: 255 Calories; 17.8 g Fats; 16.3 g Protein; 3.7 g Net Carb; 3.3 g Fiber;
Ingredients
- 2 oz tuna, packed in water
- 2 2/3 tbsp coconut flour
- 1 tsp baking powder
- 2 eggs
- 2 tbsp mayonnaise

Seasoning:
- 1/4 tsp salt
- 1/4 tsp ground black pepper

How to Prepare:
1. Turn on the oven, then set it to 375 degrees F and let it preheat.
2. Meanwhile, prepare the batter for this, add all the ingredients in a bowl, reserving mayonnaise, 1 egg, and 1/8 tsp salt, and then whisk until well combined.
3. Take a 4 by 4 inches heatproof baking pan, grease it with oil, pour in the prepared batter and bake 10 minutes until bread is firm.
4. Meanwhile, prepare tuna and for this, place tuna in a medium bowl, add mayonnaise, season with remaining salt and black pepper, and then stir until combined.
5. When done, let the bread cool in the pan for 5 minutes, then transfer it to a wire rack and cool for 20 minutes.
6. Slice the bread, prepare sandwiches with prepared tuna mixture, and then serve.

249 – Tuna Melt Jalapeno Peppers

Serves: 2; Preparation: 5 minutes; Cook time: 10 minutes;
Nutrition facts: 104 Calories; 6.2 g Fats; 7 g Protein; 2.1 g Net Carb; 1.1 g Fiber;
Ingredients
- 4 jalapeno peppers
- 1-ounce tuna, packed in water
- 1-ounce cream cheese softened
- 1 tbsp grated parmesan cheese
- 1 tbsp grated mozzarella cheese

Seasoning:
- 1 tsp chopped dill pickles
- 1 green onion, green part sliced only

How to Prepare:
1. Turn on the oven, then set it to 400 degrees F and let it preheat.
2. Prepare the peppers and for this, cut each pepper in half lengthwise and remove seeds and stem.
3. Take a small bowl, place tuna in it, add remaining ingredients except for cheeses, and then stir until combined.
4. Spoon tuna mixture into peppers, sprinkle cheeses on top, and then bake for 7 to 10 minutes until cheese has turned golden brown. Serve.

250 – Smoked Salmon Fat Bombs

Serves: 2; Preparation: 5 minutes; Cook time: 0 minutes;
Nutrition facts: 65 Calories; 4.8 g Fats; 4 g Protein; 0.5 g Net Carb; 0 g Fiber;
Ingredients
- 2 tbsp cream cheese, softened
- 1 ounce smoked salmon
- 2 tsp bagel seasoning

How to Prepare:
1. Take a medium bowl, place cream cheese and salmon in it, and stir until well combined.
2. Shape the mixture into bowls, roll them into bagel seasoning and then serve.

251 – Salmon Cucumber Rolls

Serves: 2; Preparation: 15 minutes; Cook time: 0 minutes;
Nutrition facts: 269 Calories; 24 g Fats; 6.7 g Protein; 4 g Net Carb; 2 g Fiber;
Ingredients
- 1 large cucumber
- 2 oz smoked salmon
- 4 tbsp mayonnaise
- 1 tsp sesame seeds

Seasoning:
- ¼ tsp salt
- ¼ tsp ground black pepper

How to Prepare:
4. Trim the ends of the cucumber, cut it into slices by using a vegetable peeler, and then place half of the cucumber slices in a dish.
5. Cover with paper towels, layer with remaining cucumber slices, top with paper towels, and let them refrigerate for 5 minutes.
6. Meanwhile, take a medium bowl, place salmon in it, add mayonnaise, season with salt and black pepper, and then stir until well combined.
7. Remove cucumber slices from the refrigerator, place salmon on one side of each cucumber slice, and then roll tightly.
8. Repeat with remaining cucumber, sprinkle with sesame seeds and then serve.

252 – Bacon Wrapped Mahi-Mahi

Serves: 2; Preparation: 10 minutes; Cook time: 12 minutes;
Nutrition facts: 217 Calories; 11.3 g Fats; 27.1 g Protein; 1.2 g Net Carb; 0.5 g Fiber;
Ingredients
- 2 fillets of mahi-mahi
- 2 strips of bacon
- ½ of lime, zested
- 4 basil leaves
- ½ tsp salt

Seasoning:
- ½ tsp ground black pepper
- 1 tbsp avocado oil

How to Prepare:
1. Turn on the oven, then set it to 375 degrees F and let them preheat.
2. Meanwhile, season fillets with salt and black pepper, top each fillet with 2 basil leaves, sprinkle with lime zest, wrap with a bacon strip and secure with a toothpick if needed.
3. Take a medium skillet pan, place it over medium-high heat, add oil and when hot, place prepared fillets in it and cook for 2 minutes per side.
4. Transfer pan into the oven and bake the fish for 5 to 7 minutes until thoroughly cooked. Serve.

253 – Cheesy Garlic Bread with Smoked Salmon

Serves: 2; Preparation: 10 minutes; Cook time: 1 minute;
Nutrition facts: 233 Calories; 18 g Fats; 13.8 g Protein; 1.9 g Net Carb; 1.5 g Fiber;
Ingredients
- 4 tbsp almond flour
- ½ tsp baking powder
- 2 tbsp grated cheddar cheese
- 1 egg
- 2 oz salmon, cut into thin sliced

Seasoning:
- 1 tbsp butter, unsalted
- ¼ tsp garlic powder
- 1/8 tsp salt
- ¼ tsp Italian seasoning

How to Prepare:
1. Take a heatproof bowl, place all the ingredients in it except for cheese and then stir by using a fork until well combined.
2. Fold in cheese until just mixed and then microwave for 1 minute at high heat setting until thoroughly cooked, else continue cooking for another 15 to 30 seconds.
3. When done, lift out the bread, cool it for 5 minutes and then cut it into slices.
4. Top each slice with salmon and then serve straight away

254 – Smoked Salmon Pasta Salad

Serves: 2; Preparation: 10 minutes; Cook time: 0 minutes;
Nutrition facts: 458 Calories; 38.7 g Fats; 15.4 g Protein; 6.1 g Net Carb; 1.7 g Fiber;
Ingredients
- 1 zucchini, spiralized into noodles
- 4 oz smoked salmon, break into pieces
- 2 oz cream cheese
- 2 oz mayonnaise
- 2 oz sour cream

Seasoning:
- 1/3 tsp salt
- ¼ tsp ground black pepper
- ¼ tsp hot sauce

How to Prepare:
1. Take a medium bowl, place cream cheese in it, add mayonnaise, sour cream, salt, black pepper and hot sauce and stir until well combined.
2. Add zucchini noodles, toss until well coated and then fold in salmon until just mixed. Serve.

255 – Tuna Salad Pickle Boats

Serves: 2; Preparation: 10 minutes; Cook time: 0 minutes;
Nutrition facts: 308.5 Calories; 23.7 g Fats; 17 g Protein; 3.8 g Net Carb; 3.1 g Fiber;
Ingredients
- 4 dill pickles
- 4 oz of tuna, packed in water, drained
- ¼ of lime, juiced
- 4 tbsp mayonnaise
- ¼ tsp salt
- 1/8 tsp ground black pepper
- ¼ tsp paprika
- 1 tbsp mustard paste

How to Prepare:
1. Prepare tuna salad and for this, take a medium bowl, place tuna in it, add lime juice, mayonnaise, salt, black pepper, paprika, and mustard and stir until mixed.
2. Cut each pickle into half lengthwise, scoop out seeds, and then fill with tuna salad. Serve.

256 – Shrimp Deviled Eggs

Serves: 2
Preparation: 5 minutes; Cook time: 0 minutes;
Nutrition facts: 210 Calories; 16.4 g Fats; 14 g Protein; 1 g Net Carb; 0.1 g Fiber;
Ingredients
- 2 eggs, boiled
- 2 oz shrimps, cooked, chopped
- ½ tsp tabasco sauce
- ½ tsp mustard paste
- 2 tbsp mayonnaise
- 1/8 tsp salt
- 1/8 tsp ground black pepper

How to Prepare:
1. Peel the boiled eggs, then slice in half lengthwise and transfer egg yolks to a medium bowl by using a spoon.
2. Mash the egg yolk, add remaining ingredients and stir until well combined.
3. Spoon the egg yolk mixture into egg whites, and then serve.

257 – Herb Crusted Tilapia

Serves: 2; Preparation: 5 minutes; Cook time: 10 minutes;
Nutrition facts: 520 Calories; 35 g Fats; 36.2 g Protein; 13.6 g Net Carb; 0.6 g Fiber;
Ingredients

- 2 fillets of tilapia
- ½ tsp garlic powder
- ½ tsp Italian seasoning
- ½ tsp dried parsley
- 1/3 tsp salt

Seasoning:
- 2 tbsp melted butter, unsalted
- 1 tbsp avocado oil

How to Prepare:
1. Turn on the broiler and then let it preheat.
2. Meanwhile, take a small bowl, place melted butter in it, stir in oil and garlic powder until mixed, and then brush this mixture over tilapia fillets.
3. Stir together remaining spices and then sprinkle them generously on tilapia until well coated.
4. Place seasoned tilapia in a baking pan, place the pan under the broiler and then bake for 10 minutes until tender and golden, brushing with garlic-butter every 2 minutes. Serve.

258 – Tuna Stuffed Avocado

Serves: 2; Preparation: 5 minutes; Cook time: 0 minutes;
Nutrition facts: 108.5 Calories; 8 g Fats; 6 g Protein; 0.8 g Net Carb; 2.3 g Fiber;
Ingredients
- 1 medium avocado
- ¼ of a lemon, juiced
- 5-ounce tuna, packed in water
- 1 green onion, chopped
- 2 slices of turkey bacon, cooked, crumbled

Seasoning:
- ¼ tsp salt
- ¼ tsp ground black pepper

How to Prepare:
1. Drain tuna, place it in a bowl, and then broke it into pieces with a form.
2. Add remaining ingredients, except for avocado and bacon, and stir until well combined.
3. Cut avocado into half, remove its pit and then stuff its cavity evenly with the tuna mixture. Top stuffed avocados with bacon and Serve.

259 – Garlic Butter Salmon

Serves: 2; Preparation: 10 minutes; Cook time: 15 minutes
Nutrition facts: 128 Calories; 4.5 g Fats; 41 g Protein; 1 g Net Carb; 0 g Fiber;
Ingredients
- 2 salmon fillets, skinless
- 1 tsp minced garlic
- 1 tbsp chopped cilantro
- 1 tbsp unsalted butter
- 2 tbsp grated cheddar cheese

Seasoning:
- ½ tsp salt
- ¼ tsp ground black pepper

How to Prepare:
1. Turn on the oven, then set it to 350 degrees F, and let it preheat.
2. Meanwhile, taking a rimmed baking sheet, grease it with oil, place salmon fillets on it, season with salt and black pepper on both sides.
3. Stir together butter, cilantro, and cheese until combined, then coat the mixture on both sides of salmon in an even layer and bake for 15 minutes until thoroughly cooked. Then Turn on the broiler and continue baking the salmon for 2 minutes until the top is golden brown. Serve.

260 – Salmon with Green Beans

Serves: 2; Nutrition facts: 352 Calories; 29 g Fats; 19 g Protein; 3.5 g Net Carb; 1.5 g Fiber;
Ingredients
- 6 oz green beans
- 3 oz unsalted butter
- 2 salmon fillets

Seasoning:
- ½ tsp garlic powder

- ½ tsp salt
- ½ tsp cracked black pepper

How to Prepare:
1. Take a frying pan, place butter in it and when it starts to melts, add beans and salmon in fillets in it, season with garlic powder, salt, and black pepper, and cook for 8 minutes until salmon is cooked, turning halfway through and stirring the beans frequently.
2. When done, evenly divide salmon and green beans between two plates and serve.

261 – Salmon Sheet pan

Serves: 2; Preparation: 10 minutes; Cook time: 20 minutes
Nutrition facts: 450 Calories; 23.8 g Fats; 36.9 g Protein; 5.9 g Net Carb; 2.4 g Fiber;
Ingredients
- 2 salmon fillets
- 2 oz cauliflower florets
- 2 oz broccoli florets
- 1 tsp minced garlic
- 1 tbsp chopped cilantro

Seasoning:
- 2 tbsp coconut oil
- 2/3 tsp salt
- ¼ tsp ground black pepper

How to Prepare:
1. Turn on the oven, then set it to 400 degrees F, and let it preheat.
2. Place oil in a small bowl, add garlic and cilantro, stir well, and microwave for 1 minute or until the oil has melted.
3. Take a rimmed baking sheet, place cauliflower and broccoli florets in it, drizzle with 1 tbsp of coconut oil mixture, season with 1/3 tsp salt, 1/8 tsp black pepper and bake for 10 minutes.
4. Then push the vegetables to a side, place salmon fillets in the pan, drizzle with remaining coconut oil mixture, season with remaining salt and black pepper on both sides and bake for 10 minutes until salmon is fork-tender. Serve.

262 – Bacon wrapped Salmon

Serves: 2; Preparation: 5 minutes; Cook time: 10 minutes
Nutrition facts: 190.7 Calories; 16.5 g Fats; 10.5 g Protein; 0 g Net Carb; 0 g Fiber;
Ingredients
- 2 salmon fillets, cut into four pieces
- 4 slices of bacon
- 2 tsp avocado oil
- 2 tbsp mayonnaise

Seasoning:
- ½ tsp salt
- ½ tsp ground black pepper

How to Prepare:
1. Turn on the oven, then set it to 375 degrees F and let it preheat.
2. Meanwhile, place a skillet pan, place it over medium-high heat, add oil and let it heat.
3. Season salmon fillets with salt and black pepper, wrap each salmon fillet with a bacon slice, then add to the pan and cook for 4 minutes, turning halfway through.
4. Then transfer skillet pan containing salmon into the oven and cook salmon for 5 minutes until thoroughly cooked.
5. Serve salmon with mayonnaise

263 – Stir-fry Tuna with Vegetables

Serves: 2; Preparation: 5 minutes; Cook time: 15 minutes
Nutrition facts: 99.7 Calories; 5.1 g Fats; 11 g Protein; 1.6 g Net Carb; 1 g Fiber;
Ingredients
- 4 oz tuna, packed in water
- 2 oz broccoli florets
- ½ of red bell pepper, cored, sliced
- ½ tsp minced garlic
- ½ tsp sesame seeds

Seasoning:
- 1 tbsp avocado oil
- 2/3 tsp soy sauce
- 2/3 tsp apple cider vinegar

- 3 tbsp water

How to Prepare:
1. Take a skillet pan, add ½ tbsp oil and when hot, add bell pepper and cook for 3 minutes until tender-crisp.
2. Then add broccoli floret, drizzle with water and continue cooking for 3 minutes until steamed, covering the pan.
3. Uncover the pan, cook for 2 minutes until all the liquid has evaporated, and then push bell pepper to one side of the pan.
4. Add remaining oil to the other side of the pan, add tuna and cook for 3 minutes until seared on all sides.
5. Then drizzle with soy sauce and vinegar, toss all the ingredients in the pan until mixed and sprinkle with sesame seeds. Serve.

264 – Chili-glazed Salmon

Serves: 2; Preparation: 5 minutes; Cook time: 10 minutes
Nutrition facts: 112.5 Calories; 5.6 g Fats; 12 g Protein; 3.4 g Net Carb; 0 g Fiber;
Ingredients
- 2 salmon fillets
- 2 tbsp sweet chili sauce
- 2 tsp chopped chives
- ½ tsp sesame seeds

How to Prepare:
1. Turn on the oven, then set it to 400 degrees F and let it preheat.
2. Meanwhile, place salmon in a shallow dish, add chili sauce and chives and toss until mixed.
3. Transfer prepared salmon onto a baking sheet lined with parchment sheet, drizzle with remaining sauce and bake for 10 minutes until thoroughly cooked.
4. Garnish with sesame seeds and Serve.

265 – Cardamom Salmon

Serves: 2; Preparation: 5 minutes; Cook time: 20 minutes
Nutrition facts: 143.3 Calories; 10.7 g Fats; 11.8 g Protein; 0 g Net Carb; 0 g Fiber;
Ingredients
- 2 salmon fillets
- ¾ tsp salt
- 2/3 tbsp ground cardamom
- 1 tbsp liquid stevia
- 1 ½ tbsp avocado oil

How to Prepare:
1. Turn on the oven, then set it to 275 degrees F and let it preheat.
2. Meanwhile, prepare the sauce and for this, place oil in a small bowl, and whisk in cardamom and stevia until combined.
3. Take a baking dish, place salmon in it, brush with prepared sauce on all sides, and let it marinate for 20 minutes at room temperature.
4. Then season salmon with salt and bake for 15 to 20 minutes until thoroughly cooked.
5. When done, flake salmon with two forks and then serve.

266 – Creamy Tuna, Spinach, and Eggs Plates

Serves: 2; Preparation: 5 minutes; Cook time: 0 minutes;
Nutrition facts: 212 Calories; 14.1 g Fats; 18 g Protein; 1.9 g Net Carb; 1.3 g Fiber;
Ingredients
- 2 oz of spinach leaves
- 2 oz tuna, packed in water
- 2 eggs, boiled
- 4 tbsp cream cheese, full-fat
- Seasoning:
- ¼ tsp salt
- 1/8 tsp ground black pepper

How to Prepare:
1. Take two plates and evenly distribute spinach and tuna between them.
2. Peel the eggs, cut them into half, divide them between the plates and then season with salt and black pepper.
3. Serve with cream cheese.

267 – Tuna and Avocado

Serves: 2; Preparation: 5 minutes; Cook time: 0 minutes;
Nutrition facts: 680 Calories; 65.6 g Fats; 10.2 g Protein; 2.2 g Net Carb; 9.7 g Fiber;
Ingredients
- 2 oz tuna, packed in water
- 1 avocado, pitted
- 8 green olives
- ½ cup mayonnaise, full-fat
Seasoning:
- 1/3 tsp salt
- 1/4 tsp ground black pepper
How to Prepare:
1. Cut avocado into half, then remove the pit, scoop out the flesh and distribute between two plates.
2. Add tuna and green olives and then season with salt and black pepper. Serve with mayonnaise.

268 – Baked Fish with Feta and Tomato

Serves: 2; Preparation: 5 minutes; Cook time: 15 minutes;
Nutrition facts: 427.5 Calories; 29.5 g Fats; 26.7 g Protein; 8 g Net Carb; 4 g Fiber;
Ingredients
- 2 pacific whitening fillets
- 1 scallion, chopped
- 1 Roma tomato, chopped
- 1 tsp fresh oregano
- 1-ounce feta cheese, crumbled
Seasoning:
- 2 tbsp avocado oil
- 1/3 tsp salt
- 1/4 tsp ground black pepper
- ¼ crushed red pepper
How to Prepare:
1. Turn on the oven, then set it to 400 degrees F and let it preheat.
2. Take a medium skillet pan, place it over medium heat, add oil and when hot, add scallion and cook for 3 minutes.
3. Add tomatoes, stir in ½ tsp oregano, 1/8 tsp salt, black pepper, red pepper, pour in ¼ cup water and bring it to simmer.
4. Sprinkle remaining salt over fillets, add to the pan, drizzle with remaining oil, and then bake for 10 to 12 minutes until fillets are fork-tender.
5. When done, top fish with remaining oregano and cheese and then serve.

269 – Garlic Oregano Fish

Serves: 2; Preparation: 5 minutes; Cook time: 12 minutes;
Nutrition facts: 199.5 Calories; 7 g Fats; 33.5 g Protein; 0.9 g Net Carb; 0.1 g Fiber;
Ingredients
- 2 pacific whitening fillets
- 1 tsp minced garlic
- 1 tbsp butter, unsalted
- 2 tsp dried oregano
Seasoning:
- 1/3 tsp salt
- 1/4 tsp ground black pepper
How to Prepare:
1. Turn on the oven, then set it to 400 degrees F and let it preheat.
2. Meanwhile, take a small saucepan, place it over low heat, add butter and when it melts, stir in garlic and cook for 1 minute, remove the pan from heat.
3. Season fillets with salt and black pepper, and place them on a baking dish greased with oil.
4. Pour butter mixture over fillets, then sprinkle with oregano and bake for 10 to 12 minutes until thoroughly cooked. Serve.

270 – Fish and Spinach Plate

Serves: 2
Preparation: 10 minutes; Cook time: 10 minutes;
Nutrition facts: 389 Calories; 34 g Fats; 7.7 g Protein; 10.6 g Net Carb; 2 g Fiber;
Ingredients
- 2 pacific whitening fillets
- 2 oz spinach
- ½ cup mayonnaise
- 1 tbsp avocado oil
- 1 tbsp unsalted butter

Seasoning:
- 1/2 tsp salt
- 1/3 tsp ground black pepper

How to Prepare:
1. Take a frying pan, place it over medium heat, add butter and wait until it melts.
2. Season fillets with 1/3 tsp salt and ¼ tsp black pepper, add to the pan, and cook for 5 minutes per side until golden brown and thoroughly cooked.
3. Transfer fillets to two plates, then distribute spinach among them, drizzle with oil and season with remaining salt and black pepper. Serve with mayonnaise.

271 – Fish with Kale and Olives

Serves: 2
Preparation: 5 minutes; Cook time: 12 minutes;
Nutrition facts: 454 Calories; 35.8 g Fats; 16 g Protein; 13.5 g Net Carb; 3.5 g Fiber;
Ingredients
- 2 pacific whitening fillets
- 2 oz chopped kale
- 3 tbsp coconut oil
- 2 scallion, chopped
- 6 green olives

Seasoning:
- 1/2 tsp salt
- 1/3 tsp ground black pepper
- 3 drops of liquid stevia

How to Prepare:
1. Take a large skillet pan, place it over medium-high heat, add 4 tbsp water, then add kale, toss and cook for 2 minutes until leaves are wilted but green.
2. When done, transfer kale to a strainer placed on a bowl and set aside until required.
3. Wipe clean the pan, add 2 tbsp oil, and wait until it melts.
4. Season fillets with 1/3 tsp salt and ¼ tsp black pepper, place them into the pan skin-side up and cook for 4 minutes per side until fork tender.
5. Transfer fillets to a plate, add remaining oil to the pan, then add scallion and olives and cook for 1 minute.
6. Return kale into the pan, stir until mixed, cook for 1 minute until hot and then season with remaining salt and black pepper.
7. Divide kale mixture between two plates, top with cooked fillets, and then serve.

272 – Mahi-Mahi with Chili Lime Butter

Serves: 2; Preparation: 5 minutes; Cook time: 10 minutes;
Nutrition facts: 298 Calories; 18.2 g Fats; 31.5 g Protein; 0.1 g Net Carb; 0.2 g Fiber;
Ingredients
- 3 tbsp coconut oil, divided
- ½ tsp red chili powder
- 2 mahi-mahi fillets
- 1 lime, zested

Seasoning:
- 1/3 tsp salt
- ¼ tsp ground black pepper

How to Prepare:
1. Prepare the chili-lime butter and for this, take a small bowl, add 2 tbsp coconut oil in it and then stir in red chili powder and lime zest until combined, set aside until required.
2. Take a medium skillet pan, place it over medium-high heat, add remaining oil and wait until it melts.
3. Season fillets with salt and black pepper, add to the pan and cook for 5 minutes per side until thoroughly cooked and golden brown.
4. When done, transfer fillets to the plates, top generously with prepared chili-lime butter, and then serve.

273 – Ginger Sesame Glazed Salmon

Serves: 2; Preparation: 10 minutes; Cook time: 15 minutes;
Nutrition facts: 370 Calories; 23.5 g Fats; 33 g Protein; 2.5 g Net Carb; 0 g Fiber;
Ingredients
- 2 salmon fillets
- 1 tbsp soy sauce
- 1 tsp sesame oil
- 2 tsp fish sauce
- 1 tbsp avocado oil
- 1 tsp garlic powder
- 1 tsp ginger powder
- ½ tbsp apple cider vinegar

How to Prepare:
1. Prepare the marinade and for this, take a small bowl, place soy sauce in it and stir in sesame oil, fish sauce, sesame oil, avocado oil, vinegar, ginger powder and garlic powder and stir until mixed.
2. Place salmon fillets in a shallow dish, pour prepared marinate on it, toss until coated, and let it marinate for 10 minutes.
3. When ready to cook, take a griddle pan, place it over medium heat, grease it with oil, and when hot, place marinated salmon fillets on it and then grill for 5 to 7 minutes per side until done. Serve.

274 – Tuna, Dill and Spinach Curry Bowl

Serves: 2; Preparation: 5 minutes; Cook time: 0 minutes;
Nutrition facts: 310 Calories; 28 g Fats; 12.2 g Protein; 1 g Net Carb; 0.5 g Fiber;
Ingredients
- 3 oz tuna, packed in water
- 1 green onion, sliced
- 1 tbsp diced dill pickle
- 1/3 of avocado, sliced
- 1 ounce chopped spinach
- 1 ½ tsp curry powder
- ¼ tsp of sea salt; 5 tbsp mayonnaise

How to Prepare:
1. Take a medium bowl, place mayonnaise in it, and then stir in curry powder and salt.
2. Add tuna, onion, dill pickle and spinach, toss until well coated, and then top with avocado. Serve.

275 – Mushroom with Salmon

Serves: 2; Preparation: 5 minutes; Cook time: 15 minutes;
Nutrition facts: 420 Calories; 34.2 g Fats; 25 g Protein; 1.8 g Net Carb; 0.3 g Fiber;
Ingredients
- 2 salmon fillets
- 2 oz sliced mushrooms
- 1 tbsp avocado oil
- 3 tbsp butter, unsalted
- ¼ cup of water
- 3/4 tsp salt; 1/2 tsp ground black pepper
- ¼ tsp paprika

How to Prepare:
1. Take a medium skillet pan, place it over medium heat, add oil and wait until it gets hot.
2. Season salmon with ½ tsp salt and ¼ tsp black pepper, add them to the pan and cook for 3 minutes per side until brown, set aside until done.
3. Add 2 tbsp butter into the pan and when it melts, add mushrooms, season with paprika and remaining salt and black pepper, and cook for 3 minutes until sauté.
4. Pour in water, stir well, then add remaining butter and when it melts, return pork chops into the pan and simmer for 3 minutes until cooked. Serve.

276 – Tuna Salad Cucumber Boats

Serves: 2; Preparation: 10 minutes; Cook time: 0 minutes;
Nutrition facts: 190 Calories; 14.2 g Fats; 8.8 g Protein; 3.6 g Net Carb; 2 g Fiber;

Ingredients
- 1 cucumber
- 2 oz tuna, packed in water
- 1 green onion, sliced
- 2 1/2 tbsp mayonnaise
- 1 tsp mustard paste
- ¼ tsp salt; 1/8 tsp ground black pepper

How to Prepare:
1. Prepare salad and for this, place tuna in a bowl, add onion, mayonnaise and mustard, then add salt and black pepper and stir until combined.
2. Cut cucumber from the middle lengthwise, then scrape out the inside by using a spoon and fill the space with tuna salad. Serve.

277 – Salmon with Lime Butter Sauce

Serves: 2
Preparation: 20 minutes; Cook time: 10 minutes;
Nutrition facts: 192 Calories; 18 g Fats; 6 g Protein; 4 g Net Carb; 0 g Fiber;
Ingredients
- 2 salmon fillets
- 1 lime, juiced, divided
- ½ tbsp minced garlic; 3 tbsp butter, unsalted
- 1 tbsp avocado oil
- 1/4 tsp salt
- 1/4 tsp ground black pepper

How to Prepare:
1. Prepare the fillets and for this, season fillets with salt and black pepper, place them on a shallow dish, drizzle with half of the lime juice and then it marinate for 15 minutes.
2. Meanwhile, prepare the lime butter sauce and for this, take a small saucepan, place it over medium-low heat, add butter, garlic, and half of the lime juice, stir until mixed, and then bring it to a low boil, set aside until required.
3. Then take a medium skillet pan, place it over medium-high heat, add oil and when hot, place marinated salmon in it, cook for 3 minutes per side and then transfer to a plate. Top each salmon with prepared lime butter sauce and then serve.

278 – Blackened Fish with Zucchini Noodles

Serves: 2; Preparation: 10 minutes; Cook time: 12 minutes;
Nutrition facts: 350 Calories; 25 g Fats; 27.1 g Protein; 2.8 g Net Carb; 1.6 g Fiber;
Ingredients
- 1 large zucchini
- 2 fillets of mahi-mahi
- 1 tsp Cajun seasoning
- 2 tbsp butter, unsalted
- 1 tbsp avocado oil

Seasoning:
- ½ tsp garlic powder
- 2/3 tsp salt
- ½ tsp ground black pepper

How to Prepare:
1. Spiralized zucchini into noodles, place them into a colander, sprinkle with 1/3 tsp salt, toss until mixed and set aside until required.
2. Meanwhile, prepare fish and for this, season fillets with remaining salt and ¾ tsp Cajun seasoning.
3. Take a medium skillet pan, place it over medium heat, add butter and when it melts, add prepared fillets, switch heat to medium-high level and cook for 3 to 4 minutes per side until cooked and nicely browned.
4. Transfer fillets to a plate and then reserve the pan for zucchini noodles.
5. Squeeze moisture from the noodles, add them to the skillet pan, add oil, toss until mixed, season with remaining Cajun seasoning and cook for 2 to 3 minutes until noodles have turned soft. Sprinkle with garlic powder, remove the pan from heat and distribute noodles between two plates. Top noodles with a fillet and then serve.

279 – Garlic Parmesan Mahi-Mahi

Serves: 2; Preparation: 10 minutes; Cook time: 10 minutes;
Nutrition facts: 170 Calories; 7.8 g Fats; 22.3 g Protein; 0.8 g Net Carb; 0 g Fiber;
Ingredients
- 2 fillets of mahi-mahi
- 1 tsp minced garlic
- 1/3 tsp dried thyme
- 1 tbsp avocado oil
- 1 tbsp grated parmesan cheese

Seasoning:
- 1/3 tsp salt
- 1/4 tsp ground black pepper

How to Prepare:
1. Turn on the oven, set it to 425 degrees F and let it preheat.

2. Meanwhile, take a small bowl, place oil in it, add garlic, thyme, cheese and oil and stir until mixed.
3. Season fillets with salt and black pepper, then coat with prepared cheese mixture, place fillets in a baking sheet and then cook for 7 to 10 minutes until thoroughly cooked. Serve.

280 – Salmon with Roasted Veggies

Serves: 2; Preparation: 10 minutes; Cook time: 15 minutes;
Nutrition facts: 571 Calories; 45.4 g Fats; 34.1 g Protein; 3.5 g Net Carb; 2.2 g Fiber;
Ingredients
- 2 fillets of salmon
- 4 oz asparagus spears cut
- 2 oz sliced mushrooms
- 2 oz grape tomatoes
- 2 oz basil pesto

Seasoning:
- 2/3 tsp salt
- ½ tsp ground black pepper
- 1 tbsp mayonnaise
- 1.5 oz grated mozzarella cheese
- 2 tbsp avocado oil

How to Prepare:
1. Turn on the oven, then set it to 425 degrees F and let it preheat.
2. Take a medium baking sheet lined with parchment paper, place salmon fillets on it and then season with 1/3 tsp salt and ¼ tsp ground black pepper.
3. Take a small bowl, mix together mayonnaise and pesto in it until combined, spread this mixture over seasoned salmon and then top evenly with cheese.
4. Take a medium bowl, place all the vegetables in it, season with remaining salt and black pepper, drizzle with oil and toss until coated.
5. Spread vegetables around prepared fillets and then bake for 12 to 15 minutes until fillets have thoroughly cooked. Serve.

281 – Cheesy Baked Mahi-Mahi

Serves: 2; Preparation: 10 minutes; Cook time: 25 minutes;
Nutrition facts: 241 Calories; 13.6 g Fats; 25 g Protein; 1.1 g Net Carb; 0 g Fiber;
Ingredients
- 2 fillets of mahi-mahi
- ½ tsp minced garlic
- 2 tbsp mayonnaise
- 1 tbsp grated parmesan cheese
- 1 tbsp grated mozzarella cheese

Seasoning:
- ½ tsp salt
- ¼ tsp ground black pepper
- 1 tbsp mustard paste
- ¼ of lime, juiced

How to Prepare:
1. Turn on the oven, then set it to 400 degrees F and let it preheat.
2. Meanwhile, take a baking sheet, line it with foil, place fillets on it and then season with salt and black pepper.
3. Take a small bowl, add mayonnaise, stir in garlic, lime juice and mustard until well mixed and then spread this mixture evenly on fillets.
4. Stir together parmesan cheese and mozzarella cheese, sprinkle it over fillets and then bake for 15 to 20 minutes until thoroughly cooked.
5. Then Turn on the broiler and continue cooking the fillets for 2 to 3 minutes until the top is nicely golden brown.
6. Serve.

282 – Zucchini Noodles in Creamy Salmon Sauce

Serves: 2; Preparation: 5 minutes; Cook time: 7 minutes;
Nutrition facts: 271 Calories; 22 g Fats; 13.5 g Protein; 4.5 g Net Carb; 1.5 g Fiber;
Ingredients
- 3 oz smoked salmon
- 1 zucchini, spiralized into noodles
- 1 tbsp chopped basil
- 2 oz whipping cream
- 2 oz cream cheese, softened

Seasoning:
- 1/3 tsp salt; 1/3 tsp ground black pepper
- 1 tbsp avocado oil

How to Prepare:
1. Cut zucchini into noodles, place them into a colander, sprinkle with some salt, toss until well coated and set aside for 10 minutes.

2. Meanwhile, take a small saucepan, place it over medium-low heat, add whipped cream in it, add cream cheese, stir until mixed, bring it to a simmer, and cook for 2 minutes or more until smooth.
3. Then switch heat to low heat, add basil into the pan, cut salmon into thin slices, add to the pan, season with ¼ tsp of each salt and black pepper and cook for 1 minute until hot, set aside until required.
4. Take a medium skillet pan, place it over medium-high heat, add oil and when hot, add zucchini noodles and cook for 1 to 2 minutes until fried.
5. Season zucchini with remaining salt and black pepper and then distribute zucchini between two plates.
6. Top zucchini noodles with salmon sauce and then serve.

283 – Cottage Cheese and Tuna Salad

Serves: 2; Preparation: 5 minutes; Cook time: 0 minutes;
Nutrition facts: 220 Calories; 10.8 g Fats; 23.3 g Protein; 2.4 g Net Carb; 2.9 g Fiber;
Ingredients
- 4 oz tuna, packed in water, drained
- 2 oz sliced mushroom
- 1-ounce spinach, sliced
- 3 oz cottage cheese
- 1 tbsp avocado oil
Seasoning:
- 2/3 tsp Cajun seasoning
- 1/3 tsp salt; ¼ tsp ground black pepper
- ½ tsp mustard paste
How to Prepare:
1. Take a medium bowl, place tuna in it and then add mushroom and spinach.
2. Sprinkle with Cajun seasoning, salt and black pepper, add mustard and cottage cheese, drizzle with oil and then stir until well combined. Serve.

284 – Avocado Tuna Boats

Serves: 2; Preparation: 5 minutes; Cook time: 10 minutes;
Nutrition facts: 244 Calories; 19 g Fats; 8 g Protein; 7 g Net Carb; 5 g Fiber;
Ingredients
- 4 oz tuna, packed in water, drained
- 1 green onion sliced
- 1 avocado, halved, pitted
- 3 tbsp mayonnaise
- 1/3 tsp salt; ¼ tsp ground black pepper
- ¼ tsp paprika
How to Prepare:
1. Prepare the filling and for this, take a medium bowl, place tuna in it, add green onion, salt, black pepper, paprika and mayonnaise and then stir until well combined.
2. Cut avocado in half lengthwise, then remove the pit and fill with prepared filling. Serve.

285 – Tuna Melt

Serves: 2; Preparation: 10 minutes; Cook time: 5 minutes;
Nutrition facts: 821 Calories; 72.3 g Fats; 38.4 g Protein; 2.5 g Net Carb; 2.3 g Fiber;
Ingredients
- 6 tbsp almond flour
- 2 eggs
- 3 oz tuna, packed in water, drained
- 6 tbsp mayonnaise
- 8 tsp grated cheddar cheese
Seasoning:
- 1 tsp baking powder
- 1/3 tsp salt; ¼ tsp ground black pepper
- 2 tbsp avocado oil
How to Prepare:
1. Turn on the oven, then set it to 375 degrees F and let it preheat.
2. Meanwhile, prepare the batter for this, place flour in a bowl, add baking powder, 1/8 tsp salt, oil and eggs and then whisk until well combined.
3. Take a 4 by 4 inches heatproof baking pan, pour prepared batter in it, tap the pan for few times to remove air bubbles from the batter, and then microwave for 1 minute and 30 seconds until bread is firm.
4. When done, let the bread cool in the pan for 5 minutes, then transfer it to a wire rack and cool for 10 minutes.

5. Cut the bread into four slices and then spread 2 tbsp of mayonnaise evenly on one side of each slice.
6. Take a small bowl, place tuna in it, add remaining mayonnaise, salt and black pepper, and then stir until combined.
7. Take a baking sheet, line it with parchment sheet, place mayonnaise spread slices on it, then top with tuna mixture and sprinkle cheese on top.
8. Turn on the broiler, let it preheat, then place baking sheet in it and broil for 2 minutes until cheese has melted and begin to bubbles.
9. Serve.

286 – Dinner – Smoked Salmon and Broccoli Quiche

Serves: 2; Preparation: 10 minutes; Cook time: 20 minutes;
Nutrition facts: 440 Calories; 33.4 g Fats; 26.1 g Protein; 5.6 g Net Carb; 2 g Fiber;
Ingredients
- 6 oz grated broccoli florets
- 2 oz smoked salmon, broken into pieces
- 3 eggs
- 2 oz whipping cream
- 1-ounce grated parmesan cheese
Seasoning:
- ¼ tsp salt; 1/3 tsp ground black pepper
- 1-ounce grated mozzarella cheese
- 1 tbsp avocado oil
How to Prepare:
1. Turn on the oven, then set it to 350 degrees F and let it preheat.
2. Take a medium quiche pan, grease it with avocado oil, place broccoli florets in the bottom and then top with salmon pieces.
3. Crack eggs in a medium bowl, add cream, salt, black pepper, and parmesan cheese, whisk until combined, and then pour this mixture over broccoli and salmon in the pan. Top with mozzarella cheese and then bake for 15 to 20 minutes until cooked through, and then the top has turned nicely browned.
4. When done, let the quiche cool for 5 minutes, take it out, cut it into two portions and then serve.

287 – Tuna Casserole

Serves: 2; Preparation: 5 minutes; Cook time: 10 minutes;
Nutrition facts: 233 Calories; 18 g Fats; 16.5 g Protein; 0.5 g Net Carb; 0.5 g Fiber;
Ingredients
- 5 oz tuna, packed in water, drained
- ¼ of yellow onion, chopped
- ½ tbsp mustard
- 3 tbsp mayonnaise
- 4 tbsp grated cheddar cheese
Seasoning:
- ¼ tsp salt; 1/8 tsp ground black pepper
- ¼ tsp cayenne pepper
How to Prepare:
1. Turn on the oven, then set it to 400 degrees F and let it preheat.
2. Take a medium bowl, place tuna in it, add onion, mustard, 2 tbsp cheese, salt, black pepper, and cayenne pepper and stir until well mixed.
3. Take a casserole dish, place tuna mixture in it, sprinkle remaining cheese on top and then bake for 10 minutes until hot. Serve.

288 – Tuna Zoodle Casserole

Serves: 2; Preparation: 10 minutes; Cook time: 20 minutes;
Nutrition facts: 320 Calories; 21.2 g Fats; 24.3 g Protein; 4.7 g Net Carb; 1.6 g Fiber;
Ingredients
- 1 zucchini
- 5 oz tuna, packed in water, drained
- 4 tbsp whipping cream
- 3 tbsp grated cheddar cheese
- 4 oz almond milk, unsweetened
- 1 tbsp butter, unsalted
- ½ tsp garlic powder
- 2 oz of chicken bone broth
How to Prepare:
1. Turn on the oven, then set it to 350 degrees F and let it preheat.

2. Cut zucchini into noodles, spread them on a baking sheet, and then bake for 5 to 10 minutes or more until moisture has evaporated completely, stirring every 5 minutes.
3. Meanwhile, take a medium skillet pan, place it over medium heat, add butter and when it melts, add garlic powder, cream, broth, and 2 tbsp cheddar cheese, stir until smooth and cook for 2 minutes until cheese has melted.
4. Add tuna, stir until combined, and then remove the pan from heat.
5. Take a casserole dish, spread half of the pre-baked zucchini noodles in its bottom, top with half of the tuna mixture, cover with remaining zucchini noodles, and then spread the remaining tuna mixture on it.
6. Sprinkle remaining cheese on top and then bake for 12 to 15 minutes until cheese has melted and the mixture is bubbling. Serve.

289 – Bang Bang Shrimps

Serves: 2; Preparation: 5 minutes; Cook time: 6 minutes;
Nutrition facts: 290 Calories; 23.1 g Fats; 13 g Protein; 7.2 g Net Carb; 0 g Fiber;
Ingredients
- 4 oz shrimps
- ¼ tsp paprika
- ¼ tsp apple cider vinegar
- 2 tbsp sweet chili sauce
- ¼ cup mayonnaise
- ¼ tsp salt; 1/8 tsp ground black pepper
- 2 tsp avocado oil
How to Prepare:
1. Take a medium skillet pan, place it over medium heat, add oil and wait until it gets hot.
2. Season shrimps with salt, black pepper, and paprika until coated, add them to the pan, and cook for 2 to 3 minutes per side until pink and cooked.
3. Take a medium bowl, place mayonnaise in it, and then whisk in vinegar and chili sauce until combined.
4. Add shrimps into the mayonnaise mixture, toss until coated, and then serve.

290 – Shrimp Wraps

Serves: 2; Preparation: 5 minutes; Cook time: 10 minutes;
Nutrition facts: 265 Calories; 19.9 g Fats; 13.6 g Protein; 3.2 g Net Carb; 3.3 g Fiber;
Ingredients
- 4 oz shrimps
- 2 tbsp coconut flour
- ½ tsp garlic powder
- 1 tbsp avocado oil
- 2 cabbage leaves
- ¼ tsp salt; 1/8 tsp ground black pepper
- 1 tbsp water
- 2 tbsp mayonnaise
How to Prepare:
1. Take a shallow dish, place coconut flour in it, and then stir in garlic, powder, salt, and black pepper.
2. Stir in water until smooth and then coat each shrimp in it, one at a time.
3. Take a medium skillet pan, place it over medium heat, add oil and when hot, add shrimps in it and cook for 3 minutes per side until cooked.
4. Distribute shrimps between two cabbage leaves, drizzle with mayonnaise, then roll like a wrap and serve.

291 – Creamy Shrimp and Bacon Skillet

Serves: 2; Preparation: 5 minutes; Cook time: 8 minutes;
Nutrition facts: 303 Calories; 24.4 g Fats; 17.8 g Protein; 1.5 g Net Carb; 0 g Fiber;
Ingredients
- 2 slices of bacon, chopped
- 4 oz of shrimps
- 3 oz whipping cream
- ¼ tsp salt
- 2 tsp avocado oil
- 1/8 tsp ground black pepper
How to Prepare:
1. Take a medium skillet pan, place it over medium heat and when hot, add bacon and cook for 3 minutes until cooked, but not crisp.
2. Add shrimps, season with salt and black pepper and continue cooking for 4 to 5 minutes until cooked.
3. Switch heat to the low level, add cream, stir until coated, and then cook for 1 minute until hot. Serve.

292 – Shrimp Cauliflower Rice

Serves: 2; Preparation: 5 minutes; Cook time: 12 minutes;
Nutrition facts: 180 Calories; 10.5 g Fats; 18 g Protein; 0.8 g Net Carb; 1.4 g Fiber;
Ingredients
- 4 oz shrimps
- 6 oz grated cauliflower
- 2 tsp soy sauce
- 1 tbsp avocado oil
- 1 egg, beaten
- ¼ tsp garlic powder
- 1/3 tsp salt; ¼ tsp ground black pepper

How to Prepare:
1. Take a medium skillet pan, place it over medium heat, add ½ tbsp oil and when hot, add shrimps and cook for 4 to 5 minutes until pink and cooked.
2. Sprinkle garlic powder over shrimps, continue cooking for 30 seconds and then transfer shrimps to a plate.
3. Add remaining oil into the pan and, when hot, add beaten egg and then cook for 2 to 3 minutes until scrambled to the desired level.
4. Add cauliflower, stir until mixed, season with salt and black pepper, drizzle with soy sauce and cook for 3 to 4 minutes until tender.
5. Return shrimps into the pan, toss until mixed, and then continue cooking for 1 minute until hot. Serve.

293 – Spicy Shrimps with Cabbage

Serves: 2; Preparation: 5 minutes; Cook time: 8 minutes;
Nutrition facts: 255 Calories; 15.6 g Fats; 17 g Protein; 5.8 g Net Carb; 4.8 g Fiber;
Ingredients
- 4 oz shrimps
- 1 pound cabbage, shredded
- ¼ tsp 5-spice seasoning
- 1 tbsp Sriracha sauce
- 1 tbsp grated parmesan cheese

Seasoning:
- ½ tsp garlic powder
- ¼ tsp salt; 1/8 tsp ground black pepper
- 2 tbsp avocado oil

How to Prepare:
1. Take a medium skillet pan, place it over medium heat, add 1 tbsp oil and when hot, add shrimps, season with five-spice seasoning and cook for 1 to 2 minutes per side until pink.
2. Drizzle with Sriracha sauce, toss until coated, cook for another minute and then transfer shrimps to a plate.
3. Add remaining oil into the skillet pan, add cabbage, season with salt and black pepper, toss until mixed, and then cook for 2 to 3 minutes until crisp and nicely browned.
4. Return shrimps into the pan, sprinkle with cheese, toss until mixed and cook for 1 minute until hot and cheese has melted. Serve.

294 – Coconut Crusted Tilapia Nuggets

Serves: 2; Preparation: 5 minutes; Cook time: 10 minutes;
Nutrition facts: 430 Calories; 23.2 g Fats; 37.3 g Protein; 7 g Net Carb; 10 g Fiber;
Ingredients
- 2 fillets of tilapia
- 1 egg
- 2 oz coconut flour
- 2 tbsp avocado oil

Seasoning:
- ½ tsp salt; ¼ tsp ground black pepper

How to Prepare:
1. Take a shallow bowl, crack the egg in it and then whisk until blended.
2. Take a shallow dish, place flour in it, and then stir in salt and black pepper until mixed.
3. Cut fillets into bite-size pieces, then dip each piece into egg and dredge into flour mixture until well coated.
4. Take a medium skillet pan, place it over medium heat, add oil and when hot, place nuggets in it and cook for 5 to 7 minutes per side until golden brown and cooked.
5. Serve.

Vegetables

295 – Salad Sandwiches

Serves: 2; Preparation: 5 minutes; Cook time: 0 minutes;
Nutrition facts: 187 Calories; 17 g Fats; 5 g Protein; 4 g Net Carb; 1.5 g Fiber;
Ingredients
- 1 medium avocado, peeled, pitted, diced
- 2 leaves of iceberg lettuce
- 1-ounce unsalted butter
- 2-ounce cheddar cheese, sliced

How to Prepare:
1. Rinse the lettuce leaves, pat dry with a paper towel, and then smear each leaf with butter.
2. Top lettuce with cheese and avocado and serve.

296 – Celeriac Stuffed Avocado

Serves: 2; Preparation: 10 minutes; Cook time: 0 minutes
Nutrition facts: 285 Calories; 27 g Fats; 2.8 g Protein; 4.4 g Net Carb; 2.6 g Fiber;
Ingredients
- 1 avocado
- 1 celery root, finely chopped
- 2 tbsp mayonnaise
- ½ of a lemon, juiced, zested
- 2 tbsp mayonnaise; ¼ tsp salt

How to Prepare:
1. Prepare avocado and for this, cut avocado in half and then remove its pit.
2. Place remaining ingredients in a bowl, stir well until combined and evenly stuff this mixture into avocado halves. Serve.

297 – Cobb salad

Serves: 1; Preparation: 5 minutes; Cook time: 10 minutes;
Nutrition facts: 206 Calories; 11.8 g Fats; 19.2 g Protein; 6 g Net Carb; 3 g Fiber;
Ingredients
- 1 large egg, hard-boiled, peeled, diced
- 2 oz chicken thigh
- 2 1/2 slices bacon, cooked, crumbled
- ½ of a medium avocado, diced
- ½ cup chopped lettuce
- 1 cup of water; 3 tbsp apple cider vinegar
- 1 ½ tbsp coconut oil
- ¼ tsp salt; 1/8 tsp ground black pepper

How to Prepare:
1. Cook chicken thigh and for this, place chicken thighs in an instant pot, pour in 1 cup water, and shut the pot with a lid.
2. Cook the chicken for 5 minutes at high pressure, and when done, let the pressure release naturally.
3. Meanwhile, cook the bacon and for this, take a skillet pan, place it over medium heat and when hot, add bacon slices.
4. Cook the bacon for 3 to 5 minutes until golden brown, then transfer them to a cutting board and chop the bacon, reserve the bacon grease in the pan for the next meal.
5. When chicken thigh has cooked, transfer it to a bowl and shred the chicken with two forks, reserving the chicken broth for later use.
6. Assemble the salad and for this, place lettuce in a salad plate, top with chicken, bacon, diced eggs, avocado, and chicken in horizontal rows.
7. Prepare the dressing and for this, whisk together salt, black pepper, vinegar, and oil until incorporated and then drizzle the dressing generously over the salad.

298 – Cabbage Hash Browns

Serves: 2; Preparation: 10 minutes; Cook time: 12 minutes
Nutrition facts: 336 Calories; 29.5 g Fats; 16 g Protein; 0.9 g Net Carb; 0.8 g Fiber;
Ingredients

- 1 ½ cup shredded cabbage
- 2 slices of bacon
- 1/2 tsp garlic powder
- 1 egg

Seasoning:
- 1 tbsp coconut oil
- ½ tsp salt; 1/8 tsp ground black pepper

How to Prepare:
1. Crack the egg in a bowl, add garlic powder, black pepper, and salt, whisk well, then add cabbage, toss until well mixed and shape the mixture into four patties.
2. Take a large skillet pan, place it over medium heat, add oil and when hot, add patties in it and cook for 3 minutes per side until golden brown.
3. Transfer hash browns to a plate, then add bacon into the pan and cook for 5 minutes until crispy. Serve hash browns with bacon.

299 – Cauliflower Hash Browns

Serves: 2; Preparation: 10 minutes; Cook time: 18 minutes
Nutrition facts: 347.8 Calories; 31 g Fats; 15.6 g Protein; 1.2 g Net Carb; 0.5 g Fiber;
Ingredients
- ¾ cup grated cauliflower
- 2 slices of bacon
- 1/2 tsp garlic powder
- 1 large egg white
- 1 tbsp coconut oil
- ½ tsp salt; 1/8 tsp ground black pepper

How to Prepare:
1. Place grated cauliflower in a heatproof bowl, cover with plastic wrap, poke some holes in it with a fork and then microwave for 3 minutes until tender.
2. Let steamed cauliflower cool for 10 minutes, then wrap in a cheesecloth and squeeze well to drain moisture as much as possible.
3. Crack the egg in a bowl, add garlic powder, black pepper, and salt, whisk well, then add cauliflower, and toss until well mixed and sticky mixture comes together.
4. Take a large skillet pan, place it over medium heat, add oil and when hot, drop cauliflower mixture on it, press lightly to form hash brown patties, and cook for 3 to 4 minutes per side until browned.
5. Transfer hash browns to a plate, then add bacon into the pan and cook for 5 minutes until crispy.
6. Serve hash browns with bacon.

300 – Asparagus, With Bacon and Eggs

Serves: 2; Preparation: 5 minutes; Cook time: 12 minutes
Nutrition facts: 179 Calories; 15.3 g Fats; 9 g Protein; 0.7 g Net Carb; 0.6 g Fiber;
Ingredients
- 4 oz asparagus
- 2 slices of bacon, diced
- 1 egg
- ¼ tsp salt
- 1/8 tsp ground black pepper

How to Prepare:
1. Take a skillet pan, place it over medium heat, add bacon, and cook for 4 minutes until crispy.
2. Transfer cooked bacon to a plate, then add asparagus into the pan and cook for 5 minutes until tender-crisp.
3. Crack the egg over the cooked asparagus, season with salt and black pepper, then switch heat to medium-low level and cook for 2 minutes until egg white has set.
4. Chop the cooked bacon slices, sprinkle over egg and asparagus and serve.

301 – Bell Pepper Eggs

Serves: 2; Preparation: 10 minutes; Cook time: 4 minutes
Nutrition facts: 110.5 Calories; 8 g Fats; 7.2 g Protein; 1.7 g Net Carb; 1.1 g Fiber;
Ingredients
- 1 green bell pepper,
- 2 eggs
- 1 tsp coconut oil
- ¼ tsp salt
- ¼ tsp ground black pepper

How to Prepare:
1. Prepare pepper rings, and for this, cut out two slices from the pepper, about ¼-inch, and reserve remaining bell pepper for later use.
2. Take a skillet pan, place it over medium heat, grease it with oil, place pepper rings in it, and then crack an egg into each ring.
3. Season eggs with salt and black pepper, cook for 4 minutes or until eggs have cooked to the desired level.
4. Transfer eggs to a plate and serve.

302 – Omelet-Stuffed Peppers

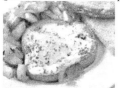

Serves: 2; Preparation: 5 minutes; Cook time: 20 minutes
Nutrition facts: 428 Calories; 35.2 g Fats; 23.5 g Protein; 2.8 g Net Carb; 1.5 g Fiber;
Ingredients
- 1 large green bell pepper, halved, cored
- 2 eggs
- 2 slices of bacon, chopped, cooked
- 2 tbsp grated parmesan cheese

Seasoning:
- 1/3 tsp salt; ¼ tsp ground black pepper

How to Prepare:
1. Turn on the oven, then set it to 400 degrees F, and let preheat.
2. Then take a baking dish, pour in 1 tbsp water, place bell pepper halved in it, cut-side up, and bake for 5 minutes.
3. Meanwhile, crack eggs in a bowl, add chopped bacon and cheese, season with salt and black pepper, and whisk until combined.
4. After 5 minutes of baking time, remove baking dish from the oven, evenly fill the peppers with egg mixture and continue baking for 15 to 20 minutes until eggs has set.

303 – Bacon Avocado Bombs

Serves: 2; Preparation: 10 minutes; Cook time: 10 minutes
Nutrition facts: 378 Calories; 33.6 g Fats; 15.1 g Protein; 0.5 g Net Carb; 2.3 g Fiber;
Ingredients
- 1 avocado, halved, pitted
- 4 slices of bacon; 2 tbsp grated parmesan cheese

How to Prepare:
1. Turn on the oven and broiler and let it preheat.
2. Meanwhile, prepare the avocado and for that, cut it in half, then remove its pit, and then peel the skin.
3. Evenly one half of the avocado with cheese, replace with the other half of avocado and then wrap avocado with bacon slices.
4. Take a baking sheet, line it with aluminum foil, place wrapped avocado on it, and broil for 5 minutes per side, flipping carefully with tong halfway.
5. When done, cut each avocado in half crosswise and serve

304 – Egg in a Hole with Eggplant

Serves: 2; Preparation: 5 minutes; Cook time: 15 minutes
Nutrition facts: 184 Calories; 14.1 g Fats; 7.8 g Protein; 3 g Net Carb; 3.5 g Fiber;
Ingredients
- 1 large eggplant
- 2 eggs
- 1 tbsp coconut oil, melted
- 1 tsp unsalted butter
- 2 tbsp chopped green onions
- ¾ tsp ground black pepper; ¾ tsp salt

How to Prepare:
1. Set the grill and let it preheat at the high setting.
2. Meanwhile, prepare the eggplant, and for this, cut two slices from eggplant, about 1-inch thick, and reserve the remaining eggplant for later use.
3. Brush slices of eggplant with oil, season with salt on both sides, then place the slices on grill and cook for 3 to 4 minutes per side.
4. Transfer grilled eggplant to a cutting board, let it cool for 5 minutes and then make a home in the center of each slice by using a cookie cutter.
5. Take a frying pan, place it over medium heat, add butter and when it melts, add eggplant slices in it and crack an egg into its each hole.
6. Let the eggs cook for 3 to 4 minutes, then carefully flip the eggplant slice and continue cooking for 3 minutes until the egg has thoroughly cooked.
7. Season egg with salt and black pepper, transfer them to a plate, then garnish with green onions and serve.

305 – Frittata with Spinach and Meat

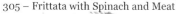

Serves: 2; Preparation: 10 minutes; Cook time: 20 minutes
Nutrition facts: 166 Calories; 13 g Fats; 10 g Protein; 0.5 g Net Carb; 0.5 g Fiber;

Ingredients
- 4 oz ground turkey
- 3 oz of spinach leaves
- 1/3 tsp minced garlic
- 1/3 tsp coconut oil
- 2 eggs

Seasoning:
- 1/3 tsp salt; ¼ tsp ground black pepper

How to Prepare:
1. Turn on the oven, then set it to 400 degrees F, and let it preheat.
2. Meanwhile, take a skillet pan, place it over medium heat, add spinach and cook for 3 to 5 minutes until spinach leaves have wilted, remove the pan from heat.
3. Take a small heatproof skillet pan, place it over medium heat, add ground turkey and cook for 5 minutes until thoroughly cooked.
4. Then add spinach, season with salt and black pepper, stir well, then remove the pan from heat and spread the mixture evenly in the pan.
5. Crack eggs in a bowl, season with salt and black pepper, then pour this mixture over spinach mixture in the pan and bake for 10 to 15 minutes until frittata has thoroughly cooked and the top is golden brown. When done, let frittata rest in the pan for 5 minutes, then cut it into slices and serve.

306 – Avocado Egg Boat with Cheddar

Serves: 2; Preparation: 5 minutes; Cook time: 15 minutes
Nutrition facts: 263.5 Calories; 21.4 g Fats; 12 g Protein; 1.3 g Net Carb; 4.6 g Fiber;
Ingredients
- 1 avocado, halved, pitted
- 2 eggs
- 2 tbsp chopped bacon
- 2 tbsp shredded cheddar cheese

Seasoning:
- 1/8 tsp salt; 1/8 tsp ground black pepper

How to Prepare:
1. Turn on the oven, then set it to 400 degrees F and let it preheat.
2. Meanwhile, prepare avocado and for this, cut it into half lengthwise and then remove the pit.
3. Scoop out some of the flesh from the center, crack an egg into each half, then sprinkle with bacon and season with salt and black pepper.
4. Sprinkle cheese over egg and avocado and then bake for 10 to 15 minutes or until the yolk has cooked to desired level. Serve.

307 – Cauliflower Fritters

Serves: 2; Preparation: 5 minutes; Cook time: 8 minutes
Nutrition facts: 92 Calories; 7.2 g Fats; 4.6 g Protein; 2 g Net Carb; 1.3 g Fiber;
Ingredients
- ½ cup cauliflower florets
- 3 tbsp shredded cheddar cheese
- ½ of egg
- 1 tbsp avocado oil

Seasoning:
- ¼ tsp salt; 1/8 tsp ground black pepper

How to Prepare:
1. Take a food processor, add cauliflower florets in it, then pulse them until finely chopped and tip the florets into a heatproof bowl.
2. Cover the bowl with a plastic wrap, pork holes by using a fork and then microwave for 2 minutes or until just tender.
3. Then add remaining ingredients except for oil and stir well until incorporated and cheese has melted.
4. Take a skillet pan, place it over medium heat, add oil and when hot, drop in ¼ of the batter, shape it into patties and cook for 3 minutes per side until crispy and browned. Serve.

308 – Brussel Sprouts Bacon Breakfast Hash

Serves: 2; Preparation: 5 minutes; Cook time: 25 minutes
Nutrition facts: 134.5 Calories; 8.2 g Fats; 10.8 g Protein; 2.8 g Net Carb; 1.6 g Fiber;
Ingredients
- 3 oz Brussel sprouts, sliced
- 2 slices of bacon, chopped
- ½ tsp minced garlic
- ¾ tbsp apple cider vinegar
- 2 eggs

How to Prepare:
1. Place a skillet pan over medium heat and when hot, add bacon and cook for 5 to 7 minutes until crispy.
2. Transfer bacon to a plate, add garlic and cook for 30 seconds until fragrant.
3. Then add Brussel sprouts, stir in vinegar and cook for 5 minutes until tender.
4. Return bacon into the pan, cook for 5 minutes until sprouts are golden brown, then create a well in the pan and cracks the egg in it.
5. Cook the eggs for 3 to 5 minutes until cooked to the desired level and then serve immediately.

309 – Cauliflower and Bacon Hash

Serves: 2; Preparation: 5 minutes; Cook time: 15 minutes
Nutrition facts: 211.5 Calories; 18.6 g Fats; 9 g Protein; 1.3 g Net Carb; 0.3 g Fiber;
Ingredients
- ½ cup chopped cauliflower florets
- 2 slices of bacon, diced
- ¼ tsp paprika
- 1 tbsp avocado oil

Seasoning:
- 1/3 tsp salt; 1/8 tsp ground black pepper
- 1 ½ tbsp water

How to Prepare:
1. Take a skillet pan, place it over medium-high heat, add bacon, and cook for 3 to 5 minutes until crispy.
2. Transfer bacon to a plate, then add cauliflower into the pan and cook for 3 minutes until golden.
3. Season with salt, black pepper, and paprika, drizzle with water, and cook for 3 to 5 minutes until cauliflower has softened.
4. Chop the bacon, add it into the pan, stir well, cook for 2 minutes and then remove the pan from heat. Serve.

310 – Bacon and Avocado Salad

Serves: 2; Preparation: 5 minutes; Cook time: 8 minutes
Nutrition facts: 147.6 Calories; 13.6 g Fats; 6 g Protein; 1.7 g Net Carb; 0.6 g Fiber;
Ingredients
- 4 slices of bacon, chopped
- 4 oz chopped lettuce
- ½ of a medium avocado, sliced
- 1 tbsp avocado oil
- 1 tbsp apple cider vinegar

How to Prepare:
1. Prepare bacon and for this, place a skillet pan over medium heat and when hot, add chopped bacon and cook for 5 to 8 minutes until golden brown.
2. Then distribute lettuce and avocado between two plates, top with bacon, drizzle with avocado oil and apple cider and serve.

311 – Spinach and Eggs Scramble

Serves: 2; Preparation: 5 minutes; Cook time: 10 minutes
Nutrition facts: 90 Calories; 7 g Fats; 5.6 g Protein; 0.7 g Net Carb; 0.6 g Fiber;
Ingredients
- 4 oz spinach
- ¼ tsp salt
- 1/8 tsp ground black pepper
- 1 tbsp unsalted butter
- 3 eggs, beaten

How to Prepare:
1. Take a frying pan, place it over medium heat, add butter and when it melts, add spinach and cook for 5 minutes until leaves have wilted.
2. Then pour in eggs, season with salt and black pepper, and cook for 3 minutes until eggs have scramble to the desired level. Serve.

312 – Breakfast Burgers with Avocado

Serves: 2; Preparation: 5 minutes; Cook time: 15 minutes
Nutrition facts: 205.2 Calories; 18.5 g Fats; 7.7 g Protein; 0.7 g Net Carb; 1.9 g Fiber;
Ingredients
- 4 strips of bacon
- 2 tbsp chopped lettuce
- 2 avocados
- 2 eggs
- 2 tbsp mayonnaise

Seasoning:
- ¼ tsp salt
- ¼ tsp sesame seeds

How to Prepare:
1. Take a skillet pan, place it over medium heat and when hot, add bacon strips and cook for 5 minutes until crispy.
2. Transfer bacon to a plate lined with paper towels, crack an egg into the pan, and cook for 2 to 4 minutes or until fried to the desired level; fry remaining egg in the same manner.
3. Prepare sandwiches and for this, cut each avocado in half widthwise, remove the pit, and scoop out the flesh.
4. Fill the hollow of two avocado halves with mayonnaise, then top each half with 1 tbsp of chopped lettuce, 2 bacon strips, and a fried egg, and then cover with the second half of avocado. Sprinkle sesame seeds on avocados and serve.

313 – Zucchini and Broccoli Fritters

Serves: 2; Preparation: 10 minutes; Cook time: 10 minutes
Nutrition facts: 191 Calories; 16.6 g Fats; 9.6 g Protein; 0.8 g Net Carb; 0.2 g Fiber;
Ingredients
- 1 ounce chopped broccoli
- 1 zucchini, grated, squeezed
- 2 eggs
- 2 tbsp almond flour
- ½ tsp nutritional yeast

Seasoning:
- 1/3 tsp salt
- ¼ tsp dried basil
- 1 tbsp avocado oil

How to Prepare:
1. Wrap grated zucchini in a cheesecloth, twist it well to remove excess moisture, and then place zucchini in a bowl.
2. Add remaining ingredients, except for oil, and then whisk well until combined.
3. Take a skillet pan, place it over medium heat, add oil and when hot, drop zucchini mixture in four portions, shape them into flat patties and cook for 4 minutes per side until thoroughly cooked. Serve.

314 – Zucchini Breakfast Hash

Serves: 2; Preparation: 5 minutes; Cook time: 15 minutes
Nutrition facts: 144.5 Calories; 12.5 g Fats; 6 g Protein; 0.9 g Net Carb; 0.5 g Fiber;
Ingredients
- 4 slices of bacon, chopped
- 1 zucchini, diced
- 2 eggs
- 2 tbsp avocado oil
- 3/4 tsp salt, divided
- ¼ tsp ground black pepper

How to Prepare:
1. Take a skillet pan, place it over medium heat, add bacon, and cook for 5 minutes until lightly brown.
2. Then add zucchini, season with ½ tsp salt, stir, cook for 10 minutes and then transfer to plate.
3. Fry eggs to desired level in avocado oil, season eggs with salt and black pepper to taste and serve with zucchini hash.

315 – Bacon, Avocado Egg Boats

Serves: 2; Preparation: 5 minutes; Cook time: 15 minutes;
Nutrition facts: 229 Calories; 18 g Fats; 11 g Protein; 1.1 g Net Carb; 4.6 g Fiber;
Ingredients
- 1 avocado, pitted
- 2 slices of turkey bacon
- 2 eggs
Seasoning:
- ¼ tsp salt; 1/8 tsp ground black pepper
How to Prepare:
1. Turn on the oven, then set it to 425 degrees F and let it preheat.
2. Meanwhile, prepare the avocado and for this, cut the avocado into half, remove the pit and then scoop out some of the flesh to make the hollow bigger.
3. Take a skillet pan, place it over medium heat and when hot, add bacon slices and cook for 3 minutes per side until crisp.
4. Transfer each slice into the hollow of each avocado half, crack the egg into each hollow and bake the egg boats for 12 to 15 minutes until the egg has cooked to the desired level. When done, season egg boats with salt and black pepper and serve.

316 – Broccoli and Mozzarella Muffins

Serves: 2; Preparation: 5 minutes; Cook time: 12 minutes;
Nutrition facts: 135 Calories; 9.5 g Fats; 9.1 g Protein; 1.4 g Net Carb; 0.6 g Fiber;
Ingredients
- 1/3 cup chopped broccoli
- 2 eggs
- 1 tbsp coconut cream
- 2 tbsp grated mozzarella cheese, full-fat
Seasoning:
- ¼ tsp salt; ¼ tsp ground black pepper
How to Prepare:
1. Turn on the oven, then set it to 350 degrees F and let it preheat.
2. Take a medium bowl, crack eggs in it and whisk in salt, black pepper, and cream until well combined.
3. Add broccoli and cheese, stir until mixed, divide the batter evenly between two silicone muffin cups, and bake for 10 to 12 minutes until firm and the top has golden brown. When done, let muffin cool for 5 minutes, then take them out and serve.

317 – Cheesy Cauliflower Muffins

Serves: 2
Preparation: 10 minutes; Cook time: 12 minutes;
Nutrition facts: 77 Calories; 5.6 g Fats; 4.6 g Protein; 1.7 g Net Carb; 0.9 g Fiber;
Ingredients
- ¾ cup chopped cauliflower florets
- 1 egg
- 1 ¾ tbsp coconut flour
- ¼ tsp Italian seasoning
- 1/3 cup grated parmesan cheese
Seasoning:
- ¼ tsp salt
- 1/8 tsp onion powder
- 1/8 tsp garlic powder
How to Prepare:
1. Turn on the oven, then set it to 375 degrees F and let it preheat.
2. Take a medium bowl, place chopped cauliflower in it, add flour, half of the cheese, onion powder, garlic powder, and Italian seasoning and stir until incorporated and smooth.
3. Take four silicone cups, fill them with prepared cauliflower mixture, sprinkle remaining cheese on top and then bake for 10 to 12 minutes until thoroughly cooked and firm.
4. Serve.

318 – Scrambled Eggs with Kale

Serves: 2; Preparation: 5 minutes; Cook time: 8 minutes;
Nutrition facts: 173 Calories; 14.5 g Fats; 8.5 g Protein; 1.2 g Net Carb; 0.1 g Fiber;
Ingredients
- 1 green onion, chopped
- ½ cup chopped kale
- 1 tbsp avocado oil
- 2 eggs
- 1 tbsp grated cheddar cheese

Seasoning:
- 1/8 tsp garlic powder; ¼ tsp salt

How to Prepare:
1. Take a medium skillet pan, place it over medium heat, add oil and when hot, add green onion and cook for 1 minute until tender-crisp.
2. Add kale, season with garlic powder and salt, stir until mixed and cook for 1 minute until kale leaves wilt.
3. Crack eggs in a bowl, whisk until well combined, then pour the egg into the pan, spread evenly, and cook for 2 minutes until it begins to set, don't stir.
4. Then scramble the eggs and continue cooking for 2 to 3 minutes until eggs have cooked to the desired level. Sprinkle with cheese and then serve.

319 – Spicy Eggs in Kale

Serves: 2; Preparation: 5 minutes; Cook time: 10 minutes;
Nutrition facts: 195 Calories; 15.5 g Fats; 9.8 g Protein; 2 g Net Carb; 3 g Fiber;
Ingredients
- 1 bunch of kale
- 2 green onion, sliced
- ½ of lime, juiced, zested
- 2 eggs
- ½ cup chicken broth

Seasoning:
- 1/3 tsp salt; 1/4 tsp ground black pepper
- 1 ½ tbsp unsalted butter

How to Prepare:
1. Take a medium frying pan, place it over medium heat, add butter and when it melts, add onion and cook for 1 minute.
2. Add kale, cook for 2 minutes until saute, then pour in broth and season with salt and black pepper.
3. Add lime zest and juice, stir until mixed, pour in chicken broth and simmer for 3 minutes until kale has turned soft.
4. Switch heat to medium-low level, make two packets in kale, crack an egg into each packet, then cover with the lid and cook for 2 to 3 minutes.
5. Remove pan from heat, let it rest for 3 minutes, then sprinkle with some black pepper and serve.

320 – Fried Eggs with Kale and Bacon

Serves: 2; Preparation: 5 minutes; Cook time: 15 minutes;
Nutrition facts: 525 Calories; 50 g Fats; 14.4 g Protein; 1.1 g Net Carb; 2.8 g Fiber;
Ingredients
- 4 slices of turkey bacon, chopped
- 1 bunch of kale, chopped
- 3 oz butter, unsalted
- 2 eggs
- 2 tbsp chopped walnuts

Seasoning:
- 1/3 tsp salt
- 1/3 tsp ground black pepper

How to Prepare:
1. Take a frying pan, place it over medium heat, add two-third of the butter in it, let it melt, then add kale, switch heat to medium-high level and cook for 4 to 5 minutes until edges have turned golden brown.
2. When done, transfer kale to a plate, set aside until required, add bacon into the pan and cook for 4 minutes until crispy.
3. Return kale into the pan, add nuts, stir until mixed and cook for 2 minutes until thoroughly warmed.
4. Transfer kale into the bowl, add remaining butter into the pan, crack eggs into the pan and fry them for 2 to 3 minutes until cooked to the desired level.
5. Distribute kale between two plates, add fried eggs on the side, sprinkle with salt and black pepper, and then serve.

321 – Eggs with Greens

Serves: 2; Preparation: 5 minutes; Cook time: 10 minutes;
Nutrition facts: 135 Calories; 11.1 g Fats; 7.2 g Protein; 0.2 g Net Carb; 0.5 g Fiber;
Ingredients
- 3 tbsp chopped parsley
- 3 tbsp chopped cilantro
- ¼ tsp cayenne pepper
- 2 eggs
- 1 tbsp butter, unsalted
- ¼ tsp salt; 1/8 tsp ground black pepper

How to Prepare:
1. Take a medium skillet pan, place it over medium-low heat, add butter and wait until it melts.
2. Then add parsley and cilantro, season with salt and black pepper, stir until mixed and cook for 1 minute.
3. Make two space in the pan, crack an egg into each space, and then sprinkle with cayenne pepper, cover the pan with the lid and cook for 2 to 3 minutes until egg yolks have set. Serve.

322 – Spicy Chaffle with Jalapeno

Serves: 2; Preparation: 5 minutes; Cook time: 10 minutes;
Nutrition facts: 153 Calories; 10.7 g Fats; 11.1 g Protein; 1 g Net Carb; 1 g Fiber;
Ingredients
- 2 tsp coconut flour
- ½ tbsp chopped jalapeno pepper
- 2 tsp cream cheese
- 1 egg
- 2 oz shredded mozzarella cheese
- ¼ tsp salt; 1/8 tsp ground black pepper

How to Prepare:
1. Switch on a mini waffle maker and let it preheat for 5 minutes.
2. Meanwhile, take a medium bowl, place all the ingredients in it and then mix by using an immersion blender until smooth.
3. Ladle the batter evenly into the waffle maker, shut with lid, and let it cook for 3 to 4 minutes until firm and golden brown. Serve.

323 – Pumpkin Smoothie

Serves: 2; Preparation: 5 minutes; Cook time: 0 minutes;
Nutrition facts: 285 Calories; 27 g Fats; 2.1 g Protein; 6.2 g Net Carb; 1.6 g Fiber;
Ingredients
- 2 tbsp whipped topping
- 4 tbsp pumpkin puree
- 1 tbsp MCT oil
- ½ cup almond milk, unsweetened
- ½ cup coconut milk, unsweetened
- ½ tsp pumpkin pie spice
- 1 ½ cup crushed ice

How to Prepare:
2. Place all the ingredients in the order into a food processor or blender, and then pulse for 2 to 3 minutes until smooth.
3. Distribute smoothie between two glasses and then serve.

324 – Bulletproof Tea

Serves: 2; Preparation: 5 minutes; Cook time: 0 minutes;
Nutrition facts: 151 Calories; 17 g Fats; 0 g Protein; 1 g Net Carb; 0 g Fiber;

Ingredients
- ¼ tsp cinnamon
- 2 cups strong tea
- 2 tbsp coconut oil
- 2 tbsp coconut milk

How to Prepare:
1. Distribute tea between two mugs, add remaining ingredients evenly and then stir until blended. Serve.

325 – Tea with Coconut

Serves: 2; Preparation: 10 minutes; Cook time: 0 minutes;
Nutrition facts: 191 Calories; 16 g Fats; 11 g Protein; 2 g Net Carb; 0 g Fiber;
Ingredients
- 2 tea bags, cinnamon-flavored
- 2 tbsp MCT oil
- ¼ cup coconut milk, unsweetened
- 2 cups boiling water

How to Prepare:
1. Pour boiling water between two mugs, add a tea into each mug and let them steep for 5 minutes.
2. Meanwhile, take a small saucepan, place it over medium heat, pour in milk and heat for 3 minutes or more until hot.
3. After 5 minutes, remove tea bags from mugs, stir in milk, and MCT oil by using a milk frother until combined and then serve.

326 – Cauliflower and Egg Plate

Serves: 2; Preparation: 5 minutes; Cook time: 12 minutes;
Nutrition facts: 193 Calories; 15.3 g Fats; 7.9 g Protein; 3.3 g Net Carb; 0.9 g Fiber;
Ingredients
- 4 oz cauliflower florets, chopped
- 1 jalapeno pepper, sliced
- 2 eggs
- 1 ½ tbsp avocado oil

Seasoning:
- ¼ tsp salt
- 1/8 tsp ground black pepper

How to Prepare:
1. Take a skillet pan, place it over medium heat, add oil and when hot, add cauliflower florets and jalapeno and then cook for 5 to 7 minutes until tender.
2. Make two spaces in the pan, crack an egg in each space, and then cook for 3 to 4 minutes until eggs have cooked to the desired level.
3. When done, sprinkle salt and black pepper over eggs and then serve.

327 – Butternut Squash and Green Onions with Eggs

Serves: 2; Preparation: 5 minutes; Cook time: 8 minutes;
Nutrition facts: 161 Calories; 11.1 g Fats; 9.3 g Protein; 2.6 g Net Carb; 1.9 g Fiber;
Ingredients
- 4 oz butternut squash pieces
- 1 green onion, sliced
- ½ tbsp butter, unsalted
- 2 tsp grated parmesan cheese
- 2 eggs

Seasoning:
- ¼ tsp salt
- ¼ tsp ground black pepper
- 1 tsp avocado oil

How to Prepare:
1. Take a skillet pan, place it over medium heat, add butter and oil and when hot, add butternut squash and green onion, season with 1/8 tsp of each salt and black pepper, stir until mixed and cook for 3 to 5 minutes until tender.
2. Make two space in the pan, crack an egg in each space, sprinkle with cheese, season with remaining salt and black pepper, cover with the lid and cook for 2 to 3 minutes until the egg has cooked to the desired level.
3. Serve.

328 – Broccoli, Asparagus and Cheese Frittata

Serves: 2; Preparation: 5 minutes; Cook time: 16 minutes;
Nutrition facts: 206 Calories; 17 g Fats; 10 g Protein; 2 g Net Carb; 1 g Fiber;
Ingredients
- ¼ cup chopped broccoli florets
- 1-ounce asparagus spear cuts
- ½ tsp garlic powder
- 2 tbsp whipping cream
- 2 eggs

Seasoning:
- 2 tsp tbsp avocado oil
- 1/8 tsp salt; 1/8 tsp ground black pepper

How to Prepare:
1. Turn on the oven, then set it to 350 degrees F and let it preheat.
2. Take a medium bowl, crack eggs in it, add salt, black pepper and cream, whisk until combined and then stir in cheese, set aside until required.
3. Take a medium skillet pan, place it over medium heat, add oil and when hot, add broccoli florets and asparagus, sprinkle with garlic powder, stir until mixed and cook for 3 to 4 minutes until tender.
4. Spread the vegetables evenly in the pan, pour egg mixture over them and cook for 1 to 2 minutes until the mixture begins to firm.
5. Transfer the pan into the oven and then cook for 10 to 12 minutes until frittata has cooked and the top has turned golden brown.
6. When done, cut the frittata into slices and then serve.

329 – Broccoli and Egg Plate

Serves: 2; Preparation: 5 minutes; Cook time: 5 minutes;
Nutrition facts: 155 Calories; 12 g Fats; 8 g Protein; 1.6 g Net Carb; 1 g Fiber;
Ingredients
- 3 oz broccoli florets, chopped
- 2 eggs
- 1 tbsp avocado oil
- ¼ tsp salt
- 1/8 tsp ground black pepper

How to Prepare:
1. Take a heatproof bowl, place broccoli florets in it, cover with a plastic wrap, microwave for 2 minutes, and then drain well.
2. Take a medium skillet pan, place it over medium heat, add oil and when hot, add broccoli florets and cook for 2 minutes until golden brown.
3. Spread broccoli florets evenly in the pan crack eggs in the pan, sprinkle with salt and black pepper, cover with the lid and cook for 2 to 3 minutes until eggs have cooked to the desired level. Serve.

330 – Radish with Fried Eggs

Serves: 2; Preparation: 5 minutes; Cook time: 10 minutes;
Nutrition facts: 187 Calories; 17 g Fats; 7 g Protein; 0.4 g Net Carb; 0.5 g Fiber;
Ingredients
- ½ bunch of radish, diced
- ½ tsp garlic powder
- 1 tbsp butter
- 1 tbsp avocado oil
- 2 eggs

Seasoning:
- 1/3 tsp salt
- ¼ tsp ground black pepper

How to Prepare:
1. Take a medium skillet pan, place it over medium heat, add butter and when it melts, add radish, sprinkle with garlic powder and ¼ tsp salt and cook for 5 minutes until tender.
2. Distribute radish between two plates, then return pan over medium heat, add oil and when hot, crack eggs in it and fry for 2 to 3 minutes until cooked to desired level.
3. Add eggs to the radish and then serve.

331 – Sunny Side Up Eggs on Creamed Spinach

Serves: 2; Preparation: 5 minutes; Cook time: 10 minutes;
Nutrition facts: 280 Calories; 23.3 g Fats; 10.2 g Protein; 2.7 g Net Carb; 2.8 g Fiber;
Ingredients

- 4 oz of spinach leaves
- 1 tbsp mustard paste
- 4 tbsp whipping cream
- 2 eggs
  Seasoning:
- ¼ tsp salt; ¼ tsp ground black pepper
- ½ tsp dried thyme
- 1 tbsp avocado oil

How to Prepare:
1. Take a medium skillet pan, place it over high heat, pour in water to cover its bottom, then add spinach, toss until mixed and cook for 2 minutes until spinach wilts.
2. Then drain the spinach by passing it through a sieve placed on a bowl and set it aside.
3. Take a medium saucepan, place it over medium heat, add spinach, mustard, thyme, and cream, stir until mixed and cook for 2 minutes.
4. Then sprinkle black pepper over spinach, stir until mixed and remove the pan from heat.
5. Take a medium skillet pan, place it over medium-high heat, add oil and when hot, crack eggs in it and fry for 3 to 4 minutes until eggs have cooked to the desired level.
6. Divide spinach mixture evenly between two plates, top with a fried egg and then serve.

332 – Creamy Kale Baked Eggs

Serves: 2; Preparation: 10 minutes; Cook time: 20 minutes;
Nutrition facts: 301.5 Calories; 25.5 g Fats; 9.8 g Protein; 4.3 g Net Carb; 4 g Fiber;
Ingredients

- 1 bunch of kale, chopped
- 1-ounce grape tomatoes, halved
- 3 tbsp whipping cream
- 2 tbsp sour cream
- 2 eggs
  Seasoning:
- ½ tsp salt; ½ tsp ground black pepper
- ½ tsp Italian seasoning
- 1 ½ tbsp butter, unsalted

How to Prepare:
1. Turn on the oven, then set it to 400 degrees F and let it preheat.
2. Meanwhile, take a medium skillet pan, place butter in it, add butter and when it melts, add kale and cook for 2 minutes until wilted
3. Add Italian seasoning, 1/3 tsp each of salt and black pepper, cream and sour cream, then stir until mixed and cook for2 minutes until cheese has melted and the kale has thickened slightly.
4. Take two ramekins, divide creamed kale evenly between them, then top with cherry tomatoes and carefully crack an egg into each ramekin.
5. Sprinkle remaining salt and black pepper on eggs and then bake for 15 minutes until eggs have cooked completely. Serve.

333 – Butter Asparagus with Creamy Eggs

Serves: 2; Preparation: 5 minutes; Cook time: 8 minutes;
Nutrition facts: 338 Calories; 28.5 g Fats; 14.4 g Protein; 4.7 g Net Carb; 1.2 g Fiber;
Ingredients

- 4 oz asparagus
- 2 eggs, blended
- 1.5 oz grated parmesan cheese
- 1-ounce sour cream
- 2 tbsp butter, unsalted
- 1/3 tsp salt; 1/8 tsp ground black pepper
- ¼ tsp cayenne pepper
- ½ tbsp avocado oil

How to Prepare:
1. Take a medium skillet pan, place it over medium heat, add butter and when it melts, add blended eggs and then cook for 2 to 3 minutes until scrambled to the desired level; don't overcook.
2. Spoon the scrambled eggs into a food processor, add 1/8 tsp salt, cayenne pepper, sour cream and cheese and then pulse for 1 minute until smooth.
3. Return skillet pan over medium heat, add oil and when hot, add asparagus, season with black pepper and remaining salt, toss until mixed and cook for 3 minutes or more until roasted.
4. Distribute asparagus between two plates, add egg mixture, and then serve.

334 – Spinach Egg Muffins

Serves: 2; Preparation: 5 minutes; Cook time: 10 minutes;
Nutrition facts: 55 Calories; 3.5 g Fats; 4.5 g Protein; 0.4 g Net Carb; 0.2 g Fiber;
Ingredients
- ½ cups chopped spinach
- 1/8 tsp dried basil
- 1/8 tsp garlic powder
- 2 large eggs
- 3 tbsp grated Parmesan cheese

Seasoning:
- ¼ tsp of sea salt; 1/8 tsp ground black pepper

How to Prepare:
1. Turn on the oven, then set it to 400 degrees F, and let preheat.
2. Meanwhile, place eggs in a bowl, season with salt and black pepper and whisk until blended.
3. Add garlic and basil, whisk in mixed and then stir in spinach and cheese until combined.
4. Take two silicone muffin cups, grease them with reserved bacon greased, fill them evenly with prepared egg mixture and bake for 8 to 10 minutes until the top has nicely browned. Serve.

335 – Broccoli and Egg Muffin

Serves: 2; Preparation: 10 minutes; Cook time: 10 minutes
Nutrition facts: 76 Calories; 5.1 g Fats; 5.7 g Protein; 1.2 g Net Carb; 0.7 g Fiber;
Ingredients
- ¼ cup broccoli florets, steamed, chopped
- 2 tbsp grated cheddar cheese
- 1/16 tsp dried thyme
- 1/16 tsp garlic powder
- 1 egg

Seasoning:
- ¼ tsp salt; 1/8 tsp ground black pepper

How to Prepare:
1. Turn on the oven, then set it to 400 degrees F and let it preheat.
2. Meanwhile, take two silicone muffin cups, grease them with oil, and evenly fill them with broccoli and cheese.
3. Crack the egg in a bowl, add garlic powder, thyme, salt, and black pepper, whisk well, then evenly pour the mixture into muffin cups and bake for 8 to 10 minutes until done. Serve.

336 – Jalapeno and Cheese Egg Muffins

Serves: 2; Preparation: 10 minutes; Cook time: 15 minutes
Nutrition facts: 108 Calories; 7.1 g Fats; 8.9 g Protein; 1.8 g Net Carb; 0.4 g Fiber;
Ingredients
- 1 jalapeno pepper, diced
- 2 tbsp sliced green onions
- 2 tbsp grated parmesan cheese
- 1 tsp all-purpose seasoning
- 2 eggs

Seasoning:
- 1/3 tsp salt; ¼ tsp ground black pepper

How to Prepare:
1. Turn on the oven, then set it to 375 degrees F, and let it preheat.
2. Meanwhile, take two silicone muffin cups, grease with oil, and evenly fill them with cheese, jalapeno pepper, and green onion.
3. Crack eggs in a bowl, season with salt, black pepper, and all-purpose seasoning, whisk well, then evenly pour the mixture into muffin cups and bake for 15 to 20 minutes or until the top is slightly brown and muffins have puffed up.
4. Serve.

337 – Cheesy Tomato and Olive Muffins

Serves: 2; Preparation: 10 minutes; Cook time: 12 minutes;
Nutrition facts: 256 Calories; 23.5 g Fats; 8.7 g Protein; 1 g Net Carb; 1.8 g Fiber;
Ingredients
- 4 1/3 tbsp almond flour
- ½ tbsp coconut flour
- 1/3 tbsp chopped tomato
- 1/3 tbsp sliced green olives
- 2 tbsp sour cream
Seasoning:
- 1/8 tsp baking powder
- 2/3 tbsp avocado oil
- 3 tbsp grated parmesan cheese
- ½ of egg
How to Prepare:
1. Turn on the oven, then set it to 320 degrees F and let it preheat.
2. Meanwhile, take a medium bowl, place flours in it, and stir in the baking powder until mixed.
3. Add eggs along with sour cream and oil, whisk until blended and then fold in cheese, tomato, and olives until just mixed.
4. Take two silicone muffin cups, add the prepared batter in it evenly and then bake for 10 to 12 minutes until cooked but slightly moist in the middle.
5. When done, let muffin cools for 5 minutes, then take them out and serve.

338 – Pumpkin Bread

Serves: 2; Preparation: 10 minutes; Cook time: 25 minutes;
Nutrition facts: 240 Calories; 17.7 g Fats; 9.4 g Protein; 1 g Net Carb; 8.4 g Fiber;
Ingredients
- 6 tbsp coconut flour
- 1 tbsp erythritol sweetener
- ¼ tsp vanilla extract, unsweetened
- 1 egg
- 2 tbsp pumpkin puree
Seasoning:
- ¼ tsp baking powder
- ¼ tsp cinnamon
- 1 tbsp chopped almonds
- 1 ½ tbsp butter, unsalted, softened
How to Prepare:
1. Turn on the oven, then set it to 350 degrees F and let it preheat.
2. Meanwhile, take a medium bowl, place butter in it, whisk in sugar and egg until fluffy.
3. Add remaining ingredients except for almonds, whisk until incorporated and smooth batter comes together and then fold in almonds until just mixed
4. Take a mini loaf pan, add the prepared batter in it and then bake for 20 to 23 minutes until firm and top have turned nicely browned.
5. When done, let the bread cool for 5 minutes, take out the bread, cut it into slices, and then serve.

339 – Buttery Broccoli and Bacon

Serves: 2; Preparation: 5 minutes; Cook time: 12 minutes;
Nutrition facts: 77 Calories; 5 g Fats; 5 g Protein; 1 g Net Carb; 2 g Fiber;
Ingredients
- 1 slice of turkey bacon
- 1 cup chopped broccoli florets
- 1/8 tsp garlic powder
- ¼ tsp Italian seasoning
- ¼ tbsp unsalted butter
Seasoning:
- 1/8 tsp salt; 1/8 tsp ground black pepper
How to Prepare:

1. Take a medium skillet pan, place it over high heat, add bacon slice and cook for 3 to 5 minutes until crispy.
2. Transfer bacon to a cutting board and then chop it into small pieces.
3. Reduce the heat to medium-low level, add broccoli florets into the pan, stir well into the bacon grease, add butter, then toss until mixed and cook for 5 minutes until tender.
4. Season the broccoli florets with salt, black pepper, and Italian seasoning, add chopped bacon, stir well and cook for 2 minutes until thoroughly heated.

340 – Broccoli Salad with Bacon

Serves: 2; Preparation: 5 minutes; Cook time: 0 minutes;
Nutrition facts: 119 Calories; 10 g Fats; 3.5 g Protein; 2 g Net Carb; 0.5 g Fiber;
Ingredients
- 1 cup broccoli florets, chopped
- 4 tbsp whipped topping
- 2 tbsp shredded cheddar cheese
- 3 slices of turkey bacon, cooked, chopped
- 1/3 tsp garlic powder

Seasoning:
- 1/8 tsp salt; 1/8 tsp dried parsley

How to Prepare:
1. Take a medium bowl, place whipped topping in it, whisk in garlic powder and parsley, and then fold in broccoli florets.
2. Top with bacon and cheddar cheese and serve.

341 – Roasted Green Beans

Serves: 2; Preparation: 5 minutes; Cook time: 25 minutes;
Nutrition facts: 119 Calories; 9 g Fats; 5 g Protein; 4.5 g Net Carb; 3 g Fiber;
Ingredients
- ½ pound green beans
- ½ cup grated parmesan cheese
- 3 tbsp coconut oil
- ½ tsp garlic powder

Seasoning:
- 1/3 tsp salt; 1/8 tsp ground black pepper

How to Prepare:
1. Turn on the oven, then set it to 425 degrees F, and let preheat.
2. Take a baking sheet, line green beans on it, and set aside until required.
3. Prepare the dressing, and for this, place remaining ingredients in a bowl, except for cheese and whisk until combined.
4. Drizzle the dressing over green beans, toss until well coated, and then bake for 20 minutes until green beans are tender-crisp.
5. Then sprinkle cheese on top of beans and continue roasting for 3 to 5 minutes or until cheese melts and nicely golden brown. Serve.

342 – Fried Cauliflower and Egg Rice

Serves: 2; Preparation: 5 minutes; Cook time: 12 minutes;
Nutrition facts: 57 Calories; 4 g Fats; 3 g Protein; 1.7 g Net Carb; 0.5 g Fiber;
Ingredients
- 8-ounce cauliflower florets, riced
- 2 green onion, sliced
- 1 large egg, beaten
- 1 tbsp soy sauce
- ½ tsp toasted sesame oil

Seasoning:
- 1 tbsp coconut oil
- ½ tsp garlic powder

How to Prepare:
1. Take a large skillet pan, place it over medium-high heat, add coconut oil and riced cauliflower, and cook for 5 minutes until softened.
2. Then add green onions, stir well and cook for 3 minutes until onions are tender.

3. Season with salt, sprinkle garlic over cauliflower, cook for 1 minute until fragrant, then pour in the egg, stir well and cook for 2 minutes until the egg has scrambled to desire level, stirring continuously. Drizzle with soy sauce and sesame oil and Serve.

343 – Spinach Zucchini Boats

Serves: 2; Preparation: 5 minutes; Cook time: 10 minutes;
Nutrition facts: 86.5 Calories; 6 g Fats; 4 g Protein; 3.5 g Net Carb; 0.5 g Fiber;
Ingredients
- 1 large zucchini
- ¾ cup spinach
- 1 ½ tbsp whipped topping
- 3 tbsp grated parmesan cheese
- ½ tsp garlic powder
- ½ tsp salt; ½ tsp ground black pepper

How to Prepare:
1. Turn on the oven, then set it to 350 degrees F, and let preheat.
2. Take a skillet pan, place it over medium heat, add spinach and cook for 5 to 7 minutes or until spinach leaves have wilted and their moisture has evaporated completely.
3. Sprinkle garlic powder, ¼ tsp each of salt and black pepper over spinach, add whipped topping and 2 tbsp cheese and stir well until the cheese has melted, remove the pan from heat.
4. Cut off the top and bottom of zucchini, then cut it in half lengthwise and make a well by scooping out pulp along the center, leaving ½-inch shell.
5. Season zucchini with remaining salt and black pepper, place them on a baking sheet and roast for 5 minutes.
6. Then fill zucchini evenly with spinach mixture, top with remaining cheese and broil for 3 minutes until cheese has melted. Serve.

344 – Green Beans with Herbs

Serves: 2; Preparation: 5 minutes; Cook time: 7 minutes;
Nutrition facts: 380 Calories; 33.7 g Fats; 15.2 g Protein; 2.4 g Net Carb; 1.4 g Fiber;
Ingredients
- 3 oz green beans
- 2 slices of bacon, diced
- 3 tbsp chopped parsley
- 3 tbsp chopped cilantro
- 1 tbsp avocado oil
- ½ tsp garlic powder; ¼ tsp salt

How to Prepare:
1. Place green beans in a medium heatproof bowl, cover with a plastic wrap, and then microwave for 3 to 4 minutes at high heat setting until tender.
2. Meanwhile, take a medium skillet pan, place it over medium heat and when hot, add bacon and cook for 3 to 4 minutes until crisp.
3. Season bacon with salt, sprinkle with garlic powder and cook for 30 seconds until fragrant, remove the pan from heat.
4. When green beans have steamed, drain them well, rinse under cold water, and then transfer to a bowl.
5. Add bacon and remaining ingredients and toss until well mixed. Serve.

345 – Broccoli with Cheddar and Bacon

Serves: 2; Preparation: 5 minutes; Cook time: 30 minutes
Nutrition facts: 530 Calories; 49.6 g Fats; 14.4 g Protein; 3.9 g Net Carb; 1.4 g Fiber;
Ingredients
- 4 oz broccoli florets
- 1/3 cup mayonnaise
- 1/3 cup grated cheddar cheese
- 2 oz crumbled bacon
- 1 tbsp avocado oil

How to Prepare:
1. Turn on the oven, then set it to 350 degrees F and let it preheat.
2. Then take a baking sheet, grease it with oil, spread broccoli florets on it and bake for 20 minutes until roasted.
3. Meanwhile, place mayonnaise in a bowl, add cheese, and stir until mixed.
4. When the broccoli has roasted, spread the mayonnaise-cheese mixture on top and continue baking for 10 minutes or until cheese is golden.
5. Serve.

346 – Broccoli, Green Beans and Bacon Stir-fry

Serves: 2; Preparation: 10 minutes; Cook time: 13 minutes
Nutrition facts: 522 Calories; 47 g Fats; 22.2 g Protein; 0.5 g Net Carb; 2.1 g Fiber;
Ingredients
- 4 oz broccoli florets
- 2 oz green beans
- 4 slices of bacon, cooked, crumbled
- 1 tbsp chopped parsley
- 1 tbsp coconut oil

Seasoning:
- ½ tsp salt; 1/8 tsp ground black pepper

How to Prepare:
1. Take a skillet pan, place it over medium heat, add bacon, and cook for 5 minutes until crispy.
2. Then transfer bacon to a cutting board, let it cool for 5 minutes, then crumble it and set aside until required.
3. Add broccoli and beans into the pan, add oil, season with salt and black pepper and cook for 5 to 7 minutes or until tender.
4. Return bacon into the pan, stir well, cook for 1 minute and then remove the pan from heat. Garnish with parsley and serve.

347 – Charred Green Beans with Pesto

Serves: 2; Preparation: 5 minutes; Cook time: 6 minutes
Nutrition facts: 265 Calories; 24.1 g Fats; 3.3 g Protein; 4.9 g Net Carb; 3.8 g Fiber;
Ingredients
- 6 oz green beans
- 2 tbsp coconut oil
- 3 tbsp basil pesto
- ½ tsp stevia

Seasoning:
- 1/8 tsp salt; 1/8 tsp ground black pepper

How to Prepare:
1. Place green beans in a heatproof bowl, cover with plastic wrap, poke holes in it with a fork, then microwave for 2 minutes and pat dry with paper towels.
2. Take a skillet pan, place it over medium-high heat, add oil and when it melts, add beans and cook for 4 to 5 minutes until slightly charred.
3. Remove pan from heat, add remaining ingredients, and stir well. Serve.

348 – Asparagus Sauté with Bacon

Serves: 2; Preparation: 5 minutes; Cook time: 10 minutes
Nutrition facts: 201 Calories; 16.1 g Fats; 9.5 g Protein; 1.7 g Net Carb; 2.8 g Fiber;
Ingredients
- 4 oz chopped asparagus
- 2 slices of bacon, chopped
- ½ tsp salt

How to Prepare:
1. Take a skillet pan, place it over medium heat, and when hot, add chopped bacon and cook for 3 minutes until sauté.
2. When done, transfer bacon to a plate, then add asparagus into the pan and cook for 5 minutes until tender.
3. Return bacon into the pan, season with salt, stir well and remove the pan from heat. Serve.

349 – Spinach Peanuts Stir-Fry

Serves: 2; Preparation: 5 minutes; Cook time: 5 minutes
Nutrition facts: 150 Calories; 11 g Fats; 7 g Protein; 4 g Net Carb; 2 g Fiber;

Ingredients
- 6 oz spinach
- 3 tbsp peanuts
- ¼ tsp salt
- 1 tbsp coconut oil

How to Prepare:
1. Take a medium pot, place it over medium heat, add oil and when hot, add spinach and cook for 3 to 5 minutes until tender-crisp.
2. Then season with salt, remove the pot from heat, sprinkle with peanuts, and stir until mixed. Serve.

350 – Coleslaw with Dill

Serves: 2; Preparation: 35 minutes; Cook time: 0 minutes
Nutrition facts: 137 Calories; 13 g Fats; 1 g Protein; 2 g Net Carb; 2 g Fiber;
Ingredients
- 1 ½ cups chopped cabbage
- 4 tbsp mayonnaise
- ½ tbsp apple cider vinegar
- ½ tbsp dried dill

Seasoning:
- ½ tsp salt; ¼ tsp stevia

How to Prepare:
1. Place mayonnaise in a bowl, add salt, dill, stevia, and vinegar and whisk until combined.
2. Add chopped cabbage, toss until well coated, and cool in the refrigerator for 30 minutes. Serve.

351 – Zucchini Noodles with Garlic and Parmesan

Serves: 2; Preparation: 10 minutes; Cook time: 6 minutes
Nutrition facts: 150 Calories; 16 g Fats; 1 g Protein; 0.5 g Net Carb; 1 g Fiber;
Ingredients
- 1 large zucchini, spiralized into noodles
- 2 tbsp unsalted butter
- 1 ½ tsp minced garlic
- 2 tbsp grated parmesan cheese
- 1/3 tsp salt; ¼ tsp red chili flakes
- ¼ tsp ground black pepper

How to Prepare:
1. Prepare zucchini noodles, and for this, cut zucchini into noodles by using a spiralizer or a vegetable peeler, and then set aside until required.
2. Take a skillet pan, place it over medium-high heat, add butter and garlic, cook for 1 minute until garlic is fragrant, then add zucchini noodles and continue cooking for 3 to 5 minutes until al dente.
3. When done, remove the skillet pan from heat, season zucchini noodles with salt, red chili flakes, and black pepper, add cheese, and stir well until mixed.

352 – Garlic and Parmesan Eggplant

Serves: 2; Preparation: 10 minutes; Cook time: 6 minutes
Nutrition facts: 136 Calories; 11 g Fats; 6 g Protein; 2 g Net Carb; 3 g Fiber;
Ingredients
- 1/3 of a medium eggplant
- 1/3 of egg
- 2 tbsp grated parmesan cheese
- ¾ tsp garlic powder
- 2 tbsp coconut oil
- ¼ tsp salt
- 1/8 tsp ground black pepper

How to Prepare:
1. Cut eggplant into 1/3-inch-thick slices, then arrange them on a plate in a single layer, sprinkle with 1/8 tsp salt, let sit for 30 minutes and then pat dry the slices of eggplant with paper towels.
2. Crack the egg in a bowl and whisk until combined.
3. Place cheese in a shallow dish, add remaining salt, black pepper, and garlic powder and stir until mixed.
4. Working on one slice at a time, first coat the eggplant slices in egg and then dredge with parmesan cheese mixture until coated, coat the remaining eggplant slices in the same manner.
5. Take a skillet pan, place it over medium heat, add oil and when it melts, add coated eggplant slices and cook for 2 to 3 minutes per side until browned and crispy.
6. When done, remove eggplant slices from the pan and then transfer them to a plate lined with paper towels. Serve.

353 – Easy Cheesy Zoodles

Serves: 2; Preparation: 5 minutes; Cook time: 10 minutes
Nutrition facts: 107 Calories; 9 g Fats; 2 g Protein; 2 g Net Carb; 1 g Fiber;
Ingredients
- 1 large zucchini, spiralized into noodles
- 1/8 tsp garlic powder
- 2 tbsp softened cream cheese
- 1 tbsp grated parmesan cheese
- ½ tbsp coconut oil
- 1/3 tsp salt; ¼ tsp ground black pepper

How to Prepare:
1. Prepare zucchini noodles, and for this, cut zucchini into noodles by using a spiralizer or a vegetable peeler.
2. Then take a skillet pan, place it over medium-high heat, add zucchini noodles and garlic, toss well until mixed, and cook for 4 minutes until slightly soft.
3. Push noodles to one side of the pan, add cream cheese into the other side of the pan, stir it until melts, then mix with noodles until coated and season with salt and black pepper. Remove pan from heat, sprinkle zoodles with parmesan cheese and serve.

354 – Keto Potatoes

Serves: 2; Preparation: 5 minutes; Cook time: 15 minutes
Nutrition facts: 88 Calories; 9 g Fats; 3 g Protein; 3.5 g Net Carb; 1 g Fiber;
Ingredients
- 1 large turnip, peeled, diced
- 1/4 of a spring onion, diced, and more for garnishing
- 2 slices of bacon, chopped
- 1 tbsp avocado oil
- 1 tbsp softened cream cheese

Seasoning:
- 1/2 tsp paprika; 1/2 tsp garlic powder
- 1/2 tsp salt; 1/2 tsp ground black pepper

How to Prepare:
1. Take a skillet pan, place it over medium-high heat add oil and when hot, add diced turnip, season with salt, black pepper, and paprika, sprinkle with garlic, stir well and cook for 5 minutes.
2. Then add onion, stir and continue cooking for 3 minutes until onions start to soften.
3. Add chopped bacon, continue cooking for 5 to 7 minutes, or until bacon is crispy and remove the pan from heat. Top with green onions and cream cheese and Serve.

355 – Garlic Spinach

Serves: 2; Preparation: 5 minutes; Cook time: 5 minutes
Nutrition facts: 155 Calories; 14 g Fats; 4 g Protein; 2 g Net Carb; 6 g Fiber;
Ingredients
- 1 tbsp coconut oil
- 8 oz of spinach leaves
- 1 ½ tsp minced garlic
- ¼ tsp salt

How to Prepare:
1. Take a frying pan, place it over medium heat, add oil and when hot, add spinach and cook for 5 minutes until its leaves wilts.
2. Then add garlic and salt, stir well and continue cooking for 2 minutes.
3. Serve.

356 – Taco Turnip Wedges

Serves: 2; Preparation: 5 minutes; Cook time: 20 minutes
Nutrition facts: 129 Calories; 12.6 g Fats; 1.7 g Protein; 4.3 g Net Carb; 2.2 g Fiber;

Ingredients
- 2 large turnips
- ¾ tsp onion powder
- ½ tsp garlic powder
- 1 ½ tbsp melted coconut oil
- 1 tbsp cream cheese

Seasoning:
- ½ tsp salt; 1 tbsp red chili powder
- 2/3 tbsp cumin
- ¼ tsp dried oregano

How to Prepare:
1. Turn on the oven, then set it to 350 degrees F, and let it preheat.
2. Prepare taco seasoning and for this, stir together salt, onion powder, garlic powder, red chili powder, cumin, and oregano and set aside until required.
3. Peel the turnips, cut into wedges, then place them in a plastic bag, add prepared taco seasoning, then add oil, seal the bag and turn it upside down until well coated.
4. Transfer the mixture onto a baking sheet, spread the wedges evenly, and bake for 20 minutes until golden brown and cooked.
5. Top with cream cheese and Serve.

357 – Roasted Cauliflower Steaks

Serves: 2; Preparation: 5 minutes; Cook time: 20 minutes
Nutrition facts: 176 Calories; 13.8 g Fats; 4.3 g Protein; 6.7 g Net Carb; 5.4 g Fiber;
Ingredients
- ¼ of a cauliflower head
- ½ tsp minced garlic
- 2 tbsp avocado oil
- 2 tbsp grated cheddar cheese

Seasoning:
- 1/8 tsp red pepper flakes
- ¼ tsp salt; 1/8 tsp ground black pepper

How to Prepare:
1. Turn on the oven, then set it to 400 degrees F and let it preheat.
2. Meanwhile, prepare cauliflower steaks and for this, cut it into two slices and place them onto a baking sheet lined with parchment paper.
3. Place oil in a small bowl, add remaining ingredients except for cheese, stir well and then brush half of the mixture on top of the cauliflower.
4. Bake cauliflower for 10 minutes, then flip them, brush with remaining avocado oil mixture, sprinkle with cheese and then continue baking for 10 minutes until roasted. Serve.

358 – Sweet and Spicy Brussel Sprouts

Serves: 2; Preparation: 5 minutes; Cook time: 12 minutes
Nutrition facts: 98.5 Calories; 7.8 g Fats; 1.7 g Protein; 3.4 g Net Carb; 2 g Fiber;
Ingredients
- 3 oz Brussel Sprouts, halved
- ¾ tbsp soy sauce
- ¾ tbsp liquid stevia
- ½ tbsp Sriracha sauce
- ¾ tsp sesame seeds
- 1 tbsp avocado oil
- ¼ tsp salt

How to Prepare:
1. Prepare the sauce, and for this, place soy sauce in a bowl, add maple syrup, Sriracha sauce, and stir until mixed.
2. Take a skillet pan, place it over medium heat, add oil and when hot, add Brussel sprouts and cook for 7 to 10 minutes until nicely golden brown.
3. Then pour in prepared sauce in the last 2 minutes of cooking, toss until well coated, and continue cooking until done.
4. Season Brussel sprouts with salt, sprinkle with sesame seeds and then serve,

359 – Bacon and Cauliflower Mac and Cheese

Serves: 2; Preparation: 5 minutes; Cook time: 20 minutes
Nutrition facts: 152.5 Calories; 14 g Fats; 2 g Protein; 1.5 g Net Carb; 0.25 g Fiber;
Ingredients
- 2 strips of bacon

- ½ cup cauliflower florets, chopped
- 3 tbsp butter, unsalted
- 3 oz whipped topping
- 3 tbsp grated cheddar cheese

Seasoning:
- ½ tsp salt; 1/8 tsp ground black pepper
- ¼ tsp cayenne pepper
- ¾ cup of water

How to Prepare:
1. Take a skillet pan, place it over medium heat and when hot, add bacon and cook for 5 minutes or until crispy.
2. Transfer bacon to a plate, pat dry with paper towels, chop the bacon and set aside until required.
3. Take a saucepan, place it over medium heat, pour in water, bring to boil, then add cauliflower florets and boil for 4 minutes.
4. When done, drain the cauliflower and then set aside until required.
5. Return saucepan over medium heat, add butter, whipped topping, salt, black pepper, and cayenne pepper, cook for 3 to 5 minutes until the butter has melted and a thick sauce comes together, stirring continuously.
6. Then add cauliflower florets in it, stir well until combined, sprinkle with cheese, and stir until cheese has melted.
7. Add bacon into the sauce, stir until combined, and remove the pan from heat. Serve.

360 – Lemon Garlic Roasted Brussels sprouts

Serves: 2; Preparation: 5 minutes; Cooking time15 6 minutes
Nutrition facts: 145 Calories; 13.4 g Fats; 1.1 g Protein; 2.8 g Net Carb; 2.3 g Fiber;
Ingredients
- 3 oz Brussel sprouts, halved
- 2 tbsp avocado oil
- ¼ tsp garlic powder
- ½ of a lemon, juiced

Seasoning:
- 1/3 tsp salt; ¼ tsp ground black pepper

How to Prepare:
1. Turn on the oven, then set it to 400 degrees F and let it preheat.
2. Meanwhile, take a sheet pan, line it with parchment sheet, place Brussel sprout halves on it and drizzle with oil and lemon juice.
3. Season Brussel sprouts with garlic powder, salt, and black pepper, toss until well mixed and cook for 10 to 15 minutes until done, tossing halfway through.

361 – Jalapeño Poppers

Serves: 2; Preparation: 5 minutes; Cook time: 10 minutes
Nutrition facts: 78.5 Calories; 4 g Fats; 1.5 g Protein; 1.3 g Net Carb; 0.2 g Fiber;
Ingredients
- 4 jalapeno peppers
- 8 strips of bacon
- 4 oz cream cheese

Seasoning:
- ¼ tsp salt; 1/8 tsp ground black pepper

How to Prepare:
1. Turn on the oven, then set it to 400 degrees F and let it preheat.
2. Meanwhile, cut each pepper in half lengthwise, remove and discard the seeds and then fill the peppers with cream cheese.
3. Wrap each pepper with bacon and cook for 10 minutes until peppers are tender and bacon is nicely golden brown. Serve.

362 – Lettuce and Avocado Salad

Serves: 2; Preparation: 5 minutes; Cook time: 0 minutes
Nutrition facts: 125.7 Calories; 11 g Fats; 1.3 g Protein; 1.7 g Net Carb; 3.7 g Fiber;
Ingredients
- 1 avocado, pitted, sliced
- 4 oz chopped lettuce
- 4 tbsp chopped chives
- ½ of a lime, juiced

- 2 tbsp avocado oil

Seasoning:
- 1/8 tsp salt; 1/8 tsp ground black pepper

How to Prepare:
1. Prepare the dressing and for this, take a small bowl, add oil, lime juice, salt, and black pepper, stir until mixed, and then slowly mix oil until combined.
2. Take a large bowl, add avocado, lettuce, and chives, and then toss gently. Drizzle with dressing, toss until well coated, and then serve.

363 – Spinach and Bacon Salad

Serves: 2; Preparation: 5 minutes; Cook time: 5 minutes
Nutrition facts: 181.5 Calories; 16.7 g Fats; 7.3 g Protein; 0.2 g Net Carb; 0.3 g Fiber;
Ingredients
- 4 oz spinach
- 4 sliced of bacon, chopped
- 2 eggs, boiled, sliced
- ¼ cup mayonnaise

How to Prepare:
1. Take a skillet pan, place it over medium heat, add bacon, and cook for 5 minutes until browned.
2. Meanwhile, take a salad bowl, add spinach in it, top with bacon and eggs and drizzle with mayonnaise. Toss until well mixed and then serve.

364 – Keto Pasta

Serves: 2; Preparation: 40 minutes; Cook time: 7 minutes
Nutrition facts: 218.3 Calories; 16.5 g Fats; 15.3 g Protein; 2 g Net Carb; 2.2 g Fiber;
Ingredients
- 4 oz grated mozzarella cheese
- 2 egg yolks
- 2 tbsp tomato sauce
- ¼ tsp salt; ¼ tsp ground black pepper

How to Prepare:
1. Take a heatproof bowl, add mozzarella in it, and microwave for 2 minutes or until it melts.
2. Whisk in yolks until combined, take a baking dish lined with parchment paper, and add cheese mixture in it.
3. Cover the cheese mixture with another parchment paper, press and spread the cheese mixture as thinly as possible, let it rest for 10 minutes until slightly firm.
4. Then uncover it, cut out thin spaghetti by using a knife and refrigerate the pasta for 45 minutes.
5. When ready to cook, take a saucepan half full with salty water, bring it to boil, add pasta and cook for 5 minutes until spaghetti is tender.
6. Drain the spaghetti, distribute it between two bowls, top with tomato sauce, season with salt and black pepper, toss until well mixed, and then serve.

365 – Spicy Sautéed Green Beans

Serves: 2; Preparation: 5 minutes; Cook time: 10 minutes
Nutrition facts: 108.5 Calories; 10.1 g Fats; 0.5 g Protein; 2.2 g Net Carb; 1.6 g Fiber;
Ingredients
- 4 oz green beans
- ½ tsp minced garlic
- ¼ tsp crushed red pepper
- 1 ½ tbsp avocado oil
- 1/3 tsp salt; ¼ tsp ground black pepper

How to Prepare:
1. Take a saucepan half full with salted water, place it over medium heat, bring the water to boil, then add green beans and cook for 4 minutes until tender.
2. Drain the beans, wipe the pan, return it over medium heat, add oil and when hot, add garlic and cook for 1 minute until fragrant.
3. Then add green beans, season with salt and black pepper, cook for 1 minute and transfer beans to a plate. Sprinkle red pepper on the green beans and serve.

366 – Bacon Wrapped Cream Cheese Stuffed Zucchini

Serves: 2; Preparation: 5 minutes; Cook time: 20 minutes
Nutrition facts: 198.8 Calories; 17.2 g Fats; 8.4 g Protein; 1.7 g Net Carb; 0.8 g Fiber;

Ingredients
- 1 zucchini, halved lengthwise
- 3 tbsp cream cheese
- 1 tbsp chopped spinach
- 1 tbsp grated mozzarella cheese
- 2 slices of bacon

Seasoning:
- ¼ tsp salt; 1/8 tsp ground black pepper
- 1/8 tsp crushed red pepper

How to Prepare:
1. Turn on the oven, then set it to 350 degrees F and let it preheat.
2. Meanwhile, cut zucchini into half lengthwise, then use a spoon to remove the seedy center and set aside until required.
3. Place remaining ingredients, except for bacon in a bowl, stir well, and then evenly stuffed this mixture into zucchini.
4. Wrap each zucchini half with a bacon slice, place them on a baking sheet lined with parchment paper and cook for 15 to 20 minutes until zucchini is tender and bacon is browned. Serve.

367 – Spinach Salad with Feta Dressing

Serves: 2; Preparation: 5 minutes; Cook time: 3 minutes
Nutrition facts: 204.3 Calories; 19.5 g Fats; 5.1 g Protein; 1.7 g Net Carb; 0.8 g Fiber;
Ingredients
- 4 oz of spinach leaves
- 3 tbsp avocado oil
- 3 oz feta cheese, crumbled
- 1 ½ tbsp apple cider vinegar

Seasoning:
- 1/8 tsp salt; 1/8 tsp ground black pepper

How to Prepare:
1. Take a skillet pan, place it over medium heat, add oil and when warmed, add cheese, cook for 1 minute until cheese has slightly melted and then stir in vinegar; remove the pan from heat. Take a bowl, add spinach in it, top with feta cheese mixture and toss until mixed. Serve.

368 – Salad Sandwiches

Serves: 2; Preparation: 5 minutes; Cook time: 0 minutes;
Nutrition facts: 187 Calories; 42.5 g Fats; 5 g Protein; 1.5 g Net Carb; 4 g Fiber;
Ingredients
- 2 cabbage leaves
- 1 avocado, pitted
- 1-ounce butter, unsalted
- 2 oz feta cheese, sliced, full-fat

How to Prepare:
1. Divide cabbage leaves into two parts, then smear them with butter and top with cheese.
2. Cut avocado in half, remove the pit, scoop out the flesh and then top it onto each cabbage. Roll the cabbage and then Serve.

369 – Garlic Butter Zucchini Noodles

Serves: 2; Preparation: 5 minutes; Cook time: 5 minutes;
Nutrition facts: 287 Calories; 25.5 g Fats; 2.9 g Protein; 7.6 g Net Carb; 3.9 g Fiber;
Ingredients
- 2 medium zucchini
- 2 tsp dried cilantro
- ½ of a lime, juiced
- 2 tbsp butter, unsalted
- 2 tbsp avocado oil

Seasoning:
- 2/3 tbsp Sriracha sauce
- 1/3 tsp red chili flakes
- ¼ tsp salt; ¼ tsp ground black pepper

How to Prepare:
1. Prepare zucchini noodles and for this, trim the ends of zucchini and then spiralize them by using a vegetable peeler or a spiralizer.

2. Take a medium skillet pan, place it over medium heat, add butter and oil and when the butter melts, add 1 tsp cilantro, lime juice, Sriracha sauce, and red pepper flakes, stir until mixed and cook for 1 minute until fragrant.
3. Add zucchini noodles, toss until coated, and then cook for 3 minutes until tender-crisp.
4. Season with salt and black pepper, then distribute zucchini between two plates, top with remaining cilantro and then serve.

370 – Sprouts and Kale Sauté

Serves: 2; Preparation: 5 minutes; Cook time: 5 minutes;
Nutrition facts: 210 Calories; 17.5 g Fats; 4.7 g Protein; 1.9 g Net Carb; 6 g Fiber;
Ingredients
- 2 oz chopped kale
- 4 oz Brussels sprouts
- 3 tbsp chopped almonds
- 1 tbsp white wine vinegar
- 1 ½ tbsp avocado oil
- 1/3 tsp salt

How to Prepare:
1. Prepare the sprout and for this, peel the leaves, starting from outside and continue peeling towards to middle until you reach the tough core.
2. Discard the core and transfer sprout leaves to a medium bowl.
3. Take a large frying pan, place it over medium heat, add oil and when hot, add sprout leaves, toss until coated with oil, and cook for 1 minute or until sauté.
4. Drizzle with vinegar, add kale, toss until mixed, and cook for 1 minute until kale leaves begin to wilt.
5. Season with salt, remove the pan from heat and garnish with almonds. Serve.

371 – Sprouts and Bacon Plate

Serves: 2; Preparation: 5 minutes; Cook time: 8 minutes;
Nutrition facts: 145 Calories; 11.2 g Fats; 5.4 g Protein; 3.2 g Net Carb; 2.2 g Fiber;
Ingredients
- 4 oz Brussels sprouts
- 1 tsp minced garlic
- 3 slices of bacon, chopped
- 1 tsp avocado oil

Seasoning:
- 1/3 tsp salt; 1/4 tsp ground black pepper

How to Prepare:
1. Take a medium skillet pan, place it over medium heat and when hot, add bacon and cook for 3 minutes per side until crisp.
2. Add sprouts, add oil, toss until mixed and cook for 10 minutes until thoroughly cooked.
3. Stir in garlic, season with salt and black pepper and continue cooking for 1 minute. Serve.

372 – Salad in Jar

Serves: 2; Preparation: 5 minutes; Cook time: 0 minutes;
Nutrition facts: 438 Calories; 38 g Fats; 13.5 g Protein; 5.5 g Net Carb; 8.5 g Fiber;
Ingredients
- 2 oz chopped kale
- 1 scallion, chopped
- 1 avocado, pitted, chopped
- 1 Roma tomato, chopped
- 4 slices of beef roast, diced

Seasoning:
- ½ cup mayonnaise

How to Prepare:
1. Take two mason jars, place kale evenly at the bottom and then top with kale, scallion, avocado, and tomato.
2. Top with beef and serve each jar with ¼ cup mayonnaise.

373 – Brussel Leaf and Spinach Skillet

Serves: 2; Preparation: 5 minutes; Cook time: 10 minutes;
Nutrition facts: 235 Calories; 19.5 g Fats; 4.6 g Protein; 4.2 g Net Carb; 5 g Fiber;

Ingredients
- 4 ounce Brussels sprouts
- 4 oz spinach
- ½ tbsp erythritol sweetener
- 2 tbsp avocado oil
- 3 tbsp almonds, chopped
- 1/3 tsp salt

How to Prepare:
1. Peel the leaves of the sprouts, starting from outside and continue peeling towards to middle until you reach the tough core, discard the core and transfer sprout leaves to a medium bowl.
2. Take a large frying pan, place it over medium heat, add oil and when hot, add sprout leaves, toss until coated with oil, and cook for 1 minute or until sauté.
3. Drizzle with vinegar, add spinach, toss until mixed, and cook for 1 minute until spinach leaves begin to wilt.
4. Season with salt, remove the pan from heat, and garnish with almonds. Serve.

374 – Garlic Broccoli-Cauliflower Rice

Serves: 2; Preparation: 5 minutes; Cook time: 10 minutes;
Nutrition facts: 91 Calories; 8 g Fats; 3 g Protein; 6 g Net Carb; 2 g Fiber;
Ingredients
- 6 oz broccoli and cauliflower, grated
- ½ tsp garlic powder
- 2 tbsp butter, unsalted
- 2 tbsp grated parmesan cheese
- 3 tbsp water

Seasoning:
- 1/3 tsp salt; 1/4 tsp ground black pepper

How to Prepare:
1. Take a medium heatproof bowl, place broccoli and cauliflower, and drizzle with water.
2. Cover with a plastic wrap, microwave for 2 minutes at high heat setting, then uncover the bowl and carefully drain the broccoli and cauliflower rice.
3. Take a frying pan, place it over medium heat, add butter and when it melts, add broccoli and cauliflower rice and cook for 2 to 3 minutes until beginning to brown.
4. Season with salt and black pepper, sprinkle with cheese and then serve.

375 – Oven Fried Cheddar Cauliflower and Broccoli Florets

Serves: 2
Preparation: 5 minutes; Cook time: 15 minutes;
Nutrition facts: 185 Calories; 14.1 g Fats; 7.7 g Protein; 3.9 g Net Carb; 2 g Fiber;
Ingredients
- 6 oz cauliflower and broccoli florets
- ½ tsp garlic powder
- 1 tbsp coconut oil, melted
- 2 tbsp grated cheddar cheese
- ½ egg, beaten

Seasoning:
- ¼ tsp salt

How to Prepare:
1. Turn on the oven, then set it to 400 degrees F and let it preheat.
2. Take a small bowl, crack the egg in it, add garlic powder, salt, and coconut oil and whisk until blended.
3. Take a medium bowl, place add florets in it, pour egg batter on florets, toss until well coated, and then mix in cheese.
4. Take a baking sheet, grease it with oil, spread florets mixture on it in a single layer, and then bake for 10 to 15 minutes until vegetables have turned tender and nicely browned. Serve.

376 – Garlic Brussels sprouts with Bacon

Serves: 2; Preparation: 5 minutes; Cook time: 15 minutes;
Nutrition facts: 202 Calories; 15.1 g Fats; 7.7 g Protein; 3.9 g Net Carb; 2.4 g Fiber;
Ingredients
- 3 slices of bacon
- 4 oz Brussels sprouts, halved
- 2 green onions, diced
- ¾ tbsp butter, unsalted

- 2 tbsp chicken broth
- ½ tsp garlic powder
- ¼ tsp salt
- ¾ tbsp avocado oil

How to Prepare:
1. Take a medium skillet pan, place it over medium heat, add oil and wait until it gets hot.
2. Cut bacon slices into squares, add to the skillet pan and cook for 2 to 3 minutes until bacon fat starts to render.
3. Transfer bacon pieces to a plate lined with paper towels and then set aside until required.
4. Add butter into the skillet pan and when it starts to brown, add onion, sprinkle with garlic powder and cook for 1 minute or more until semi-translucent.
5. Add sprouts, season with salt, stir until mixed and cook for 2 to 3 minutes until beginning to brown.
6. Pour in chicken broth, stir until mixed and cook for 5 to 7 minutes until broth is absorbed, covering the pan.
7. Then make a hole in the center of pan by pushing sprouts to the side of the pan, add bacon and stir until well mixed. Serve.

377 – Cheesy Spicy Broccoli and Cauliflower Rice

Serves: 2; Preparation: 5 minutes; Cook time: 12 minutes;
Nutrition facts: 288 Calories; 25.3 g Fats; 5.8 g Protein; 5.5 g Net Carb; 3.9 g Fiber;
Ingredients

- 3 oz cauliflower florets, grated
- 3 oz broccoli florets, chopped
- ½ tbsp BBQ spice
- 1 ½ tbsp avocado oil
- 2 tbsp grated cheddar cheese

How to Prepare:
1. Take a medium pot, place it over medium-low heat, add ¾ tbsp oil and when hot, stir in the cauliflower and cook for 5 to 7 minutes until tender and golden brown.
2. Meanwhile, take a medium heatproof bowl, place broccoli florets in it, cover with a plastic wrap, and then microwave for 2 minutes until steams.
3. Drain the steamed broccoli florets, add it to the pot, add oil and cheese, sprinkle with BBQ spice, stir well and cook for 2 minutes until cheese has melted.

378 – Sprouts Gratin with Bacon

Serves: 2; Preparation: 10 minutes; Cook time: 30 minutes;
Nutrition facts: 196 Calories; 15 g Fats; 8 g Protein; 5 g Net Carb; 3 g Fiber;
Ingredients

- 4 oz Brussels sprouts, halved
- 2 slices of bacon, chopped, cooked
- 2 tbsp almond milk, unsweetened
- 2 tbsp coconut cream
- 3 tbsp grated cheddar cheese

Seasoning:
- 1/3 tsp salt; 1/3 tsp ground black pepper
- ½ tbsp butter, unsalted
- 1 tbsp avocado oil

How to Prepare:
1. Turn on the oven, then set it to 400 degrees F and let it preheat.
2. Take a baking pan, line it with aluminum foil, place Brussels sprouts in it, drizzle with oil, and season with 1/4 tsp each of salt and black pepper.
3. Spread sprouts in a single layer and then roast for 15 to 20 minutes until crispy and edges turned browned, stirring halfway.
4. Meanwhile, prepare the sauce, and for this, take a medium heatproof bowl, place butter in it, and then microwave for 1 minute or more until it melts.
5. Add milk and cream, whisk until combined, and microwave for 1 minute until hot.
6. Add 2 tbsp of cheese along with remaining salt and black pepper and stir until mixed.
7. When sprouts have roasted, transfer them into a small pan, pour prepared sauce over sprouts, sprinkle with bacon and remaining cheese, and then bake for 5 to 10 minutes until bubbly and top have turned golden brown. Serve.

379 – Buttery Bacon Brussel Sprouts

Serves: 2; Preparation: 5 minutes; Cook time: 10 minutes;
Nutrition facts: 278 Calories; 24.7 g Fats; 7.6 g Protein; 3.9 g Net Carb; 2.4 g Fiber;
Ingredients

- 4 oz Brussels sprouts, halved

- 3 slices of turkey bacon, chopped
- 1 tsp garlic powder
- ¼ of a lime, zested
- 3 tbsp butter, unsalted

Seasoning:
- 1 tbsp chopped walnut

How to Prepare:
1. Take a small saucepan half full with water, place it over medium heat, and bring it to a boil.
2. Add sprouts, cook for 5 minutes until just cooked and then drain into a colander.
3. Take a frying pan, place it over medium heat, add butter and when it melts, add bacon and cook for 3 to 4 minutes until crispy.
4. Sprinkle with ½ tsp garlic, cook for 30 seconds until fragrant, and then sprinkle with lime zest.
5. Add sprouts, stir until mixed, toss until well coated, and cook for 1 minute until hot. Garnish with walnuts and serve.

380 – Broccoli and Cauliflower Nuggets

Serves: 2; Preparation: 10 minutes; Cook time: 10 minutes;
Nutrition facts: 483.5 Calories; 46.7 g Fats; 9.7 g Protein; 2.2 g Net Carb; 3.9 g Fiber;
Ingredients
- 2 tbsp almond flour
- 4 oz broccoli and cauliflower florets
- 2 tbsp grated cheddar cheese
- 2 tbsp ground flaxseed meal
- ½ of an egg

Seasoning:
- 1/3 tsp salt; ¼ tsp ground black pepper
- 2 tbsp avocado oil
- ¼ cup mayonnaise

How to Prepare:
1. Place cauliflower and broccoli florets into a medium heatproof bowl, cover with a plastic wrap, and then microwave for 2 to 3 minutes at high heat setting until steamed.
2. Drain the florets, transfer them to a food processor, add cheese, flaxseed, salt, black pepper, and egg, and then pulse for 1 to 2 minutes until smooth.
3. Tip the mixture into a bowl, shape it into small balls, flatten them into the shape of nugget and then coat with almond flour.
4. Take a frying pan, place it over medium heat, add oil and when hot, place prepared nuggets on it, and then cook for 3 minutes per side until golden brown.
5. Serve nuggets with mayonnaise.

381 – Roasted Cabbage Wedges

Serves: 2; Preparation: 5 minutes; Cook time: 20 minutes;
Nutrition facts: 120 Calories; 9 g Fats; 2 g Protein; 3 g Net Carb; 2 g Fiber;
Ingredients
- 2 slices of cabbage
- ½ tsp onion powder
- 1/3 tsp garlic powder
- 1/3 tsp salt
- 2 tbsp avocado oil

Seasoning:
- ¼ tsp ground black pepper

How to Prepare:
1. Turn on the oven, then set it to 400 degrees F and let it preheat.
2. Place cabbage slices on a baking sheet lined with parchment sheet, brush each side with oil.
3. Place onion powder in a small bowl, add garlic salt and black pepper, stir until mixed, sprinkle this mixture over cabbage slices and then bake for 15 to 20 minutes until golden brown and cooked, turning halfway. Serve.

382 – Cauliflower Oatmeal

Serves: 2; Preparation: 5 minutes; Cook time: 10 minutes;
Nutrition facts: 125 Calories; 9.1 g Fats; 6.4 g Protein; 1.2 g Net Carb; 2.5 g Fiber;
Ingredients
- 1 ½ cup grated cauliflower
- 2 tbsp peanut butter
- ½ cup almond milk, unsweetened
- 1 strawberry, sliced

Seasoning:
- ¼ tsp stevia
- 1 tsp cinnamon

How to Prepare:
1. Take a medium saucepan, place it over medium-high heat, add grated cauliflower, stir in stevia and cinnamon, pour in milk, stir until mixed and bring it to a boil.
2. Then switch heat to medium-low level, cook for 4 to 5 minutes until thickened, and remove the pan from heat.
3. Divide oatmeal between two bowls, top with peanut butter and berry, and then serve.

383 – Cabbage Chips with Almond Butter

Serves: 2; Preparation: 5 minutes; Cook time: 6 hours;
Nutrition facts: 158 Calories; 12 g Fats; 3.6 g Protein; 1.5 g Net Carb; 33.5 g Fiber;
Ingredients
- 6 oz cabbage leaves, torn into 3-inch pieces
- 2 tbsp almond butter
- 1 tbsp hemp seeds
- ½ tsp garlic powder
- 2 tbsp avocado oil

Seasoning:
- 1 ½ tbsp soy sauce
- ½ tbsp fish sauce

How to Prepare:
1. Take a medium bowl, place all the ingredients in it except for cabbage, and stir until smooth paste comes together.
2. Add cabbage leaves, mix well by using hands until well coated, spread cabbage leaves on a dehydrator and let them dehydrate at 145 degrees F for 6 hours until cabbage has dried and turn crispy. Serve.

384 – Southern Fried Cabbage

Serves: 2; Preparation: 5 minutes; Cook time: 12 minutes;
Nutrition facts: 90 Calories; 5.8 g Fats; 6.1 g Protein; 1.6 g Net Carb; 1 g Fiber;
Ingredients
- 4 slices of bacon, chopped
- 1 cup shredded cabbage
- 2 green onions, chopped

Seasoning:
- 1/3 tsp salt; 1/4 tsp ground black pepper

How to Prepare:
6. Take a medium skillet pan, place it over medium heat and when hot, add chopped bacon and cook for 3 to 4 minutes until crisp.
7. Transfer bacon to a pan, switch heat to the low level, add green onion and cook for 2 minutes.
8. Add cabbage, switch heat to medium level, stir until mixed and cook for 5 to 7 minutes until crispy.
9. Remove pan from heat, add chopped bacon and stir well until mixed. Season cabbage with salt and black pepper and then serve.

385 – Scrambled Cauliflower

Serves: 2; Preparation: 5 minutes; Cook time: 12 minutes;
Nutrition facts: 128 Calories; 10.8 g Fats; 6.3 g Protein; 0.4 g Net Carb; 0.5 g Fiber;
Ingredients
- 1/3 cup grated cauliflower
- 1 egg, beaten
- 1 tbsp butter, unsalted
- 2 tsp shredded mozzarella cheese
- 1 tsp cream cheese

Seasoning:
- ¼ tsp salt; ¼ tsp cayenne pepper

How to Prepare:
1. Place cauliflower florets in a heatproof bowl, cover with plastic wrap, and then microwave for 2 to 3 minutes until tender.
2. Drain the cauliflower, transfer in a bowl, mash by using a fork, then add remaining ingredients except for butter and stir until well combined.
3. Take a medium skillet pan, place it over medium heat, add butter and when it melts, add cauliflower mixture and cook for 3 minutes until bottom turns golden brown.
4. Then flip cauliflower mixture, continue cooking for 3 to 5 minutes until done and serve.

386 – Balsamic Grilled Zucchini

Serves: 2; Preparation: 5 minutes; Cook time: 8 minutes;
Nutrition facts: 76 Calories; 5 g Fats; 1.6 g Protein; 5.6 g Net Carb; 1.6 g Fiber;
Ingredients
- 1 zucchini, sliced lengthwise
- 1/3 tsp garlic powder
- 1 tsp Italian seasoning
- 2 tbsp balsamic vinegar
- 2 tsp avocado oil
- ¼ tsp salt

How to Prepare:
1. Take a griddle pan, place it over medium-low heat, brush it with oil and let it preheat.
2. Meanwhile, brush zucchini slices with oil and then sprinkle with garlic powder, Italian seasoning, and salt.
3. Place zucchini slices on the griddle pan and cook for 2 to 3 minutes per side, then brush zucchini with vinegar and cook for another minute. Serve.

387 – Microwave Spinach Muffin

Serves: 2; Preparation: 5 minutes; Cook time: 2 minutes;
Nutrition facts: 150.5 Calories; 9.1 g Fats; 11.2 g Protein; 1.5 g Net Carb; 2 g Fiber;
Ingredients
- 4 tsp coconut flour
- 2 tbsp cooked spinach
- ½ tsp dried basil
- 2 tsp grated mozzarella cheese
- 2 eggs

Seasoning:
- ¼ tsp salt; 1/8 tsp ground black pepper
- 1/16 tsp baking soda

How to Prepare:
1. Take a medium bowl, place all the ingredients in it, and whisk until well combined.
2. Take two ramekins, grease them with oil, distribute the prepared batter in it and then microwave for 1 minute and 45 seconds until done.
3. When done, take out muffin from the ramekin, cut in half, and then serve.

388 – Balsamic Swiss chard

Serves: 2; Preparation: 5 minutes; Cook time: 5 minutes;
Nutrition facts: 172 Calories; 13.8 g Fats; 2.5 g Protein; 7.4 g Net Carb; 2 g Fiber;
Ingredients
- ½ bunch of Swiss chards, leaves chopped
- 1/2 tbsp minced garlic
- 1 ½ tbsp avocado oil
- 3 tbsp balsamic vinegar
- ¼ tsp salt; 1/8 tsp ground black pepper

How to Prepare:
1. Take a medium skillet pan, place it over medium heat, add oil and when hot, add garlic and cook for 30 seconds until fragrant.
2. Then add chards, drizzle with vinegar, stir until mixed and cook for 3 to 5 minutes until chard leaves wilt.
3. Season chard with salt and black pepper and then serve.

389 – Cauliflower Tator Tots with Kale

Serves: 2; Preparation: 10 minutes; Cook time: 20 minutes;
Nutrition facts: 260 Calories; 19.4 g Fats; 10.1 g Protein; 4.9 g Net Carb; 4.6 g Fiber;
Ingredients
- 6 oz cauliflower florets

- 1 tbsp kale powder
- 2 tbsp almond flour
- 1 egg
- 2 1/2 cups water

Seasoning:
- 1/3 tsp salt
- 1/8 tsp ground black pepper
- 2/3 tbsp garlic powder
- 2 tbsp avocado oil

How to Prepare:
1. Turn on the oven, then set it to 350 degrees F and let it preheat.
2. Meanwhile, take a medium pot, place it over medium heat, pour in water, and bring it to a boil.
3. Then add cauliflower florets, cook for 4 minutes until tender, drain the florets and cool completely.
4. Dice the cauliflower florets, add kale powder, flour, salt, black pepper, and garlic powder, stir until combined, and then whisk in the egg until smooth batter comes together.
5. Place spoonful of the cauliflower batter into a baking sheet lined with parchment paper, spray with oil, and then bake for 15 to 25 minutes until golden brown and cooked. Serve straight away with hot sauce.

390 – Pesto Stuffed Mushroom

Serves: 2; Preparation: 5 minutes; Cook time: 15 minutes;
Nutrition facts: 409 Calories; 33.1 g Fats; 24.2 g Protein; 2.8 g Net Carb; 0.4 g Fiber;
Ingredients
- 2 cremini mushrooms
- 2 strips of bacon, halved lengthwise
- 2 tsp cream cheese, softened
- 2 tbsp basil pesto

How to Prepare:
1. Turn on the oven, then set it to 375 degrees F and let it preheat.
2. Meanwhile, take a small bowl, place cream cheese in it, add pesto and stir until combined.
3. Remove the stalk from each mushroom, then stuff mushroom caps with cream cheese mixture, wrap each mushroom with two bacon strips and secure with toothpicks. Place wrapped mushroom onto a baking sheet and then bake for 10 to 15 minutes until done. Serve.

391 – Roasted and Cheesy Butternut Squash

Serves: 2; Preparation: 5 minutes; Cook time: 10 minutes;
Nutrition facts: 190 Calories; 15.1 g Fats; 2.8 g Protein; 6 g Net Carb; 3.3 g Fiber;
Ingredients
- 8 oz butternut squash pieces
- ½ tsp garlic powder
- ¼ tsp ground black pepper
- 1 tbsp grated mozzarella cheese
- 1 tsp chopped cilantro

Seasoning:
- 2 tbsp avocado oil
- ½ tsp salt

How to Prepare:
1. Turn on the oven, then set it to 425 degrees F and let it preheat.
2. Meanwhile, take a rimmed baking sheet, spread butternut squash pieces on it, drizzle with oil and sprinkle with garlic powder, salt, and black pepper.
3. Toss until well coated and then bake for 12 minutes until done, stirring halfway.
4. Then sprinkle cheese on top and continue baking for 2 minutes until cheese has melted. Sprinkle with cilantro and then Serve.

392 – Warm Kale Salad

Serves: 2; Preparation: 5 minutes; Cook time: 5 minutes;
Nutrition facts: 245 Calories; 24 g Fats; 5 g Protein; 2.5 g Net Carb; 1 g Fiber;
Ingredients
- ½ bunch of kale, chopped
- 2 tbsp avocado oil
- 2 oz whipped topping

- 2 tbsp mayonnaise
- 2 oz feta cheese

Seasoning:
- ½ tsp garlic powder
- 1 tsp mustard paste
- 1/3 tsp salt; 1/4 tsp ground black pepper
- 2 tbsp butter, unsalted

How to Prepare:
1. Prepare the dressing and for this, take a medium bowl, place garlic, salt, black pepper, topping, mustard, mayonnaise, and oil in it and then stir until mixed.
2. Take a frying pan, place it over medium heat, add butter and when it melts, add kale and cook for 2 minutes until sauté and bright green.
3. Transfer kale to a bowl, pour prepared dressing on it, stir until mixed, and then top with feta cheese. Serve.

393 – Caprese Salad

Serves: 2; Preparation: 5 minutes; Cook time: 0 minutes;
Nutrition facts: 163 Calories; 10.3 g Fats; 10.2 g Protein; 4 g Net Carb; 1.5 g Fiber;
Ingredients
- 2 Roma tomatoes
- 6 basil leaves
- 1/2 tbsp balsamic vinegar
- 4 oz mozzarella cheese, cut into pieces

How to Prepare:
1. Cut each tomato into three slices, and then top with tomato slice, a mozzarella cheese piece and a basil leaf.
2. Drizzle with vinegar and then serve.

394 – Spinach Tortilla Wraps with Cream Cheese

Serves: 2; Preparation: 10 minutes; Cook time: 10 minutes;
Nutrition facts: 150 Calories; 11.4 g Fats; 7.9 g Protein; 1.1 g Net Carb; 1.5 g Fiber;
Ingredients
- 3 oz spinach
- ¼ tsp psyllium husk powder
- 2 eggs
- 2 tsp avocado oil
- 2 tsp cream cheese
- 1/8 tsp salt

How to Prepare:
1. Place spinach leaves in a heatproof bowl, cover with plastic wrap, and then microwave for 2 minutes until steamed.
2. Then drain spinach, squeeze moisture as much as possible, and place it in a blender.
3. Add all the remaining ingredients except for oil and then pulse for 2 minutes until smooth.
4. Take a pancake pan, place it over medium heat, add 1 tsp oil, and when hot, switch heat to lower level, add half of the spinach mixture, spread it evenly into a tortilla shape and then cook for 2 to 3 minutes until edges begin to brown.
5. Flip the tortilla, continue cooking for 2 to 3 minutes until done, and then transfer to a plate.
6. Cook another tortilla in the same manner, then spread with cream cheese and serve.

395 – Spinach with Eggs

Serves: 2; Preparation: 5 minutes; Cook time: 10 minutes;
Nutrition facts: 175 Calories; 14 g Fats; 8.4 g Protein; 1.5 g Net Carb; 1.1 g Fiber;
Ingredients
- 3 oz spinach, chopped
- 1 green onion, sliced
- 2 eggs
- 1 tsp grated parmesan cheese
- 1 tsp grated mozzarella cheese
- 1/3 tsp salt; 1/4 tsp ground black pepper
- 1 tsp avocado oil
- 1 tbsp butter, unsalted

How to Prepare:
1. Take a skillet pan, place it over medium heat, add butter and oil and when hot, add spinach and green onion and cook for 3 to 5 minutes until tender.
2. Make two space in the pan, crack an egg in each space, sprinkle with cheeses, salt and black pepper, cover with lid and cook for 3 to 4 minutes until egg has cooked to desired level. Serve.

396 – Eggplant Parmesan

Serves: 2
Preparation: 10 minutes; Cook time: 25 minutes;
Nutrition facts: 355 Calories; 25 g Fats; 14.1 g Protein; 6 g Net Carb; 12 g Fiber;
Ingredients
- 1 large eggplant, sliced
- 1 egg
- 2 oz marinara sauce
- 2 tbsp grated parmesan cheese

Seasoning:
- 2 tbsp almond flour
- 2 tbsp avocado oil
- 1/2 tsp salt
- 1/4 tsp ground black pepper
- ½ tsp garlic powder

How to Prepare:
1. Turn on the oven, then set it to 425 degrees F and let it preheat.
2. Cut eggplant into round slices, brush with oil and then sprinkle with garlic powder, salt, and black pepper.
3. Crack the egg in a bowl and beat with a whisker; then take a shallow dish and add almond flour in it.
4. Dip each slice of eggplant in egg, dredge in almond flour, and place it over a baking sheet lined with parchment sheet and sprayed with oil.
5. Repeat with remaining eggplant slices and then bake for 7 to 10 minutes per side until golden brown and cooked.
6. Top eggplant slices with marinara sauce, sprinkle with cheese, and continue baking for 3 minutes until cheese has melted. Serve.

397– Sautéed Greens with Garlic Butter

Serves: 2; Preparation: 5 minutes; Cook time: 8 minutes;
Nutrition facts: 241 Calories; 22.7 g Fats; 1.8 g Protein; 3.6 g Net Carb; 3 g Fiber;
Ingredients
- 4 oz green beans
- 4 oz asparagus cuts
- 4 tbsp butter, unsalted
- ½ tbsp minced garlic
- 1/3 tsp salt; 1/4 tsp ground black pepper

How to Prepare:
1. Take a medium saucepan half full with water, place it over high heat, bring the water to boil, add green beans and asparagus, cook for 3 minutes, drain and then set aside until required.
2. Take a frying pan, place it over medium heat, add butter and when it melts, stir in garlic and cook for 30 seconds until fragrant.
3. Add vegetables, toss until mixed, cook for 2 minutes until hot and then season with salt and black pepper. Serve.

398 – Green Beans Casserole with Bacon and Cheese

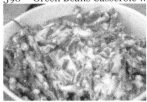

Serves: 2; Preparation: 5 minutes; Cook time: 10 minutes;
Nutrition facts: 182 Calories; 15 g Fats; 9 g Protein; 2 g Net Carb; 1 g Fiber;
Ingredients
- 2 slices of bacon, chopped
- 4 oz green beans
- 1 tbsp butter, unsalted
- 4 tbsp sour cream
- 1 tbsp shredded cheddar cheese
- ½ tsp garlic powder
- ¼ tsp salt; ¼ tsp ground black pepper
- ¾ tsp Italian seasoning

How to Prepare:
1. Turn on the oven, then set it to 350 degrees F and let it preheat.
2. Take a medium skillet pan, place it over medium heat and when hot, place chopped bacon in it and cook for 3 minutes until crisp.
3. Transfer bacon to a plate lined with paper towels, then add beans in the bean and cook for 3 to 5 minutes until tender.
4. Switch heat to medium-low level, add butter, sprinkle with garlic powder, cook for 1 minute and then remove the pan from heat.
5. Add bacon into the pan along with cheese and cream, season with salt and black pepper and stir until combined.
6. Take a casserole dish, grease it with oil, transfer bean mixture in it, sprinkle Italian seasoning on top and then bake for 6 to 10 minutes until bubbly. Serve.

399 – Cauliflower Caprese Salad

Serves: 2; Preparation: 5 minutes; Cook time: 2 minutes;
Nutrition facts: 300 Calories; 25.3 g Fats; 9.8 g Protein; 6 g Net Carb; 2.4 g Fiber;
Ingredients
- 4 oz grape tomatoes
- 4 oz cauliflower florets
- 2 tbsp basil pesto
- 2 oz mozzarella cheese
- 2 tbsp mayonnaise

How to Prepare:
1. Take a medium bowl, place cauliflower florets in it, cover with a plastic wrap and then microwave for 2 minutes or more until steamed.
2. Drain the cauliflower well, place them in a medium bowl, add remaining ingredients and toss until well mixed. Serve.

400 – Berries, Avocado and Spinach Salad

Serves: 2; Preparation: 5 minutes; Cook time: 0 minutes;
Nutrition facts: 322 Calories; 28.3 g Fats; 4.8 g Protein; 3.8 g Net Carb; 7.6 g Fiber;
Ingredients
- 3 oz mixed berries
- 6 oz spinach
- ½ of avocado, pitted, sliced
- 2 tbsp coconut milk, unsweetened
- 1-ounce feta cheese, crumbled

Seasoning:
- ¼ tsp salt; ¼ tsp ground black pepper
- 2 tbsp avocado oil
- 1 tbsp apple cider vinegar
- 1 tsp sliced almond

How to Prepare:
1. Prepare the salad dressing and for this, take a small bowl and mix together milk, oil, vinegar, salt and black pepper until combined.
2. Take a medium bowl, place berries, spinach and avocado, drizzle with prepared salad dressing and toss until combined.
3. Garnish salad with almonds and feta cheese and then serve.

401 – Vegetable Sandwich

Serves: 2; Preparation: 10 minutes; Cook time: 15 minutes;
Nutrition facts: 421 Calories; 33.6 g Fats; 11.6 g Protein; 7.7 g Net Carb; 11.2 g Fiber;
Ingredients
- 6 tbsp coconut flour
- 2 oz green beans
- 2 oz spinach
- ½ of avocado, slices
- 2 eggs

Seasoning:
- 1/8 tsp salt; 1/8 tsp ground black pepper
- 3 tbsp avocado oil
- 1 tsp baking powder

How to Prepare:
1. Turn on the oven, then set it to 375 degrees F and let it preheat.
2. Meanwhile, prepare the batter for this, take a medium bowl, place flour in it, add baking powder and 2 tbsp of oil, add eggs in it and then whisk well until incorporated.
3. Take a 4 by 4 inches heatproof baking pan, grease it with oil, pour in the prepared batter and bake 10 to 15 minutes until bread is firm.
4. Meanwhile, prepare the vegetable and for this, take a medium skillet pan, place it over medium heat, add remaining oil and when hot, add green beans, season with remaining salt and black pepper and cook for 3 to 4 minutes until tender to the desired level.
5. When the bread has baked, take it out, then cut it into four slices and place avocado slices on two slices of bread.
6. Top avocado with green beans and spinach, cover with the remaining slices of bread and then serve.

402 – Roasted Tomato Salad

Serves: 2; Preparation: 5 minutes; Cook time: 15 minutes;
Nutrition facts: 135 Calories; 13.5 g Fats; 0.3 g Protein; 1.5 g Net Carb; 0.8 g Fiber;
Ingredients
- 4 oz grape tomatoes, halved
- 1 green onion, sliced
- ½ tsp salt
- ½ tbsp apple cider vinegar
- 2 tbsp avocado oil
- ¼ tsp ground black pepper

How to Prepare:
1. Turn on the oven, then set it to 450 degrees F and let it preheat.
2. Take a rimmed baking sheet, line it with foil, place tomatoes in it, drizzle with 1 ½ tbsp oil and then season with salt and black pepper.
3. Roast the tomatoes for 10 to 15 minutes until tender, stirring halfway, and then transfer tomatoes to a dish.
4. Sprinkle green onion on top of tomatoes, drizzle with vinegar and remaining oil and let the salad rest for 5 minutes. Serve.

403 – Asparagus and Tomato Salad

Serves: 2; Preparation: 5 minutes; Cook time: 5 minutes;
Nutrition facts: 259 Calories; 21.5 g Fats; 8.9 g Protein; 2.3 g Net Carb; 4.1 g Fiber;
Ingredients
- 2 oz asparagus
- ½ of avocado, sliced
- 2 oz grape tomatoes, halved
- 2 tbsp pecans, chopped
- 1 egg, boiled

Seasoning:
- ¼ tsp salt; 1/8 tsp ground black pepper
- 1 tbsp apple cider vinegar
- 1 tbsp avocado oil

How to Prepare:
1. Take a small bowl, place it over medium heat, fill it half full with water, bring it to a boil, then add asparagus and boil for 2 minutes.
2. Drain the asparagus, place them in a medium bowl and add avocado, tomato, and pecans.
3. Peel the egg, cut it into slices, and add to the salad bowl.
4. Stir together vinegar and oil, drizzle it over salad and then sprinkle with salt and black pepper and toss gently until combined. Serve.

404 – Broccoli and Cottage Cheese Balls

Serves: 2; Preparation: 10 minutes; Cook time: 10 minutes;
Nutrition facts: 202 Calories; 14.4 g Fats; 10.4 g Protein; 3.7 g Net Carb; 2.8 g Fiber;
Ingredients
- 2 tbsp almond flour
- 1 ½ tsp flaxseed
- 3.5 oz broccoli, grated
- 3.5 oz cottage cheese
- ½ of egg

Seasoning:
- 1 tbsp grated mozzarella cheese
- ¼ tsp salt; 1/8 tsp ground black pepper
- 1/3 tsp paprika

How to Prepare:
1. Take a heatproof bowl, place broccoli florets in it, cover with a plastic wrap, microwave for 2 minutes until tender and then drain well.
2. Place broccoli into a medium bowl, add remaining ingredients except for almond flour and flaxseed, stir until well mixed and then shape the mixture into four balls.
3. Take a shallow dish, stir together almond flour and flaxseed until mixed and then roll broccoli balls in the mixture until evenly coated.
4. Take a skillet pan, place it over medium heat, grease it with avocado oil and when hot, place balls in it and cook for 3 to 4 minutes per side until thoroughly cooked and golden brown. Serve.

405 – Cauliflower Hash Brown

Serves: 2; Preparation: 5 minutes; Cook time: 12 minutes;
Nutrition facts: 175 Calories; 15.1 g Fats; 6 g Protein; 1 g Net Carb; 2.1 g Fiber;
Ingredients
- 4 oz grated cauliflower florets
- 1 green onion, sliced
- 1 tbsp butter, unsalted
- 1 tbsp avocado oil
- 1 egg
- 1/3 tsp salt; ¼ tsp ground black pepper

How to Prepare:
1. Take a medium bowl, place cauliflower florets in it, add green onion, egg, salt and black pepper, stir until well combined and set the mixture aside for 10 minutes.
2. Then take a medium skillet pan, place it over medium heat, add butter and oil and when it melts, scoop one-fourth portion of prepared mixture in the pan, shape it like a pancake and then cook for 2 to 3 minutes per side until cooked and nicely browned. Transfer hash brown to a plate and then repeat with the remaining batter.

406 – Broccoli and Cheddar Deviled Eggs

Serves: 2; Preparation: 10 minutes; Cook time: 0 minutes;
Nutrition facts: 99 Calories; 6.5 g Fats; 8 g Protein; 0.8 g Net Carb; 0.2 g Fiber;
Ingredients
- 2 eggs, boiled
- 1 tbsp chopped broccoli florets
- 1/3 tsp mustard paste
- ¼ tsp apple cider vinegar
- 1 tbsp grated cheddar cheese
- 1/8 tsp ground black pepper

How to Prepare:
1. Peel the boiled eggs, then slice in half lengthwise and transfer egg yolks to a medium bowl by using a spoon.
2. Mash the egg yolk, add remaining ingredients and stir until well combined.
3. Spoon the egg yolk mixture into egg whites and then serve.

407 – Loaded Radish

Serves: 2; Preparation: 5 minutes; Cook time: 10 minutes;
Nutrition facts: 371 Calories; 29 g Fats; 20 g Protein; 3 g Net Carb; 3 g Fiber;
Ingredients
- ½ bunch of radish, peeled, diced
- 2 slices of bacon, chopped, cooked
- 1 green onion, chopped
- 2 oz sliced mushrooms
- 2 tbsp grated cheddar cheese
- ½ tsp garlic powder
- 1/3 tsp salt; ¼ tsp ground black pepper
- 1 tbsp avocado oil

How to Prepare:
1. Take a medium skillet pan, place it over medium heat, add oil and when hot, add radish and mushroom, sprinkle with garlic powder, salt and black pepper, stir until mixed and cook for 5 to 8 minutes until nicely browned and tender.
2. When done, sprinkle cheese and bacon on top of vegetables, then cover with the lid and let the vegetables sit for 2 minutes until cheese has melted. Garnish with green onions and then serve.

408 – Swiss chard with Nested Eggs

Serves: 2; Preparation: 5 minutes; Cook time: 10 minutes;
Nutrition facts: 202 Calories; 15.8 g Fats; 8.4 g Protein; 3 g Net Carb; 2.4 g Fiber;
Ingredients

- ¾ bunch of Swiss chard
- 2 tbsp apple cider vinegar
- 1 ½ tbsp avocado oil
- 2 eggs
- ¼ tsp salt; ¼ tsp ground black pepper
- ¼ tsp garlic powder

How to Prepare:
1. Separate ribs and leaves of chards, chop the ribs and then chop its leaves.
2. Take a medium skillet pan, place it over medium heat, add oil and when hot, add chard ribs and cook for 3 to 4 minutes until caramelized and tender.
3. Sprinkle with garlic powder, salt, and black pepper, stir until mixed, add chard leaves and then cook for 2 to 3 minutes until wilted.
4. Stir in vinegar, continue cooking until chard leaves are completely wilted, then switch heat to medium-low level, crack eggs on top of chards, cover with the lid and cook for 3 to 4 minutes until eggs have cooked to the desired level. When done, sprinkle some salt and black pepper over eggs and then serve.

409 – Garlic Butter Cauliflower Rice with Spinach

Serves: 2; Preparation: 5 minutes; Cook time: 5 minutes;
Nutrition facts: 165 Calories; 13.6 g Fats; 4.4 g Protein; 1.3 g Net Carb; 4 g Fiber;
Ingredients
- 4 oz spinach
- 8 oz grated cauliflower
- 1 tsp garlic powder
- 2 tbsp butter, unsalted
- 1 tbsp avocado oil
- 1/3 tsp salt; ¼ tsp ground black pepper
- ¼ tsp paprika

How to Prepare:
1. Take a medium skillet pan, place it over medium heat, add oil and when it melts, add cauliflower, sprinkle with garlic powder, salt, black pepper, and paprika, stir until mixed and then cook for 2 minutes until combined.
2. Add lime juice, oil, spinach, cook for 1 minute until spinach leaves wilt, and then remove the pan from heat. Divide rice between two plates and then serve.

410 – Bok Choy Stir-Fry with Green Beans

Serves: 2; Preparation: 5 minutes; Cook time: 8 minutes;
Nutrition facts: 210 Calories; 15.4 g Fats; 5.5 g Protein; 4.2 g Net Carb; 5.9 g Fiber;
Ingredients
- 1 pound bok choy, destemmed, sliced
- 4 oz green beans
- 1 tsp garlic powder
- 2 tbsp soy sauce
- 2 tbsp sesame oil

How to Prepare:
1. Take a medium skillet pan, place it over medium heat, add oil and when hot, add bok choy and green beans, sprinkle with garlic powder and cook for 3 to 4 minutes until vegetables are almost cooked.
2. Drizzle soy sauce over vegetables, toss until well coated, and continue cooking until tender. Serve.

411 – Grilled Squash Salad

Serves: 2; Preparation: 5 minutes; Cook time: 8 minutes;
Nutrition facts: 245 Calories; 21 g Fats; 7.8 g Protein; 3.6 g Net Carb; 2 g Fiber;
Ingredients
- 1 large summer squash
- 4 basil leaves
- 1 tbsp apple cider vinegar
- 2 tbsp avocado oil
- 2 oz mozzarella cheese, cubed
- 1/3 tsp salt; ¼ tsp ground black pepper

How to Prepare:
1. Peel the squash, then cut it into 1/4-inch thick slices, place them in a medium bowl, drizzle with 1 tbsp oil, season with salt and black pepper and toss until well coated.
2. Take a grill pan, place it over medium-high heat, grease it with oil and when hot, place squash slices on it, and then cook for 2 to 3 minutes per side until slightly charred and tender.
3. Transfer grilled squash slices to a plate, cool for 5 minutes, then top with cheese and drizzle with vinegar and remaining oil and scatter with basil leaves. Serve.

412 – Parmesan Roasted Grape Tomatoes

Serves: 2; Preparation: 5 minutes; Cook time: 5 minutes;
Nutrition facts: 130 Calories; 10.8 g Fats; 2.2 g Protein; 3 g Net Carb; 1.4 g Fiber;
Ingredients

- 8 oz grape tomatoes, halved
- 1/3 tsp garlic powder
- 1 tsp chopped cilantro
- 1 ½ tbsp avocado oil
- 2 tbsp grated parmesan cheese

How to Prepare:
1. Turn on the broiler and then let it preheat.
2. Meanwhile, take a sheet pan, line it with parchment paper, and then spread cherry tomatoes in it cut-side up. Stir together garlic powder, cilantro, oil, and cheese, spread this mixture evenly on top of tomato halves, and then broil for 4 to 5 minutes until the top has turned nicely browned. Serve.

413 – Cheddar, Bacon and Tomato Egg Cups

Serves: 2; Preparation: 5 minutes; Cook time: 16 minutes;
Nutrition facts: 170 Calories; 11.7 g Fats; 12.7 g Protein; 1.8 g Net Carb; 0.3 g Fiber;
Ingredients

- 2 slices of bacon
- 2 tbsp chopped tomatoes
- 1 green onion, chopped
- 2 eggs
- 2 tbsp grated cheddar cheese
- 1/8 tsp salt; 1/8 tsp ground black pepper
- 2 tbsp coconut milk, unsweetened

How to Prepare:
1. Turn on the oven, then set it to 350 degrees F and let it preheat.
2. Meanwhile, take a medium skillet pan, place it over medium heat and when hot, add bacon and cook for 2 minutes per side until cooked and browned.
3. Transfer bacon to a cutting board and then chop, set aside until required.
4. Take a medium bowl, crack eggs in it, add milk, salt, and black pepper and whisk until combined.
5. Take two silicone muffin cups, divide bacon between them, and then add 1 tbsp tomato and green onion into each cup.
6. Pour in egg mixture, sprinkle cheese on top and then bake the muffins for 10 to 12 minutes until firm and top have turned nicely browned.

414 – Green Beans with Cream Cheese

Serves: 2; Preparation: 5 minutes; Cook time: 5 minutes;
Nutrition facts: 103 Calories; 8.4 g Fats; 1.2 g Protein; 1.6 g Net Carb; 2.3 g Fiber;
Ingredients

- 6 oz green beans
- ½ tbsp garlic powder
- ¼ tsp salt; 1/8 tsp ground black pepper
- 2 tbsp cream cheese
- 1 tsp avocado oil
- 1 tbsp butter, unsalted

How to Prepare:
1. Take a medium skillet pan, place it over medium heat, add oil and when hot, add green beans and cook for 2 minutes until hot.
2. Add butter and cream cheese, stir until mixed, and then cook for 3 minutes until softened.
3. Season green beans with salt and black pepper, sprinkle with garlic powder and remove the pan from heat. Distribute green beans between two plates and then serve.

415 – Moroccan Roasted Green Beans

Serves: 2; Preparation: 5 minutes; Cook time: 15 minutes;
Nutrition facts: 112.5 Calories; 10.3 g Fats; 0.8 g Protein; 2.2 g Net Carb; 2 g Fiber;

Ingredients
- 5 oz green beans
- ½ tsp salt
- ½ tbsp Moroccan spice mix
- 1 ½ tbsp avocado oil

How to Prepare:
1. Turn on the oven, then set it to 400 degrees F and let it preheat.
2. Take a medium bowl, place green beans in it, add oil, salt, spice mix and toss until well coated.
3. Spread green beans on a sheet pan and then bake for 15 minutes until roasted, stirring halfway. Serve.

416 – Onion Rings

Serves: 2; Preparation: 10 minutes; Cook time: 12 minutes;
Nutrition facts: 210 Calories; 16 g Fats; 9.2 g Protein; 5 g Net Carb; 1.8 g Fiber;
Ingredients
- ½ of yellow onion
- 2 slices of bacon, chopped, cooked
- 1 ½ tbsp coconut flour
- 1 ½ tbsp almond flour
- 1 egg

Seasoning:
- ¼ tsp garlic powder
- 1/8 tsp salt; ¼ tsp paprika
- 1 tbsp avocado oil
- 1 ½ tbsp almond milk

How to Prepare:
1. Turn on the oven, then set it to 400 degrees F and let it preheat.
2. Take a small bowl, crack the egg in it and whisk until blended.
3. Take a shallow dish, place coconut flour in it and then stir in salt until mixed.
4. Take a separate shallow dish, add almond flour and bacon in it and then stir in garlic powder and paprika until mixed.
5. Prepare the onion rings and for this, cut onion into ¼-inch thick rings, coat each ring with coconut flour mixture, dip into egg, coat with almond flour mixture and then place on a baking sheet lined with foil
6. Repeat with the remaining onion rings, spray with oil and then bake for 10 to 12 minutes until golden brown and crisp. Serve.

417 – Egg Nest in Braised Cabbage

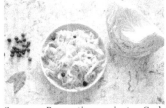

Serves: 2; Preparation: 5 minutes; Cook time: 8 minutes;
Nutrition facts: 163 Calories; 12.1 g Fats; 8 g Protein; 2.7 g Net Carb; 2 g Fiber;
Ingredients
- 1 cup shredded cabbage
- 1 tbsp apple cider vinegar
- 2 eggs
- 1 tbsp avocado oil

Seasoning:
- 1/8 tsp salt; 1/8 tsp ground black pepper

How to Prepare:
1. Take a medium frying pan, place it over medium-high heat, add oil and when hot, add cabbage, season with salt, toss until mixed and cook for 2 to 3 minutes until cabbage is nicely golden brown.
2. Sprinkle with black pepper, drizzle with vinegar, then shape cabbage into two mounds and make a well in each mound by using the back of a spoon.
3. Crack an egg in each well, switch heat to the medium low level, cover with the lid, and cook eggs for 1 to 2 minutes until cooked to the desired level. When done, sprinkle some salt and black pepper over eggs and then Serve.

418 – Loaded Egg and Bacon Salad with Cabbage

Serves: 2; Preparation: 10 minutes; Cook time: 0 minutes;
Nutrition facts: 391 Calories; 34 g Fats; 15.6 g Protein; 5 g Net Carb; 1.8 g Fiber;
Ingredients
- 2 slices of bacon, chopped, cooked
- 1 cup chopped cabbage leaves
- 1-ounce grape tomatoes, halved

- 3 eggs, boiled
- 4 tbsp mayonnaise
- ¼ tsp salt; 1/8 tsp ground black pepper

How to Prepare:
1. Prepare the egg salad, and for this, peel the eggs, then chop them and place them in a medium bowl.
2. Add mayonnaise, season with salt and black pepper, and then stir until mixed.
3. Divide cabbage leaves between two plates, top with prepared egg salad, and then sprinkle with bacon and tomatoes. Serve.

419 – Green Olives Deviled Eggs

Serves: 2; Preparation: 5 minutes; Cook time: 0 minutes;
Nutrition facts: 209 Calories; 19.3 g Fats; 7.3 g Protein; 1.4 g Net Carb; 0.2 g Fiber;
Ingredients
- 2 eggs, boiled
- 1 tbsp chopped green olives
- ¼ tsp paprika; 2 tbsp mayonnaise
- 1 tbsp cream cheese, softened

How to Prepare:
1. Peel the boiled eggs, then slice in half lengthwise and transfer egg yolks to a medium bowl by using a spoon.
2. Mash the egg yolk, add remaining ingredients and stir until well combined. Spoon the egg yolk mixture into egg whites and then serve.

420 – Tomato and Avocado Salad

Serves: 2; Preparation: 10 minutes; Cook time: 0 minutes;
Nutrition facts: 173 Calories; 15.3 g Fats; 1.3 g Protein; 3 g Net Carb; 3.8 g Fiber;
Ingredients
- 2 tomatoes, sliced
- ¼ of avocado, pitted, sliced
- ¼ of lime, juiced
- 1 ½ tbsp avocado oil
- 1-ounce basil pesto
- ¼ tsp salt; 1/8 tsp ground black pepper

How to Prepare:
3. Cut avocado into slices, place them on a plate, drizzle with lime juice and toss.
4. Cut tomato into slices, place them in a separate plate, sprinkle with salt, and toss until coated.
5. Assemble the salad and for this, layer avocado and tomato slice on each other, then drizzle with vinegar, pesto and oil and sprinkle with some more salt and black pepper. Serve.

421 – Green Onion and Tomato Deviled Eggs

Serves: 2; Preparation: 10 minutes; Cook time: 0 minutes;
Nutrition facts: 159 Calories; 12.6 g Fats; 9.1 g Protein; 1.7 g Net Carb; 0.3 g Fiber;
Ingredients
- 1 slice of bacon, chopped, cooked
- 1-ounce grape tomatoes, minced
- 1 stalk of green onion, chopped
- 1 tbsp mayonnaise
- 2 eggs, boiled
- 1/8 tsp salt; 1/8 tsp ground black pepper

How to Prepare:
1. Peel the boiled eggs, then slice in half lengthwise and transfer egg yolks to a medium bowl by using a spoon.
2. Mash the egg yolk, add remaining ingredients and stir until well combined. Spoon the egg yolk mixture into egg whites, and then serve.

422 – Mushroom, Spinach and Bacon Egg Cups

Serves: 2; Preparation: 10 minutes; Cook time: 20 minutes;
Nutrition facts: 213 Calories; 15.7 g Fats; 14.4 g Protein; 2.3 g Net Carb; 1.4 g Fiber;
Ingredients

- 4 slices of bacon
- 1-ounce sliced mushrooms
- 2 oz spinach
- 2 eggs
- 2 tbsp coconut milk, unsweetened

Seasoning:
- ¼ tsp salt
- 1/8 tsp ground black pepper
- 2 tsp avocado oil
- 2 tbsp grated mozzarella cheese

How to Prepare:
1. Turn on the oven, then set it to 400 degrees F and let it preheat.
2. Take two silicon muffin cups, place two slices of bacon into each cup, wrap them in a circle around the cup, and then bake for 8 minutes.
3. Meanwhile, take a medium skillet pan, place it over medium heat, add oil and when hot, add mushroom and cook for 3 to 4 minutes until golden brown and cooked.
4. Then add spinach, stir until mixed and continue cooking for 2 minutes until wilted, set aside until required.
5. Take a small bowl, crack the egg in it, add salt, black pepper, and milk and whisk until combined.
6. When the bacon has baked, drain the grease, rearrange the slices around the edges of cups, fill evenly with cooked vegetables, and then pour in egg batter. Sprinkle cheese on top of each muffin and then bake for 10 minutes until firm and cooked. Serve.

423 – Mushroom Pie

Serves: 2; Preparation: 5 minutes; Cook time: 25 minutes;
Nutrition facts: 274 Calories; 18 g Fats; 23 g Protein; 4 g Net Carb; 2 g Fiber;
Ingredients
- 3 oz sliced mushroom
- 1 green onion, sliced
- 4 eggs
- 2 tbsp yogurt
- 2 tbsp grated parmesan cheese
- ¼ tsp salt; 1/8 tsp ground black pepper
- 1/8 tsp dried thyme
- 1 tbsp avocado oil

How to Prepare:
1. Turn on the oven, then set it to 400 degrees F and let it preheat.
2. Meanwhile, take a medium skillet pan, place it over medium heat, add oil and when hot, add mushrooms and cook for 4 to 5 minutes until all the moisture has evaporated and nicely browned.
3. Meanwhile, crack eggs in a medium bowl, add yogurt, salt, black pepper, and thyme, whisk until beaten, and then stir in green onion and cheese until combined.
4. Take a pie dish, grease it with oil, spread mushroom mixture in the bottom, then cover with egg mixture and bake for 15 to 20 minutes until frittata has turned firm and browned on top. When done, let frittata cool for 5 minutes, then cut it into slices and serve.

424 – Broccoli and Cheddar Fritters

Serves: 2; Preparation: 5 minutes; Cook time: 8 minutes;
Nutrition facts: 303 Calories; 22.7 g Fats; 16.3 g Protein; 4.1 g Net Carb; 2.6 g Fiber;
Ingredients
- 2 slices of bacon, chopped, cooked
- 4 oz broccoli florets, chopped
- 1 tbsp coconut flour
- 2 oz grated cheddar cheese
- 1 egg
- ½ tsp Cajun seasoning
- 1 tbsp avocado oil

How to Prepare:
1. Take a medium heatproof bowl, place broccoli florets in it, drizzle with 1 tbsp water, cover the bowl with a plastic wrap, and then microwave for 2 to 3 minutes at high heat setting until tender.
2. Drain the broccoli, pat dry with paper towels, then transfer broccoli into a bowl and stir in flour and Cajun seasoning until mixed.
3. Add egg and cheddar cheese and then stir until well combined.
4. Take a medium skillet pan, place it over medium heat, add oil and when hot, spoon broccoli mixture in it in the form of mounds and then cook for 2 to 3 minutes per side until golden brown. Serve.

425 – Broccoli and Cheddar Loaf

Serves: 2; Preparation: 5 minutes; Cook time: 15 minutes;
Nutrition facts: 222 Calories; 15.5 g Fats; 14.4 g Protein; 3.7 g Net Carb; 2.4 g Fiber;

Ingredients
- 3 tbsp grated broccoli
- 1 ½ tbsp coconut flour
- ¾ tsp baking powder
- 2 eggs
- 2 oz grated cheddar cheese
- ½ tsp salt

How to Prepare:
1. Turn on the oven, then set it to 350 degrees F and let it preheat.
2. Meanwhile, take a medium bowl, place all the ingredients in it and whisk until incorporated and smooth.
3. Take a mini loaf pan, line it with parchment paper, pour the prepared batter in it and then bake for 12 to 15 minutes until firm and puffed.
4. When done, let the bread cool for 5 minutes, then cut it into slices and serve.

426 – Sauteed Kale with Garlic and Avocado Oil

Serves: 2; Preparation: 5 minutes; Cook time: 5 minutes;
Nutrition facts: 160 Calories; 14.6 g Fats; 1.5 g Protein; 3.5 g Net Carb; 0.3 g Fiber;
Ingredients
- ¾ bunch of kale, destemmed, leaves sliced
- 1 tsp sliced garlic
- ¼ tsp salt
- ¼ tsp red chili flakes
- 2 tbsp avocado oil

How to Prepare:
1. Take a medium skillet pan, place it over medium heat, add oil and when hot, add garlic and red chili flakes and cook for 1 minute until fragrant.
2. Add kale, toss until well coated, and cook for 3 minutes until sauté.
3. Then season kale with salt and black pepper, continue cooking for 1 to 2 minutes until cooking liquid has evaporated completely and then serve.

427 – Lime Roasted Spicy Broccoli

Serves: 2; Preparation: 5 minutes; Cook time: 10 minutes;
Nutrition facts: 210 Calories; 17.3 g Fats; 6.2 g Protein; 4.5 g Net Carb; 2.3 g Fiber;
Ingredients
- 6 oz broccoli florets
- ¼ of lime, juiced, zested
- 1 tsp dried basil
- 2 tbsp grated parmesan cheese
- 2 tbsp avocado oil

Seasoning:
- 1 tsp garlic powder
- 1/3 tsp salt; ¼ tsp red chili flakes

How to Prepare:
1. Turn on the oven, then set it to 425 degrees F and let it preheat.
2. Meanwhile, take a medium bowl, place florets in it, drizzle with oil and lime juice, add all the spices along with lime zest and toss until well coated.
3. Spread broccoli florets onto a baking sheet lined with foil, sprinkle cheese on top and then bake for 10 to 15 minutes until golden brown and tender. Serve.

428 – Broccoli and Cheese soup

Serves: 2; Preparation: 5 minutes; Cook time: 10 minutes;
Nutrition facts: 145.5 Calories; 12.5 g Fats; 6.5 g Protein; 2 g Net Carb; 0.5 g Fiber;
Ingredients
- ¾ cup broccoli florets
- ½ tsp garlic powder
- ½ cup shredded cheddar cheese
- ¼ cup whipped topping
- 1 cup chicken broth, reserved

Seasoning:
- ½ tsp salt; ½ tsp cracked black pepper

How to Prepare:

1. Take a large pot, place it over medium heat, pour in reserved chicken broth, and stir in whipped topping.
2. Add broccoli florets, season with salt and black pepper and cook for 10 minutes until florets are tender.
3. Remove the pot from heat and use an immersion blender to puree the soup until smooth.
4. Then return the pot to low heat, add ¼ cup cheese, stir until it melts, then add remaining cheese and stir until it melts.
5. Ladle soup into bowls and serve.

429 – Zucchini Noodle Carbonara

Serves: 2; Preparation: 10 minutes; Cook time: 10 minutes;
Nutrition facts: 114 Calories; 7 g Fats; 8 g Protein; 1.5 g Net Carb; 1.5 g Fiber;
Ingredients
- 2 large zucchini
- 1 large egg
- 1 egg yolk
- ¼ cup grated cheddar cheese
- 3 slices of turkey bacon, diced

Seasoning:
- 1/4 tsp sea salt; 1/2 tsp fresh ground black pepper

How to Prepare:
1. Prepare zucchini noodles, and for this, cut off the bottom and top of zucchini and then use a spiralizer to convert into noodles.
2. Take a baking sheet, line it with a paper towel, then lay the zucchini noodles on them, sprinkle with salt, and let sit for 5 minutes.
3. Then wrap zucchini noodles in a cheesecloth and squeeze well to remove its liquid as much as possible and set aside until required.
4. Prepare the sauce and for this, crack the egg in a bowl, add egg yolk and cheese and whisk until well combined.
5. Take a skillet pan, place it over medium heat, add bacon slices, and cook for 3 to 5 minutes until crispy.
6. Then add zucchini noodles and cook for 3 minutes until warmed through.
7. Switch heat to a low level, pour in egg mixture, stir well and remove the pan from heat.
8. Stir the zucchini noodle until the egg is just cooked and then sprinkle with black pepper. Serve.

430 – Cheese and Cauliflower Soup

Serves: 2; Preparation: 5 minutes; Cook time: 15 minutes;
Nutrition facts: 123.5 Calories; 9.3 g Fats; 4.5 g Protein; 1.2 g Net Carb; 0.4 g Fiber;
Ingredients
- 4 ounce chopped cauliflower
- 2 slices of turkey bacon
- 1 ¾ tbsp whipped topping
- 1 1/2 cups chicken broth
- 4-ounce shredded parmesan cheese

Seasoning:
- ½ tsp salt; ½ tsp ground black pepper
- ¼ tsp garlic powder

How to Prepare:
1. Take a medium pot, place it over medium-high heat, then add turkey bacon and cook for 5 minutes until crispy.
2. Transfer bacon to a plate, crumble it and reserve the grease from the pot.
3. Add cauliflower into the pot, pour in chicken broth, season with salt and black pepper, add garlic powder and bring the mixture to boil.
4. Then lower heat to medium-low level and simmer cauliflower for 5 to 7 minutes until tender.
5. Remove pot from the heat, puree the mixture with an immersion blender, then add cheese and whipped topping and stir until well combined.
6. Ladle soup into bowls, top with bacon and serve.

431 – Avocado Stuffed Egg Salad

Serves: 2; Preparation: 10 minutes; Cook time: 0 minutes
Nutrition facts: 131.8 Calories; 11.7 g Fats; 3.6 g Protein; 0.6 g Net Carb; 2.4 g Fiber;
Ingredients
- 2 tbsp mayonnaise
- 2 large eggs, hard-boiled
- 1 green onion, chopped
- 1 avocado
- 1/8 tsp ground black pepper; ¼ tsp salt

How to Prepare:

1. Peel the eggs, then dice them and place them in a bowl.
2. Add remaining ingredients except for avocado and stir until well mixed.
3. Cut avocado in half, remove its pit, and then fill the avocado halved with prepared egg salad. Serve.

432 – Broccoli and Bacon Stir-Fry

Serves: 2; Preparation: 5 minutes; Cook time: 15 minutes
Nutrition facts: 481 Calories; 38 g Fats; 30 g Protein; 2.7 g Net Carb; 2.1 g Fiber;
Ingredients
- 6-oz broccoli florets, chopped
- 4 oz ground turkey
- 2 green onions, chopped
- 2 slices of bacon, cooked, crumbled
- ¼ tsp dried thyme
- ½ tsp salt; ¼ tsp ground black pepper

How to Prepare:
1. Take a skillet pan, place it over medium heat, add bacon slices, and cook for 5 minutes until crispy.
2. Transfer bacon to a cutting board, cool for 5 minutes, then crumble it and set aside until required.
3. Add turkey into the pan, cook for 3 minutes until turkey is no longer pink, then add broccoli and onions, season with salt, black pepper, and thyme, stir well and continue cooking for 5 to 7 minutes until thoroughly cooked.
4. When done, top with bacon and serve.

433 – Buttery Garlic Green Beans

Serves: 2; Preparation: 5 minutes; Cook time: 12 minutes
Nutrition facts: 224 Calories; 21.7 g Fats; 1.1 g Protein; 3.9 g Net Carb; 2.3 g Fiber;
Ingredients
- 6 oz green beans
- 1 tsp minced garlic
- 1/8 tsp lemon pepper seasoning
- ½ cup of water
- 2 tbsp mayonnaise
- 2 tbsp unsalted butter
- 1/3 tsp salt

How to Prepare:
1. Take a medium skillet pan, place it over medium heat, pour in water, and bring it to boil.
2. Switch heat to medium-low level, add green beans and cook for 5 minutes until beans start to soften.
3. Drain the beans, return them to the pan and place the pan over medium heat.
4. Add butter, stir, cook the beans for 3 minutes, then add garlic and continue cooking for 1 minute until fragrant.
5. Season green beans with lemon pepper and salt and cook for 3 minutes until beans have cooked and then serve straight away with mayonnaise.

434 – Pesto Zucchini Noodles

Serves: 2
Preparation: 5 minutes; Cook time: 3 minutes
Nutrition facts: 384 Calories; 33 g Fats; 14.4 g Protein; 1.7 g Net Carb; 6 g Fiber;
Ingredients
- 2 zucchini, spiralized into noodles
- 2 tbsp coconut oil
- 1/3 tsp salt
- 4 tbsp pesto sauce
- 2 tbsp chopped peanuts

How to Prepare:
1. Prepare zucchini noodles, and for this, cut zucchini into noodles by using a spiralizer or vegetable peeler.
2. Take a skillet pan, place it over medium heat, and add zucchini and cook for 3 minutes until it begins to soften.
3. Then add peanuts, season with salt, add pesto sauce and stir until well mixed. Serve.

435 – Broccoli Cheese Casserole

Serves: 2; Preparation: 10 minutes; Cook time: 25 minutes
Nutrition facts: 163 Calories; 11 g Fats; 11.4 g Protein; 4 g Net Carb; 1 g Fiber;
Ingredients

- 6 oz broccoli florets
- 2 eggs
- 1 tbsp whipped topping
- 4 tbsp grated cheddar cheese
- ¼ tsp all-purpose seasoning
- 1/8 tsp ground black pepper

How to Prepare:
1. Turn on the oven, then set it to 375 degrees F, and let it preheat.
2. Meanwhile, cut broccoli into 1-inch pieces, then place them in a pot, pour in enough water to cover them and bring to boil over medium-high heat.
3. Switch heat to medium level, simmer broccoli for 4 to 5 minutes until tender-crisp and bright green and then drain them into a colander, set aside until cooled.
4. In the meantime, crack eggs in a bowl, add whipped topping, seasoning, and black pepper and beat until well combined.
5. Take a casserole dish, place cooled broccoli florets in it, sprinkle cheese on top, evenly pour in eggs, stir gently with a fork, and bake for 15 to 20 minutes until eggs have puffed up and the top is slightly browned. Serve.

436 – Cream of Asparagus Soup

Serves: 2; Preparation: 10 minutes; Cook time: 17 minutes
Nutrition facts: 124 Calories; 12.1 g Fats; 4.1 g Protein; 5 g Net Carb; 1.8 g Fiber;
Ingredients

- 0.5-ounce spinach
- 4 oz chopped asparagus
- ½ tsp garlic powder
- 4 oz whipped topping
- 1 ½ cup water; ½ tbsp coconut oil
- ½ tsp salt; ¼ tsp ground black pepper

How to Prepare:
1. Place a medium saucepan over medium heat, add oil and when hot, add asparagus, season with salt and black pepper and cook for 4 minutes until bright green.
2. Add garlic, stir well, cook for 1 minute until fragrant, then add water, stir well and bring the mixture to boil.
3. Switch heat to medium-low level, simmer for 10 minutes until asparagus is tender, then add spinach and continue cooking for 2 minutes.
4. Remove the pan from heat, puree the soup using an immersion blender and stir in whipped topping until combined. Serve.

437 – Green Beans with Almonds

Serves: 2; Preparation: 5 minutes; Cook time: 6 minutes
Nutrition facts: 157 Calories; 12.6 g Fats; 3.1 g Protein; 4.1 g Net Carb; 3.8 g Fiber;
Ingredients

- 6 oz green beans
- 1 tbsp lemon juice
- 1 tsp minced garlic
- 3 tbsp sliced almonds
- ¼ tsp salt
- 1 tbsp avocado oil

How to Prepare:
1. Place green beans in a heatproof bowl, cover it with plastic wrap, poke holes in it by using a fork and then microwave for 2 minutes until beans are tender-crisp.
2. Drain the beans, place them in another bowl, drizzle with lemon juice, season with salt and toss well until mixed.
3. Take a skillet pan, place it over medium heat, add oil and when hot, add sliced almonds and cook for 3 minutes until slightly browned.
4. Add garlic, stir well, cook for 1 minute until fragrant and light brown and then transfer the almond-garlic mixture into green beans bowl. Toss well until mixed. Serve.

438 – Broccoli Fritters

Serves: 2; Preparation: 10 minutes; Cook time: 10 minutes
Nutrition facts: 170.5 Calories; 14 g Fats; 6.8 g Protein; 3.1 g Net Carb; 2 g Fiber;

Ingredients
- 6 oz broccoli florets, chopped
- 1 tsp garlic powder
- 1 egg
- 1 tbsp grated parmesan cheese
- 2 tbsp mayonnaise
- 1 tsp onion powder
- 2/3 tsp salt; ¼ tsp ground black pepper

How to Prepare:
1. Turn on the oven, then set it to 400 degrees F, and let it preheat.
2. Place chopped broccoli florets in a bowl, add them in a food processor and pulse for 1 minute until finely chopped.
3. Tip broccoli in a bowl, add remaining ingredients, and stir until well combined.
4. Take a baking sheet, grease it with oil, then drop scoops of prepared broccoli mixture, shape it into patties and bake for 7 to 10 minutes until golden brown. Serve fritters with mayonnaise.

439 – Cabbage with Crispy Bacon

Serves: 2; Preparation: 5 minutes; Cook time: 10 minutes;
Nutrition facts: 425 Calories; 39 g Fats; 10 g Protein; 4.5 g Net Carb; 3 g Fiber;
Ingredients
- 4 oz green cabbage, chopped
- 4 slices of bacon
- 2 oz butter, unsalted
- 1/3 tsp salt; 1/4 tsp ground black pepper

How to Prepare:
1. Take a medium skillet pan, place it over medium heat and when hot, add bacon and cook for 3 minutes per side until crisps.
2. Transfer bacon to a cutting board, let it cool for 5 minutes and then chop it.
3. Add butter to the pan and when it melts, add cabbage, toss until mixed and fry for 4 to 5 minutes until golden brown and softened.
4. Season cabbage with salt and black pepper, return bacon into the pan, stir until mixed and remove the pan from heat.
5. Distribute cabbage and bacon between two plates and then serve.

440 – Baked Sprouts Casserole

Serves: 2; Preparation: 10 minutes; Cook time: 25 minutes;
Nutrition facts: 235 Calories; 19.7 g Fats; 9.3 g Protein; 3.1 g Net Carb; 1.6 g Fiber;
Ingredients
- 2 slices of bacon, cooked, crumbled
- 2 oz Brussels sprouts, halved
- 3 tbsp coconut cream
- ½ of egg
- 4 tbsp grated mozzarella cheese, full-fat
- ¼ tsp salt; 1/8 tsp ground black pepper
- ¼ tsp paprika
- ¾ tbsp avocado oil

How to Prepare:
1. Turn on the oven, then set it to 400 degrees F and let it preheat.
2. Take a medium bowl, add sprouts in it, drizzle with oil, season with salt and black pepper and toss until well coated.
3. Spread sprouts into a casserole dish and then bake for 15 minutes until tender.
4. Meanwhile, take a separate medium bowl, crack the egg in it, add cheese cream, paprika and whisk until well combined.
5. When sprouts have cooked, top them with crumbled bacon, let the mixture cool for 5 minutes, then top with egg mixture and bake for 7 to 10 minutes until the top has turned nicely browned. Serve.

441 – Garlic and Buttery Brussel Sprouts with Bacon

Serves: 2; Preparation: 5 minutes; Cook time: 18 minutes;
Nutrition facts: 312 Calories; 12 g Fats; 11 g Protein; 4 g Net Carb; 4 g Fiber;
Ingredients
- 6 oz Brussel sprouts, halved
- 1-ounce turkey bacon, chopped
- 1 tbsp butter, unsalted
- 2 ½ tbsp grated parmesan cheese
- 2 oz coconut cream
Seasoning:
- ½ tsp garlic powder

- ¼ tsp salt; 1/8 tsp ground black pepper

How to Prepare:
1. Turn on the oven, then set it to 375 degrees F and let it preheat.
2. Take a medium skillet pan, place it over medium heat and when hot, add chopped bacon and cook for 3 to 5 minutes until browned.
3. Transfer bacon to a plate lined with paper towels, drain most of the bacon fat from the skillet, then add butter and wait until it melts.
4. Add Brussel sprouts, toss until coated, season with salt and black pepper and cook for 3 to 4 minutes until beginning to crisp.
5. Sprinkle with garlic, cook for 30 seconds until fragrant, then switch heat to the low level and pour cream over sprouts.
6. Simmer for 2 minutes, then sprinkle with bacon and cheese and bake for 5 to 7 minutes until cheese has melted and golden brown.

442 – Broccoli and Cauliflower in Cheese

Serves: 2; Preparation: 5 minutes; Cook time: 8 minutes;
Nutrition facts: 183.5 Calories; 15.5 g Fats; 7 g Protein; 4.5 g Net Carb; 2.5 g Fiber;
Ingredients
- 4 oz broccoli and cauliflower florets, medium chopped
- 2 tbsp chopped oregano
- 3 tbsp butter, unsalted
- 3 tbsp grated parmesan cheese
- 1 ounce whipped cream

Seasoning:
- 1/3 tsp salt; 1/4 tsp ground black pepper

How to Prepare:
1. Take a medium skillet pan, place it over medium-high heat, add butter and when it melts, add broccoli and cauliflower and cook for 3 to 4 minutes until golden brown.
2. Sprinkle with oregano, season with salt and black pepper, add cheese and cream, stir until well combined and cook for 1 to 2 minutes until cheese has melted. Serve.

443 – Bacon Braised Cabbage

Serves: 2; Preparation: 5 minutes; Cook time: 10 minutes;
Nutrition facts: 150 Calories; 10.7 g Fats; 9.1 g Protein; 2.1 g Net Carb; 1.2 g Fiber;
Ingredients
- 4 strips of bacon, sliced
- 1 cup sliced cabbage
- 1 tsp avocado oil
- 2 tbsp water

Seasoning:
- 1/3 tsp salt; 1/4 tsp ground black pepper

How to Prepare:
1. Take a skillet pan, place it over medium heat and when hot, add bacon pieces and cook for 4 to 5 minutes until browned on all sides.
2. Add cabbage, stir in water and then cook for 4 to 5 minutes until the cabbage has turned soft.
3. Drizzle with oil, season with salt and black pepper, continue cooking for 2 minutes and then Serve.

444 – Cheesy Stuffed Tomatoes with Pork

Serves: 2; Preparation: 10 minutes; Cook time: 10 minutes;
Nutrition facts: 286 Calories; 23.3 g Fats; 14.7 g Protein; 3.4 g Net Carb; 1.5 g Fiber;
Ingredients
- 2 tomatoes
- 3 oz ground pork
- ½ tsp dried parsley
- 4 tbsp grated parmesan cheese
- 1 tbsp avocado oil

Seasoning:
- ¼ tsp salt
- 1/8 tsp ground black pepper

How to Prepare:
1. Turn on the oven, then set it to 350 degrees F and let it preheat.
2. Take a medium skillet pan, place it over medium heat and when hot, add pork, season with salt and black pepper and cook for 3 to 4 minutes until golden brown, set aside until required.
3. Prepare tomatoes, and for this, rinse them, pat dry with a paper towel, cut a thin at the end, then slice the top part and scoop out seeds from the tomatoes.
4. Place 1 tbsp of cheese into each tomato, top with cooked pork, cover with remaining cheese and then bae for 3 to 5 minutes until cheese has melted. Serve.

445 – Strawberry, Spinach and Cream Cheese Salad

Serves: 2
Preparation: 5 minutes; Cook time: 0 minutes;
Nutrition facts: 170 Calories; 15.8 g Fats; 1.2 g Protein; 1.7 g Net Carb; 1.5 g Fiber;
Ingredients
- 2 oz spinach leaves
- 2 oz strawberries, sliced
- 1 tbsp chopped walnuts
- 2 tsp cream cheese
- 2 tbsp avocado oil

Seasoning:
- 1/16 tsp salt
- 1/16 tsp ground black pepper
- 1/8 tsp stevia

How to Prepare:
3. Prepare the dressing and for this, take a small bowl, place oil in it and stir in stevia, salt, and black pepper until combined.
4. Take a salad bowl, place spinach, berries, and walnuts in it, drizzle with prepared salad dressing and toss until mixed. Serve.

446 – Coconut Lime Cauliflower Rice

Serves: 2; Preparation: 5 minutes; Cook time: 8 minutes;
Nutrition facts: 175 Calories; 14.4 g Fats; 3.8 g Protein; 2.4 g Net Carb; 4 g Fiber;
Ingredients
- 4 oz grated cauliflower
- ½ of lime, juiced, zested
- 1 green onion, sliced
- 1 tbsp avocado oil
- 2 oz coconut milk, unsweetened

Seasoning:
- ½ tsp garlic powder
- ¼ tsp salt; 1/8 tsp ground black pepper

How to Prepare:
1. Take a medium skillet pan, place it over medium heat, add oil and when hot, add green onion and cook for 1 minute.
2. Sprinkle with garlic powder, add cauliflower, stir until mixed and cook for 1 minute.
3. Pour in milk, continue cooking for 5 minutes until cauliflower has absorbed all the milk, and then remove the pan from heat.
4. Stir in lime juice and zest, season with salt and black pepper, and then serve.

447 – Creamed Spinach

Serves: 2; Preparation: 5 minutes; Cook time: 10 minutes;
Nutrition facts: 307 Calories; 28 g Fats; 10 g Protein; 2 g Net Carb; 3 g Fiber;
Ingredients
- 4 oz of spinach leaves
- 1 tbsp avocado oil
- 1 tbsp butter, unsalted
- 2 tbsp grated mozzarella cheese
- 2 tbsp whipped topping

Seasoning:
- ¼ tsp salt; 1/8 tsp ground black pepper

How to Prepare:
1. Take a frying pan, place it over medium heat, add oil and when hot, add spinach, season with salt and black pepper and cook for 3 to 4 minutes until wilted.
2. Add butter and cream, stir until mixed and cook for 2 minutes until mixture begins to thicken.
3. Stir in cheese, cook for 1 minute, then remove the pan from heat and serve.

448 – Spinach Bowl with Bacon and Feta

Serves: 2; Preparation: 5 minutes; Cook time: 5 minutes;
Nutrition facts: 140 Calories; 11.5 g Fats; 4.9 g Protein; 1.4 g Net Carb; 0.6 g Fiber;
Ingredients
- 2 oz spinach leaves
- 2 strips of bacon, chopped
- 1 tbsp avocado oil
- 1 tsp balsamic vinegar
- 2 tbsp crumbled feta cheese
- ½ tsp garlic powder

How to Prepare:
1. Take a frying pan, place it over medium heat and when hot, add bacon and cook for 3 to 4 minutes until crispy and golden brown.
2. Transfer bacon to a plate lined with paper towels and then set aside until required.
3. Prepare the dressing and for this, take a small heatproof bowl, add garlic powder, oil, and vinegar in it, stir until combined, and then microwave for 30 seconds until warm. Take a medium bowl, place spinach in it, pour in warm salad dressing, then add bacon and toss until mixed.
4. Top salad with feta cheese and then serve.

449 – Creamed Kale with Mushrooms

Serves: 2; Preparation: 5 minutes; Cook time: 10 minutes;
Nutrition facts: 254 Calories; 23.3 g Fats; 5.5 g Protein; 3.1 g Net Carb; 0.6 g Fiber;
Ingredients
- ½ bunch of kale
- 3 mushrooms, sliced
- 1 ounce whipped topping
- 2 oz cream cheese
- 2 tbsp grated parmesan cheese

Seasoning:
- 1/3 tsp salt; 1/8 tsp ground black pepper
- ¼ tsp garlic powder
- 1 ½ tbsp butter, unsalted

How to Prepare:
1. Take a medium skillet pan, place it over medium heat, add butter and when it melts, add kale and cook for 3 minutes until tender.
2. Add remaining ingredients, stir until mixed, switch heat to the low level, and simmer for 5 to 7 minutes until mushrooms have turned tender. Serve.

450 – Spinach and Feta Wrap

Serves: 2; Preparation: 5 minutes; Cook time: 10 minutes;
Nutrition facts: 190 Calories; 15.4 g Fats; 9.3 g Protein; 1.6 g Net Carb; 0.8 g Fiber;
Ingredients
- 2 eggs
- 1 egg white
- 2-ounce spinach, chopped
- 2 tsp crumbled feta cheese
- 2 tbsp diced tomato

Seasoning:
- ¼ tsp salt; 1 tsp sesame oil
- 1 tbsp avocado oil

How to Prepare:
1. Prepare the wrap and for this, crack eggs in a medium bowl, add egg white and sesame oil, and then whisk well until foamy.
2. Take a medium skillet pan, place it over medium-low heat, add ½ tbsp avocado oil and when hot, pour in half of the egg batter, spread it evenly, and cook for 2 to 3 minutes until center is firm, covering with the lid.
3. Then flip the egg, continue cooking for 2 to 3 minutes until done, and when done, transfer egg wrap to a plate and cook another wrap in the same manner.
4. Add remaining oil into the pan and when hot, add spinach and cook for 2 minutes until leaves have turned tender.
5. Distribute spinach between egg wraps, top with feta and tomato, then roll up the wrap and serve.

451 – Three-Cheese Stuffed Jalapeno Pepper

Serves: 2; Preparation: 5 minutes; Cook time: 10 minutes;
Nutrition facts: 93.3 Calories; 6.3 g Fats; 5.8 g Protein; 2.2 g Net Carb; 1.1 g Fiber;
Ingredients
- 4 jalapeno pepper
- 1 tbsp feta cheese
- 1 tbsp grated parmesan cheese
- 1 tbsp grated mozzarella cheese
- 1 slice of bacon, chopped

Seasoning:
- ¼ tsp garlic powder; 1/8 tsp ground black pepper
- ½ tsp dried parsley

How to Prepare:
1. Turn on the oven, then set it to 425 degrees F and let it preheat.
2. Prepare the peppers, and for this, cut peppers into half lengthwise and then remove the seeds.
3. Take a medium bowl, place all the cheeses in it, add parsley, garlic powder, and black pepper and stir until combined.
4. Spoon the cheese mixture into the pepper, sprinkle with bacon, arrange them on a baking sheet lined with parchment sheet and then bake for 8 to 10 minutes until done. Serve.

452 – Aromatic Greens

Serves: 2; Preparation: 5 minutes; Cook time: 8 minutes;
Nutrition facts: 110 Calories; 8.7 g Fats; 1.8 g Protein; 1 g Net Carb; 2.8 g Fiber;
Ingredients
- 1 tbsp chopped jalapeno pepper
- ½ bunch of chard, chopped
- ½ bunch of kale, chopped
- 3 tbsp coconut milk, unsweetened

Seasoning:
- 1 tbsp avocado oil
- 1/3 tsp salt; ¼ tsp garlic powder
- 1 tsp whipped topping

How to Prepare:
1. Take a medium skillet pan, place it over medium heat, add oil and when hot, add green onions, sprinkle with garlic powder and cook for 2 minutes.
2. Season with salt, cook for 2 minutes until softened, then add jalapeno, kale, and chards and cook for 3 to 4 minutes until leaves wilt.
3. Add 2 tbsp coconut milk, toss until mixed, then transfer the mixture into a bowl, add remaining coconut milk and whipped topping and stir until mixed. Serve.

453 – Coconut Cauliflower Rice with Green Onions

Serves: 2; Preparation: 5 minutes; Cook time: 5 minutes;
Nutrition facts: 120 Calories; 10.7 g Fats; 1.7 g Protein; 1.1 g Net Carb; 2.1 g Fiber;
Ingredients
- 3 oz grated cauliflower florets
- 2 green onions, sliced
- 2 tbsp shredded coconut, unsweetened
- 1 tbsp avocado oil
- 3 oz coconut milk, unsweetened

How to Prepare:
1. Take a medium skillet pan, place it over medium heat, add oil and when hot, add grated cauliflower and cook for 3 minutes until golden brown.
2. Add coconut, pour in milk, stir until mixed and cook for 1 to 2 minutes until hot and creamy. Remove pan from heat, garnish cauliflower rice with green onions. Serve.

454 – Lime Garlic Mushrooms

Serves: 2; Preparation: 5 minutes; Cook time: 12 minutes;
Nutrition facts: 110 Calories; 10.2 g Fats; 1.3 g Protein; 1 g Net Carb; 0.6 g Fiber;

Ingredients
- 4 oz cremini mushroom, halved
- 1 tsp garlic powder
- ½ tsp dried parsley
- 1 ½ tbsp avocado oil
- ½ of lime, juiced, zested

Seasoning:
- 1/3 tsp salt; ¼ tsp ground black pepper

How to Prepare:
1. Turn on the oven, then set it to 400 degrees F and let it preheat.
2. Remove stems from the mushrooms, then place them in a bowl, drizzle with oil and lime juice, sprinkle with garlic powder, and toss until coated.
3. Take a rimmed baking sheet, spread mushrooms on it, roast for 12 minutes, turning halfway through until mushrooms have turned tender and then remove from oven.
4. Season mushrooms with salt and black pepper, sprinkle with lime zest and then serve.

455 – Buttered Mushrooms and Asparagus

Serves: 2; Preparation: 5 minutes; Cook time: 10 minutes;
Nutrition facts: 165 Calories; 15.2 g Fats; 1.5 g Protein; 1.6 g Net Carb; 1.1 g Fiber;
Ingredients
- 2 ounce asparagus spears
- 3 oz sliced mushroom
- 1 ½ tbsp butter, unsalted
- 1 tbsp avocado oil
- ½ tsp garlic powder
- 1/3 tsp salt; 1/4 tsp ground black pepper

How to Prepare:
1. Turn on the oven, then set it to 400 degrees F and let it preheat.
2. Take a small baking dish and place mushrooms slices and asparagus spears in it.
3. Take a small bowl, place butter in it, microwave for 20 seconds until it melts and then stir in oil, salt and black pepper until mixed.
4. Drizzle butter mixture over mushrooms and asparagus, toss until mixed and then bake for 6 to 8 minutes until tender, stirring halfway. Serve.

456 – Cauliflower Tortilla with Butternut Squash

Serves: 2; Preparation: 10 minutes; Cook time: 20 minutes;
Nutrition facts: 171 Calories; 12.2 g Fats; 8 g Protein; 3.6 g Net Carb; 2.7 g Fiber;
Ingredients
- 3 oz grated cauliflower
- 1 egg
- 4 oz butternut squash
- 2 slices of bacon, chopped
- 1 tbsp avocado oil
- 1/8 tsp dried oregano
- ¼ tsp paprika
- 1/2 tsp salt; 1/4 tsp ground black pepper

How to Prepare:
1. Turn on the oven, then set it to 375 degrees F and let it preheat.
2. Prepare the wraps and for this, place grated cauliflower in a heatproof bowl, cover with plastic wrap, and then microwave for 2 to 3 minutes until tender.
3. Drain the cauliflower, squeeze moisture as much as possible by wrapping cauliflower in a cheesecloth, then place it in a bowl, add oregano, 1/8 tsp paprika, ¼ tsp salt, and 1/8 tsp black pepper, and egg and stir until well combined.
4. Divide the mixture into two portions, shape each portion into a ball, place it on a baking sheet lined with parchment and spread into a circle.
5. Bake cauliflower circles for 4 minutes per side until cooked and then remove from oven.
6. While tortilla baked, prepare the butternut squash and for this, take a medium skillet pan and place butternut squash in it.
7. Add bacon in the pan, drizzle with oil, season with remaining paprika, salt and black pepper, toss until mixed and then bake for 12 minutes until cooked, stirring halfway. Top each cauliflower tortilla with butternut squash mixture and then serve.

457 – Stuffed Baby Bella Mushrooms

Serves: 2; Preparation: 10 minutes; Cook time: 8 minutes;
Nutrition facts: 249 Calories; 22.4 g Fats; 5.5 g Protein; 3.9 g Net Carb; 1 g Fiber;
Ingredients
- 6 oz baby bella mushrooms, destemmed

- 2 tbsp butter, unsalted
- 1 tbsp grated parmesan cheese
- 1 tbsp grated mozzarella cheese
- 2 oz cream cheese, softened
- ¼ tsp salt; 1/8 tsp ground black pepper
- ½ tsp dried parsley

How to Prepare:
1. Turn on the oven, then set it to 350 degrees F and let it preheat.
2. Then place prepared mushroom on a baking sheet, cap-side up and then roast for 3 to 5 minutes.
3. Meanwhile, place butter in a small heatproof bowl, microwave for 20 seconds until it melts and then stir in parsley, salt and black pepper.
4. When mushrooms have roasted, take them out of the oven and then brush generously with butter mixture.
5. Stir together cream cheese, parmesan and mozzarella cheese until combined, stuff this mixture into the mushrooms, sprinkle with some more black pepper and then bake for 2 to 3 minutes until cheese has turned golden brown. When done, sprinkle mushrooms with some more parsley and then serve.

458 – Garlic Mushroom Zoodles

Serves: 2; Preparation: 10 minutes; Cook time: 10 minutes;
Nutrition facts: 211 Calories; 19.3 g Fats; 2.6 g Protein; 3.6 g Net Carb; 2.1 g Fiber;
Ingredients
- 1 zucchini, spiralized into noodles
- 3 oz sliced mushrooms
- ½ tsp garlic powder
- 2 tbsp avocado oil
- 1 tbsp grated parmesan cheese

Seasoning:
- 1/3 tsp salt; 1/4 tsp ground black pepper
- ¼ tsp red chili flakes

How to Prepare:
1. Prepare zucchini noodles, and for this, cut zucchini into noodles by using a spiralizer or a vegetable peeler, and then set aside until required.
2. Take a medium skillet pan, place it over medium heat, add 1 tbsp oil and when hot, add zucchini noodles, cook for 3 to 5 minutes until al dente and then transfer zucchini noodles to a plate.
3. Add remaining oil into the pan and when hot, add mushroom and cook for 2 to 3 minutes until sauté and begin to golden brown.
4. Sprinkle with garlic powder and continue cooking for 2 minutes until mushrooms are caramelized.
5. Return zucchini noodles into the pan, season with salt, black pepper and red chili flakes, toss until well mixed and cook for 1 minute until hot.
6. Garnish with cheese and then serve.

459 – Southern Collard Greens

Serves: 2; Preparation: 5 minutes; Cook time: 25 minutes;
Nutrition facts: 186 Calories; 14.7 g Fats; 6.8 g Protein; 3.2 g Net Carb; 2.3 g Fiber;
Ingredients
- 2 slices of bacon, chopped
- ½ bunch collard greens
- 1/8 tsp red pepper flakes
- 1 ½ tbsp avocado oil
- ½ cup chicken stock

Seasoning:
- 1/4 tsp salt; 1/4 tsp ground black pepper

How to Prepare:
1. Take a skillet pan, place it over high heat, add oil and when hot, add bacon and cook for 2 to 3 minutes until crisp.
2. Transfer bacon to a plate, set aside until required, then add oil into the pan, and when hot, add collard greens and cook for 3 minutes until leaves wilt.
3. Sprinkle with red pepper, salt, and black pepper, pour in the stock, stir well and cook for 15 to 20 minutes until leaves have turned tender.
4. Then remove the pan from heat, stir bacon into the greens and then serve.

460 – Sautéed Mushrooms

Serves: 2; Preparation: 5 minutes; Cook time: 8 minutes;
Nutrition facts: 181 Calories; 17.7 g Fats; 4 g Protein; 0.4 g Net Carb; 0.3 g Fiber;

Ingredients
- 2 oz baby Bella mushrooms, sliced
- 3 oz sliced mushrooms
- 1 tbsp butter, unsalted
- 2 tsp avocado oil
Seasoning:
- ¼ tsp garlic powder
- ¼ tsp salt; ¼ tsp ground black pepper
- 1/3 tsp dried rosemary

How to Prepare:
1. Take a medium skillet pan, place it over medium heat, add 1 tsp oil and when hot, add all the mushrooms and then season with salt and black pepper.
2. Add ½ tbsp butter, sprinkle with rosemary and garlic powder, stir well and cook for 5 to 7 minutes until nicely browned and cooked.
3. When done, remove the pan from heat, add remaining butter and then distribute between two plates. Serve.

461 – Mexican Cauliflower Rice

Serves: 2; Preparation: 5 minutes; Cook time: 6 minutes;
Nutrition facts: 120 Calories; 10.1 g Fats; 2.5 g Protein; 0.5 g Net Carb; 2 g Fiber;
Ingredients
- 6 oz grated cauliflower
- 1 tsp ground cumin
- ½ tsp salt
- ¼ tsp chipotle chili powder
- 1 ½ tbsp avocado oil
Seasoning:
- ¼ tsp salt; 1/8 tsp ground black pepper

How to Prepare:
1. Take a medium skillet pan, place it over medium heat, add oil and when hot, add cauliflower, stir until mixed and cook for 1 minute.
2. Add remaining ingredients, stir until mixed, continue cooking for 5 minutes until cauliflower has turned soft, and then remove the pan from heat.
3. Taste to adjust seasoning and then serve.

462 – Caprese Zucchini Noodles Salad

Serves: 2; Preparation: 10 minutes; Cook time: 0 minutes;
Nutrition facts: 312 Calories; 27.4 g Fats; 7.7 g Protein; 4.6 g Net Carb; 2.4 g Fiber;
Ingredients
- 1 zucchini, spiralized into noodles
- 6 basil leaves
- 2 oz grape tomatoes, halved
- ¼ of lime, juiced
- 2 oz grated mozzarella cheese
Seasoning:
- ¼ tsp garlic powder
- 1/3 tsp salt; ¼ tsp ground black pepper
- 3 tbsp avocado oil

How to Prepare:
1. Prepare the salad dressing and for this, take a small bowl, add oil in it and then stir in lime juice, garlic powder, salt, and black pepper until combined.
2. Take a medium bowl, place zucchini noodles in it, add cherry tomatoes, basil leaves, and cheese, drizzle with prepared salad dressing and then toss until combined.

463 – Cheesy Cheddar Cauliflower Rice

Serves: 2; Preparation: 5 minutes; Cook time: 12 minutes;
Nutrition facts: 310 Calories; 25 g Fats; 15.2 g Protein; 2.5 g Net Carb; 2 g Fiber;
Ingredients
- 6 oz grated cauliflower
- 2 slices of bacon, chopped
- 1 tbsp butter, unsalted
- 3 tbsp cream cheese

- 2 oz grated cheddar cheese

Seasoning:
- ½ tsp salt; 1/3 tsp ground black pepper

How to Prepare:
1. Take a medium skillet pan, place it over medium heat and when hot, add chopped bacon and then cook for 2 to 3 minutes until crisp.
2. Transfer bacon to a plate, add cauliflower into the pan, sprinkle with salt and black pepper, stir until mixed and cook for 3 to 5 minutes until tender-crisp.
3. Switch heat to medium-low heat, add cheese and cream cheese, stir until well mixed, and cook for 2 to 3 minutes until cheese has melted.
4. When done, distribute cauliflower between two plates, top with bacon, and then serve.

464 – Tomato Soup

Serves: 2; Preparation: 5 minutes; Cook time: 15 minutes;
Nutrition facts: 300 Calories; 27 g Fats; 8.2 g Protein; 4.2 g Net Carb; 1 g Fiber;
Ingredients
- 1-ounce grape tomatoes, halved
- 6 oz diced tomatoes in juice
- 1-ounce whipping cream
- 1 tbsp grated cheddar cheese
- 1 tbsp grated mozzarella cheese

Seasoning:
- ½ tsp salt; ¼ tsp ground black pepper
- ½ tsp paprika
- 2 tbsp butter, unsalted
- 1 cup of water

How to Prepare:
1. Take a medium saucepan, place it over medium heat, add butter and when it melts, add tomatoes and cook for 2 minutes until stir-fry.
2. Cover with a lid, switch heat to the low level, stir in salt, black pepper, and paprika, pour in water, cover with the lid and cook for 5 to 8 minutes or more until tomatoes have turned very tender.
3. When tomatoes have cooked, remove the pan from heat, add half of cheeses and then pulse the soup until smooth.
4. Return pan over medium-low heat, stir in cream, and then cook the soup for 2 minutes until hot. Ladle soup into bowls, top with remaining cheeses, and then serve.

465 – Pumpkin Soup

Serves: 2; Preparation: 5 minutes; Cook time: 18 minutes;
Nutrition facts: 221 Calories; 20.3 g Fats; 1.1 g Protein; 5.8 g Net Carb; 2.4 g Fiber;
Ingredients
- 2 green onions, sliced
- 1 tbsp butter, unsalted
- 1 tbsp avocado oil
- 6 oz pumpkin puree
- 3 oz coconut milk, unsweetened

Seasoning:
- ½ tsp salt; ¼ tsp ground black pepper
- ¼ tsp curry powder
- ¼ tsp dried thyme
- 1 cup water

How to Prepare:
1. Take a medium saucepan, place it over medium heat, add butter and oil and when hot, add onion and cook for 1 to 2 minutes until sauté.
2. Then add remaining ingredients, stir until mixed, and bring the mixture to a boil.
3. Switch heat to medium-low level, simmer soup for 15 minutes until thickened slightly and then remove it from heat.
4. When done, ladle soup into two bowls, drizzle with more coconut milk and then serve.

466 – Smothered Green Beans

Serves: 2; Preparation: 5 minutes; Cook time: 8 minutes;
Nutrition facts: 181 Calories; 14.5 g Fats; 6.6 g Protein; 3.1 g Net Carb; 1.7 g Fiber;
Ingredients
- 4.5 oz green beans

- 2 slices of bacon, chopped
- 1 ½ tbsp butter, unsalted
- 2 tbsp water
- 2 tbsp grated cheddar cheese

Seasoning:
- ¼ tsp garlic powder
- 1/3 tsp salt; ¼ tsp ground black pepper

How to Prepare:
1. Take a medium skillet pan, place it over medium heat and when hot, add bacon and cook for 3 minutes until nicely brown and crisp.
2. Transfer bacon to a plate lined with paper towel, then add butter and when it melts, add green beans and then season with salt and black pepper.
3. Sprinkle garlic powder over green beans, stir until coated and cook for 2 to 3 minutes until sauté.
4. Add water, continue cooking for 2 minutes or more until green beans have turned tender-crisp.
5. Transfer green beans into a casserole dish and then sprinkle cheese and bacon on top.
6. Turn on the broiler, let it preheat, then place casserole dish in it and broil green beans for 1 minute until cheese have melted and golden brown. Serve.

467 – Cheesy Portobello Mushroom with Butter Sauce

Serves: 2; Preparation: 10 minutes; Cook time: 10 minutes;
Nutrition facts: 260 Calories; 19.4 g Fats; 13.3 g Protein; 5.3 g Net Carb; 1 g Fiber;
Ingredients
- 2 Portobello mushroom caps
- 2 eggs
- 1 tsp chopped cilantro
- 3 tbsp grated mozzarella cheese
- 1 tbsp grated parmesan cheese

Seasoning:
- 1 tsp minced garlic
- ¼ tsp salt; ¼ tsp ground black pepper
- 1 ½ tbsp butter, unsalted
- 1 tbsp cream cheese

How to Prepare:
1. Turn on the oven, then set it to 450 degrees F and let it preheat.
2. Remove gills from the mushroom caps, place them on a rimmed baking sheet cap-side up, and then bake for 5 minutes until the mushroom release some water.
3. Meanwhile, take a small heatproof bowl, place butter in it, add garlic and cilantro, and then microwave wave for 30 to 60 seconds until butter has melted, stirring every 20 seconds.
4. When mushroom caps have baked, let them cool for 5 minutes and then brush inside out generously with the butter mixture.
5. Take a small bowl, place cream cheese in it, stir in mozzarella cheese, salt, and black pepper and then spoon the cheese mixture onto the edges of the mushroom caps to form a small hole in the middle of the cap.
6. Separate egg yolks and egg whites, carefully place an egg yolk in the hole of each mushroom, sprinkle parmesan cheese and black pepper on yolk, and then bake for 5 minutes until cheese has melted and yolks have cooked to the desired level.
7. Serve.

468 – Lime Garlic Bok Choy

Serves: 2; Preparation: 5 minutes; Cook time: 6 minutes;
Nutrition facts: 160 Calories; 13.8 g Fats; 2.3 g Protein; 2.7 g Net Carb; 2.8 g Fiber;
Ingredients
- 1 pound bok choy, destemmed, quartered
- 1 tsp minced garlic
- ¼ tsp red pepper flakes
- 1/3 of lime, cut into wedges
- 2 tbsp avocado oil

Seasoning:
- ¼ tsp salt

How to Prepare:
1. Take a medium skillet pan, place it over medium heat, add oil and when hot, add bok choy, sprinkle with garlic powder, stir until mixed, and then cook for 2 minutes until golden brown.
2. Spread bok choy in a single layer, sprinkle with salt and red pepper flakes, and continue cooking for 2 minutes until bok coy begins to brown, don't stir.
3. Flip the bok choy, continue cooking for 2 minutes until leaves have wilted, and white bottoms become tender-crisp.
4. Distribute bok choy between two plates and then serve with lime wedges

469 – Creamy Sauteed Mushrooms with Parmesan

Serves: 2; Preparation: 5 minutes; Cook time: 10 minutes;
Nutrition facts: 384 Calories; 36 g Fats; 7 g Protein; 7 g Net Carb; 1 g Fiber;
Ingredients
- 6 oz sliced mushroom
- 2 tbsp butter, salted
- 4 tbsp grated parmesan cheese
- 2 tbsp cream cheese, softened
- 2 tbsp sour cream

Seasoning:
- ½ tsp garlic powder
- ¼ tsp salt; 1/8 tsp ground black pepper

How to Prepare:
1. Take a medium skillet pan, place it over medium-high heat, add butter and when it melts, add mushroom and cook for 4 to 5 minutes until golden brown and tender.
2. Sprinkle with garlic, cook for 1 minute until fragrant, add cheese, cream cheese, and sour cream and then cook for 1 minute until cheese has melted and smooth mixture comes together. Switch heat to medium-low level, cook for 2 to 3 minutes until thick sauce comes together, and then serve.

470 – Parmesan Cauliflower Rice

Serves: 2; Preparation: 5 minutes; Cook time: 7 minutes;
Nutrition facts: 330 Calories; 22.3 g Fats; 19.9 g Protein; 8.4 g Net Carb; 2 g Fiber;
Ingredients
- 8 oz grated cauliflower
- 4 oz grated parmesan cheese
- ½ tsp garlic powder
- ½ tsp salt
- 1 tbsp avocado oil
- 1/8 tsp ground black pepper

How to Prepare:
1. Take a medium skillet pan, place it over medium heat and when hot, add cauliflower into the pan, sprinkle with garlic powder, salt, and black pepper, stir until mixed and cook for 5 to 7 minutes until tender and golden brown. Remove pan from heat, stir in cheese until combined, then distribute cauliflower between two plates,Serve.

471 – Cheesy Green Beans and Mushroom Casserole

Serves: 2
Preparation: 5 minutes; Cook time: 12 minutes;
Nutrition facts: 360 Calories; 33.2 g Fats; 8.1 g Protein; 5.5 g Net Carb; 1.8 g Fiber;
Ingredients
- 1.5 oz sliced mushroom
- 4 oz green beans
- 5 tbsp whipping cream
- 2 tbsp grated mozzarella cheese
- 2 tbsp grated parmesan cheese

Seasoning:
- ½ tsp garlic powder
- ¼ tsp salt; 1/8 tsp ground black pepper
- 1 tbsp butter, unsalted
- 1 tbsp avocado oil

How to Prepare:
1. Turn on the oven, then set it to 350 degrees F and let it preheat.
2. Meanwhile, take a medium skillet pan, place it over medium heat, add oil and when hot, add green beans and cook for 3 minutes until sauté.
3. Transfer green beans to a bowl, add butter into the pan and when it melts, add mushrooms and cook for 3 minutes or until mushrooms begin to release their juices and golden brown.
4. Stir in cream, switch heat to the low level, cook for 2 minutes until slightly thick, add green beans and then season with salt and black pepper.
5. Transfer the mixture to a medium baking dish, sprinkle with cheeses and then bake for 10 minutes until cheese has melted and the mixture is bubbling.

472 – Loaded Cauliflower Casserole

Serves: 2; Preparation: 10 minutes; Cook time: 10 minutes;
Nutrition facts: 290 Calories; 22.8 g Fats; 10.8 g Protein; 9.4 g Net Carb; 1.4 g Fiber;
Ingredients
- 2 slices of bacon, chopped, cooked
- 7 oz cauliflower florets
- 1-ounce cream cheese, softened
- 4 oz sour cream
- 2 tbsp grated cheddar cheese
- 2 green onions, diced
- ½ tsp garlic powder
- ½ tsp salt; ¼ tsp ground black pepper

How to Prepare:
1. Turn on the oven, then set it to 350 degrees F and let it preheat.
2. Meanwhile, take a medium heatproof bowl, place florets in it, drizzle with 1 tbsp water, cover the bowl with a plastic wrap and microwave for 2 minutes, or more until florets turned soft.
3. Then uncover the bowl, mash florets by using a fork, and then stir in sour cream, cream cheese, and cheese until cheese has melted.
4. Add onion and bacon, sprinkle with salt, black pepper, and garlic powder and stir until mixed.
5. Take a casserole dish, place cauliflower in it and then bake for 10 minutes until thoroughly cooked. Serve immediately.

473 – Stewed Cabbage

Serves: 2; Preparation: 5 minutes; Cook time: 18 minutes;
Nutrition facts: 140 Calories; 10.6 g Fats; 4.7 g Protein; 3.3 g Net Carb; 1.8 g Fiber;
Ingredients
- 2 slices of bacon, chopped, cooked
- 1 ½ cup chopped cabbage
- 1 tomato, diced
- 1 tbsp avocado oil
- 3 tbsp chicken bone broth
- ¼ tsp salt; 1/8 tsp ground black pepper
- ¼ tsp red pepper flakes

How to Prepare:
1. Take a medium pot, place it over medium heat, add oil and when hot, add cabbage and tomatoes, switch heat to medium-high level and cook for 7 to 10 minutes until the cabbage has released its moisture.
2. Add chicken broth, continue cooking for 10 minutes until some of the cooking liquid has evaporated and cabbage has turned very soft.
3. Season cabbage with salt and black pepper, stir in bacon, and then serve.

474 – Cauliflower Creamed Spinach

Serves: 2; Preparation: 10 minutes; Cook time: 10 minutes;
Nutrition facts: 233 Calories; 19.5 g Fats; 6.3 g Protein; 4.5 g Net Carb; 3 g Fiber;
Ingredients
- 5 oz spinach
- 8 oz cauliflower florets
- 1 green onion, chopped
- 2 tbsp grated mozzarella cheese; 2 tbsp whipping cream
- 1 1/2 tbsp butter, unsalted
- ½ tbsp avocado oil
- ¼ tsp salt; 1/8 tsp ground black pepper

How to Prepare:
1. Turn on the broiler and then let it preheat.
2. Meanwhile, take a medium heatproof bowl, place cauliflower florets in it, drizzle with 1 tbsp water, cover the bowl with a plastic wrap and microwave for 2 minutes or more until florets turned soft.
3. Meanwhile, take a medium skillet pan, place it over medium heat, add ½ tbsp butter and avocado oil and when hot, add spinach and cook for 3 minutes until wilted and thoroughly warmed.
4. Transfer cauliflower florets into a food processor by using a slotted spoon, add butter and cream and pulse until smooth.
5. Transfer cauliflower mixture into a bowl, add spinach mixture, sprinkle with salt and black pepper, add cheese and stir until combined.
6. Transfer cauliflower mixture into a small baking dish, place it under the broiler and then cook for 3 minutes until bubbly and the top has turned nicely golden brown.

475 – Mushroom, Mayonnaise, and Cheese Frittata

Serves: 2; Preparation: 10 minutes; Cook time: 20 minutes;
Nutrition facts: 531 Calories; 50.6 g Fats; 14.6 g Protein; 3.4 g Net Carb; 0.6 g Fiber;
Ingredients
- 4 oz sliced mushrooms
- 2 eggs
- 1-ounce cheddar cheese, grated
- 1-ounce parmesan cheese, grated
- ¼ cup mayonnaise

Seasoning:
- ¼ tsp salt; 1/8 tsp ground black pepper
- 2 tbsp butter, unsalted

How to Prepare:
1. Turn on the oven, then set it to 350 degrees F and let it preheat.
2. Meanwhile, take a medium skillet pan, place it over medium heat, add butter and when it melts, add mushrooms, switch heat to medium-low level and cook for 3 to 5 minutes until nicely browned.
3. Meanwhile, take a medium bowl, crack eggs in it, add salt, black pepper, cheeses, mayonnaise and whisk until combined.
4. Take a baking dish, place mushrooms in it, pour egg mixture over them and then bake for 15 to 20 minutes until eggs have cooked and the top is golden brown. When done, let frittata cool for 5 minutes, then cut it into slices and serve.

476 – Broccoli Cheese Casserole

Serves: 2; Preparation: 5 minutes; Cook time: 12 minutes;
Nutrition facts: 201 Calories; 15.3 g Fats; 7.3 g Protein; 4.8 g Net Carb; 2 g Fiber;
Ingredients
- 6 oz broccoli florets, chopped
- 1-ounce cream cheese
- 2 tbsp sour cream
- 2 tbsp shredded cheddar cheese
- 2 tbsp shredded parmesan cheese

Seasoning:
- ¼ tsp salt; 1/8 tsp ground black pepper
- 1/3 tsp Italian seasoning

How to Prepare:
1. Turn on the oven, then set it to 350 degrees F and let it preheat.
2. Take a medium bowl, place broccoli florets in it, drizzle with 1 tbsp water, cover with a plastic wrap, and then microwave for 2 minutes until tender-crisp.
3. Then drain the broccoli and transfer it into a baking dish, set aside until required.
4. Take a medium bowl, add cream cheese, sour cream, cheeses, salt, black pepper, and Italian seasoning and stir until well mixed.
5. Spoon cream cheese mixture over broccoli, stir until well combined, and then bake for 8 to 10 minutes until the top has turned golden brown. Serve.

477 – Turmeric Cauliflower and Bacon Rice

Serves: 2; Preparation: 5 minutes; Cook time: 8 minutes;
Nutrition facts: 133 Calories; 10.5 g Fats; 5 g Protein; 2.6 g Net Carb; 1.7 g Fiber;
Ingredients
- 2 slices of bacon, chopped
- 6 oz grated cauliflower
- 1/8 tsp ginger powder
- ¼ tsp onion powder
- ¼ tsp ground turmeric

Seasoning:
- 1/3 tsp salt; ¼ tsp garlic powder
- 1 tbsp avocado oil

How to Prepare:
1. Take a medium skillet pan, place it over medium heat and when hot, add bacon and cook for 3 minutes until tender and crisp.
2. Then add cauliflower, add oil and cook for 2 minutes.
3. Then sprinkle all the spices over cauliflower, toss until mixed, and then continue cooking for 3 minutes until thoroughly cooked.
4. Serve.

Snacks

478 – Breakfast Omelet Sandwich

Serves: 2; Preparation: 10 minutes; Cook time: 20 minutes
Nutrition facts: 377 Calories; 32.3 g Fats; 15.1 g Protein; 3.2 g Net Carb; 3.4 g Fiber;
Ingredients

- 2 2/3 tbsp coconut flour
- 1 tsp baking powder
- 3 tbsp avocado oil
- 3 eggs
- 2 egg whites

Seasoning:

- ¼ tsp salt; 1/8 tsp ground black pepper
- 1/8 tsp paprika

How to Prepare:
1. Turn on the oven, then set it to 375 degrees F and let it preheat.
2. Meanwhile, prepare the batter for this, add flour, 2 tbsp avocado oil, baking powder, 2 eggs, and 1/8 tsp in a bowl and then whisk until well combined.
3. Take a 4 by 4 inches heatproof baking pan, grease it with oil, pour in the prepared batter and bake 10 minutes until bread is firm.
4. Meanwhile, prepare omelet and for this, crack the remaining egg in a bowl, add egg whites, black pepper, paprika, and remaining salt and whisk until combined.
5. Take a skillet pan, place it over medium heat, add oil and when hot, pour in egg mixture, cook for 2 minutes, then flip it and continue cooking for 2 minutes until done, set aside until required. When done, let the bread cool in the pan for 5 minutes, then transfer it to a wire rack and cool for 20 minutes.
6. Cut bread into four slices, divide omelet into two, sandwich it between bread slices and serve.

479 – Chaffles

Serves: 2; Preparation: 5 minutes; Cook time: 10 minutes;
Nutrition facts: 142 Calories; 9.8 g Fats; 10.3 g Protein; 2.3 g Net Carb; 1 g Fiber;
Ingredients

- 2 tsp coconut flour
- ½ cup shredded mozzarella cheese, full-fat
- 1 egg

How to Prepare:
1. Switch on a mini waffle maker and let it preheat for 5 minutes.
2. Meanwhile, take a medium bowl, place all the ingredients in it and then mix by using an immersion blender until smooth.
3. Ladle the batter evenly into the waffle maker, shut with lid, and let it cook for 3 to 4 minutes until firm and golden brown. Serve.

480 – Mozzarella Garlic Chaffles

Serves: 2; Preparation: 5 minutes; Cook time: 10 minutes;
Nutrition facts: 208 Calories; 16 g Fats; 11 g Protein; 2 g Net Carb; 2 g Fiber;
Ingredients

- 1/4 tsp baking powder
- ½ tsp minced garlic
- 1 egg
- 2/3 cup shredded mozzarella cheese, full-fat
- 1/2 tsp Italian seasoning

How to Prepare:
1. Switch on a mini waffle maker and let it preheat for 5 minutes.
2. Meanwhile, take a medium bowl, place all the ingredients in it and then mix by using an immersion blender until smooth.
3. Ladle the batter evenly into the waffle maker, shut with lid, and let it cook for 3 to 4 minutes until firm and golden brown. Serve.

481 – Yogurt Chaffles

Serves: 2; Preparation: 5 minutes; Cook time: 4 minutes;
Nutrition facts: 140 Calories; 9.9 g Fats; 8.9 g Protein; 2.5 g Net Carb; 0.6 g Fiber;
Ingredients

- 2 tbsp coconut flour
- ½ tsp Psyllium husk
- 1 egg
- 1/3 cup shredded mozzarella cheese, full-fat
- 1 tbsp Greek yogurt, full-fat
- ¼ tsp baking powder

How to Prepare:
1. Switch on a mini waffle maker and let it preheat for 5 minutes.
2. Meanwhile, take a medium bowl, crack eggs in it and whisk by using a fork until blended.
3. Then add remaining ingredients except for cheese, stir until smooth batter comes together, stir in cheese and let the batter stand for 3 minutes.
4. Ladle the batter evenly into the waffle maker, shut with lid, and let it cook for 3 to 4 minutes until firm and golden brown. Serve.

482 – Garlic Parmesan Chaffles

Serves: 2; Preparation: 5 minutes; Cook time: 10 minutes;
Nutrition facts: 208 Calories; 16 g Fats; 11 g Protein; 2 g Net Carb; 2 g Fiber;
Ingredients

- 1/4 tsp baking powder
- 1 tsp garlic powder
- 1 egg
- 2/3 cup shredded parmesan cheese, full-fat
- 1/2 tsp Italian seasoning

How to Prepare:
1. Switch on a mini waffle maker and let it preheat for 5 minutes.
2. Meanwhile, take a medium bowl, place all the ingredients in it and then mix by using an immersion blender until smooth.
3. Ladle the batter evenly into the waffle maker, shut with lid, and let it cook for 3 to 4 minutes until firm and golden brown. Serve.

483 – Spicy Flaxseed Wraps

Serves: 2; Preparation: 5 minutes; Cook time: 10 minutes;
Nutrition facts: 270 Calories; 24.3 g Fats; 4.7 g Protein; 0.4 g Net Carb; 7.7 g Fiber;
Ingredients

- 1/3 cup ground flaxseeds
- 1/8 tsp ginger powder
- 1/8 tsp garlic powder
- ½ cup of water
- 2 tbsp avocado oil
- ¼ tsp salt

How to Prepare:
1. Take a small saucepan, place it over medium heat, pour in water, and bring it to a boil.
2. Remove pan from heat, add garlic, ginger, salt, and flaxseeds and stir until well combined and the dough comes together.
3. Transfer dough to a clean working space lined with parchment paper, divide it into two portions and shape each portion into a ball.
4. Working on each dough ball at a time, cover with another piece of parchment paper and then roll 0.1-inch thick round wrap and when done, remove the parchment paper on top.
5. Take a medium skillet pan, place it over medium-high heat, add 1 tbsp oil and when hot, place a prepared wrap and cook for 2 minutes per side until golden.
6. Repeat with the other wrap and serve it straight away or with favorite filling.

484 – Breakfast Crepe with Berries

Serves: 2; Preparation: 5 minutes; Cook time: 12 minutes;
Nutrition facts: 231 Calories; 20 g Fats; 8 g Protein; 6 g Net Carb; 1 g Fiber;
Ingredients

- 2 oz cream cheese, softened
- 2 eggs
- ¼ tsp cinnamon
- 2 oz berries medley
- 1 tbsp whipped topping

Seasoning:
- 1 tbsp avocado oil

How to Prepare:
1. Place softened cream cheese in a bowl, add egg and cinnamon and then whisk by using a hand blender until smooth.
2. Take a medium skillet pan, place it over medium heat, add oil and when hot, pour in half of the crepe batter, spread it evenly, and cook for 3 minutes per side until golden brown. Transfer crepe to a plate and then cook another crepe by using the remaining batter.
3. Top crepe with berries and whipped topping and then serve.

485 – Spicy Psyllium Husk Wrap

Serves: 2; Preparation: 5 minutes; Cook time: 8 minutes;
Nutrition facts: 131 Calories; 9 g Fats; 7.3 g Protein; 1.1 g Net Carb; 3.1 g Fiber;
Ingredients
- 1 1/2 tbsp whole psyllium husks
- 1/8 tsp onion powder
- 1/8 tsp garlic powder
- 1/8 tsp baking powder
- 4 egg whites
- ¼ tsp salt
- 4 tsp avocado oil

How to Prepare:
1. Take a medium bowl, place egg whites in it, add remaining ingredients, and whisk until smooth batter comes together.
2. Take a medium skillet pan, place it over medium heat, add 1 tsp oil and when hot, pour in one-fourth portion of the batter, spread it evenly in the form of round crepe and then cook for 90 seconds per side until golden brown.
3. Transfer wrap to a plate and repeat with the remaining batter to cook three more wraps by using 1 tsp of oil every time. Serve.

486 – Breakfast Cloud Bread

Serves: 2; Preparation: 5 minutes; Cook time: 15 minutes;
Nutrition facts: 98 Calories; 9 g Fats; 4 g Protein; 0.2 g Net Carb; 0 g Fiber;
Ingredients
- ¼ tsp onion powder
- ¼ tsp dried oregano
- 1/16 tsp salt
- 2 eggs
- 2 oz cream cheese, softened

How to Prepare:
1. Turn on the oven, then set it to 300 degrees F and let it preheat.
2. Separate egg whites and yolks between two medium bowls, then add cream cheese into the egg whites and beat until stiff peaks form.
3. Add salt into the egg yolks, add onion powder and oregano, beat until smooth, and then gently fold egg whites in it until just incorporated.
4. Take a baking sheet, line with parchment paper, scoop mixture on it in the form of four circular discs and then bake for 12 to 15 minutes until golden. Serve.

487 – Pumpkin Pancake

Serves: 2; Preparation: 5 minutes; Cook time: 12 minutes;
Nutrition facts: 210 Calories; 17.5 g Fats; 5.2 g Protein; 4 g Net Carb; 3.8 g Fiber;
Ingredients
- 2 ¾ tbsp coconut flour
- 2/3 tsp baking powder
- 2 tbsp pumpkin puree
- 1 tbsp avocado oil and more for frying
- 1 egg
- 1 1/3 tbsp erythritol sweetener

How to Prepare:
1. Take a medium bowl, place all the ingredients in it, and whisk until smooth batter comes together.
2. Take a medium skillet pan, place it over medium heat, add 1 tbsp oil and when hot, pour in one-fourth pancake batter, spread it evenly, and then cook for 2 to 3 minutes per side until cooked. Repeat with the remaining batter and then Serve.

488 – Herbed Coconut Flour Bread

Serves: 2; Preparation: 5 minutes; Cook time: 3 minutes;
Nutrition facts: 309 Calories; 26.1 g Fats; 9.3 g Protein; 4.3 g Net Carb; 5 g Fiber;
Ingredients
- 4 tbsp coconut flour
- ½ tsp baking powder
- ½ tsp dried thyme
- 2 tbsp whipping cream
- 2 eggs
- ½ tsp oregano
- 2 tbsp avocado oil

How to Prepare:
1. Take a medium bowl, place all the ingredients in it and then whisk until incorporated and smooth batter comes together.
2. Distribute the mixture evenly between two mugs and then microwave for 1 minute and 30 seconds until cooked.
3. When done, take out bread from the mugs, cut it into slices, and then serve.

489 – Parmesan Chips

Serves: 2; Preparation: 5 minutes; Cook time: 4 minutes;
Nutrition facts: 31 Calories; 2 g Fats; 3 g Protein; 0 g Net Carb; 0 g Fiber;
Ingredients
- 2 oz grated parmesan cheese
- ¼ tsp ground black pepper

How to Prepare:
6. Turn on the oven, then set it to 400 degrees F and let it preheat.
7. Take a baking sheet, line it with parchment paper, spoon grated parmesan on it, about 2-inch apart, and then spread into 2-inch round.
8. Sprinkle black pepper over the cheese and then bake for 3 to 4 minutes until cheese has melted and turned crisp.
9. When done, let cheese chips cool completely and then serve.

490 – Crepe with Avocado

Serves: 2; Preparation: 5 minutes; Cook time: 10 minutes;
Nutrition facts: 198 Calories; 16.7 g Fats; 5.4 g Protein; 2.4 g Net Carb; 4 g Fiber;
Ingredients
- 1/2 of avocado, sliced
- 4 tsp coconut flour
- 8 tsp almond milk, unsweetened
- 2 egg whites
- 2 tbsp mayonnaise
- 1/16 tsp baking powder
- 1/16 tsp garlic powder; 1/8 tsp salt

How to Prepare:
1. Take a medium bowl, place flour in it, add remaining ingredients except for avocado and mayonnaise and whisk until well combined.
2. Take a skillet pan, place it over medium heat, spray with avocado oil and when hot, pour one-fourth of the batter in the pan, spread it as thin as possible, and then cook for 1 to 2 minutes per side until golden brown.
3. Transfer crepe to a plate and cook three more crepes in the same manner. Serve crepes with avocado and mayonnaise.

491 – Keto Cornbread

Serves: 2; Preparation: 5 minutes; Cook time: 2 minutes;
Nutrition facts: 116.2 Calories; 10.4 g Fats; 4.3 g Protein; 1.1 g Net Carb; 1.5 g Fiber;

Ingredients
- 1 ¾ oz almond flour
- ¼ tsp baking powder
- 1/8 tsp salt
- 1 tbsp melted butter
- 1 egg

How to Prepare:
1. Take a small bowl, place butter and egg in it, whisk until combined and then whisk in flour, baking powder, and salt until smooth batter comes together.
2. Take a small microwave proof container, spoon prepared batter in it, and then microwave for 1 minute and 45 seconds at high heat setting until cooked.
3. When done, cut bread into slices, then spread with butter and serve.

492 – Flax Seed Bread Sandwich

Serves: 2; Preparation: 10 minutes; Cook time: 10 minutes;
Nutrition facts: 191 Calories; 15.1 g Fats; 4.8 g Protein; 1.2 g Net Carb; 7.1 g Fiber;
Ingredients
- 4 oz ground flaxseed
- 2 tsp coconut flour
- ½ tsp baking soda
- 1 tsp apple cider vinegar
- 2 tbsp almond milk, unsweetened

Seasoning:
- ¼ tsp sesame seeds
- ¼ tsp pumpkin seeds
- ¼ tsp sunflower seeds
- Peanut butter for serving

How to Prepare:
1. Take a medium bowl, place flaxseed in it, add flour, baking soda, vinegar, and milk and mix by using hand until smooth dough ball comes together.
2. Take a shallow dish, place sesame seeds, pumpkin seeds and sunflower seeds in it and then stir until mixed.
3. Divide dough ball into two pieces, roll each piece into a loaf and then press into seed mixture until evenly coated on both sides.
4. Place dough onto a heatproof plate, microwave for 1 minute and then cool breads for 5 minutes.
5. Slice each bread into half, then spread with peanut butter and serve.

493 – Cheesy Jalapeno Cornbread

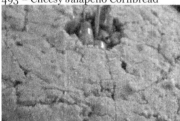

Serves: 2; Preparation: 5 minutes; Cook time: 2 minutes;
Nutrition facts: 131 Calories; 11.1 g Fats; 4.8 g Protein; 1.1 g Net Carb; 0.9 g Fiber;
Ingredients
- 1 jalapeno pepper, chopped
- 1 ¾ oz almond flour
- ¼ tsp baking powder
- 1 egg
- 1 tbsp grated parmesan cheese

Seasoning:
- 1 tbsp melted butter
- 1/8 tsp salt; 1/8 tsp ground black pepper

How to Prepare:
1. Take a small bowl, place butter and egg in it, whisk until combined, and then whisk in remaining ingredients until smooth batter comes together.
2. Take a small microwave proof container, spoon prepared batter in it, and then microwave for 1 minute and 45 seconds at high heat setting until cooked. When done, cut bread into slices, then spread with butter and serve.

494 – Cheese Cup

Serves: 2; Preparation: 5 minutes; Cook time: 5 minutes;
Nutrition facts: 125 Calories; 8.1 g Fats; 9.5 g Protein; 1.1 g Net Carb; 1.7 g Fiber;
Ingredients
- 4 tsp coconut flour
- 1/16 tsp baking soda
- 1 tbsp grated mozzarella cheese
- 1 tbsp grated parmesan cheese

- 2 eggs

Seasoning:
- ¼ tsp salt
- ½ tsp dried basil
- ½ tsp dried parsley

How to Prepare:
1. Take a medium bowl, place all the ingredients in it, and whisk until well combined.
2. Take two ramekins, grease them with oil, distribute the prepared batter in it and then microwave for 1 minute and 45 seconds until done.
3. When done, take out muffin from the ramekin, cut in half, and then serve.

495 – Cinnamon Mug Cake

Serves: 2; Preparation: 5 minutes; Cook time: 5 minutes;
Nutrition facts: 298 Calories; 28.8 g Fats; 6.7 g Protein; 1.3 g Net Carb; 1.7 g Fiber;
Ingredients
- 3 tbsp almond flour
- 1 tbsp erythritol sweetener
- 3 tbsp butter, unsalted
- 2 tbsp cream cheese
- 1 egg

Seasoning:
- 1 tsp baking soda
- ¾ tsp cinnamon

How to Prepare:
1. Take a heatproof mug, place 2 tbsp butter in it, and then microwave for 30 seconds or more until butter melts.
2. Then add remaining ingredients, reserving cream cheese and remaining butter, stir until mixed and microwave for 1 minute and 20 seconds until done.
3. Run a knife along the side of the mug and then take out the cake. Melt the remaining butter, top it over the cake, then top with cream cheese, cut cake in half, serve.

496 – Spicy Dosa

Serves: 2; Preparation: 5 minutes; Cook time: 8 minutes;
Nutrition facts: 181 Calories; 16.5 g Fats; 6 g Protein; 2 g Net Carb; 0 g Fiber;
Ingredients
- 3.5 oz almond flour
- ½ tsp ground cumin
- ½ tsp ground coriander
- 1.5 oz grated mozzarella cheese
- 4 oz coconut milk, unsweetened
- ¼ tsp salt; 2 tsp avocado oil

How to Prepare:
1. Take a medium bowl, place all the ingredients in it except for oil, and stir until well combined and smooth batter comes together.
2. Take a medium skillet pan, place it over medium heat, add 1 tsp oil and when hot, pour in half of the prepared batter, spread it evenly in a circular shape, then switch heat to the low level and cook for 2 minutes per side until golden brown and cooked.
3. Transfer dosa to a plate, then repeat with the remaining batter and serve.

497 – Garlic Cheese Balls

Serves: 2
Preparation: 10 minutes; Cook time: 0 minutes;
Nutrition facts: 335 Calories; 28.7 g Fats; 12.4 g Protein; 5.8 g Net Carb; 0 g Fiber;
Ingredients
- 2 bacon sliced, cooked, chopped
- ½ tsp minced garlic
- 2 oz cream cheese, softened
- 2 tbsp sour cream
- 3 tbsp grated parmesan cheese
- ½ tsp Italian seasoning

How to Prepare:
1. Take a medium bowl, place cheese in it, then add remaining ingredients except for bacon and stir until mixed.
2. Cover the bowl, let it refrigerate for 1 hour until chilled, and then shape the mixture into four balls.
3. Roll the balls in chopped bacon until coated, refrigerate for 30 minutes until firm, and then serve.

498 – Cheddar and Green Onion Biscuits

Serves: 2; Preparation: 5 minutes; Cook time: 8 minutes;
Nutrition facts: 272 Calories; 23 g Fats; 11.5 g Protein; 4.5 g Net Carb; 0.7 g Fiber;
Ingredients
- 1 tsp chopped green onion
- 2 ½ tbsp coconut flour
- 2 ½ tbsp melted butter, unsalted
- 2 oz grated cheddar cheese
- 1 egg
- 1/8 tsp baking powder; ½ tsp garlic powder
- ¼ tsp salt; 1/8 tsp ground black pepper

How to Prepare:
1. Turn on the oven, then set it to 400 degrees F and let it preheat.
2. Take a medium bowl, place flour in it, and then stir in garlic powder, baking powder, salt, and black pepper.
3. Take a separate medium bowl, crack the egg in it, whisk in butter until blended, and then whisk this mixture into the flour until incorporated and smooth.
4. Fold in green onion and cheese, then drop the mixture in the form of mounds onto a cookie sheet greased with oil and bake for 8 minutes until lightly browned.
5. When done, brush biscuit with some more melted butter and then serve.

499 – Basil Wrapped Cheese Balls

Serves: 2; Preparation: 10 minutes; Cook time: 0 minutes;
Nutrition facts: 428 Calories; 31.4 g Fats; 28.9 g Protein; 7.5 g Net Carb; 0 g Fiber;
Ingredients
- 2 oz grated cheddar cheese
- 3 oz grated mozzarella cheese
- 3 oz grated parmesan cheese
- ¼ tsp ground black pepper
- 8 basil leaves

How to Prepare:
1. Take a medium bowl, place all the cheeses in it, add black pepper, stir until blended, then cover the bowl and let it refrigerate for 30 minutes until firm.
2. Then shape the mixture into 1-inch long eight balls, then place each ball on the wide end of a basil leaf and roll it up. Serve immediately.

500 – Double Cheese Chips

Serves: 2; Preparation: 10 minutes; Cook time: 10 minutes;
Nutrition facts: 468 Calories; 34.2 g Fats; 30.3 g Protein; 9.3 g Net Carb; 0 g Fiber;
Ingredients
- 3 oz grated cheddar cheese
- 5 oz grated parmesan cheese
- 1/8 tsp onion powder
- 1/8 tsp ground cumin
- 1/8 tsp red chili powder; 1/8 tsp salt

How to Prepare:
1. Turn on the oven, then set it to 400 degrees F and let it preheat.
2. Take a medium bowl, place cheeses in it, add salt, onion powder, cumin, and red chili powder and stir until mixed.
3. Take a baking pan, line it with parchment paper, spread cheese mixture on it in an even layer, and then bake for 10 minutes until cheese has melted and begin to crisp.
4. When done, remove the baking pan from the oven, let it cool completely and then cut it into triangles. Serve.

501 – Bacon Caprese with Parmesan

Serves: 2; Preparation: 5 minutes; Cook time: 8 minutes;
Nutrition facts: 198 Calories; 17.4 g Fats; 4.4 g Protein; 3.9 g Net Carb; 1.5 g Fiber;

Ingredients
- 2 slices of bacon
- 2 Roma tomato, sliced
- 1 tsp balsamic vinegar
- 2 tbsp avocado oil
- 1 tbsp grated parmesan cheese
- ½ tsp salt; ½ tsp ground black pepper

How to Prepare:
1. Take a frying pan, place it over medium heat and when hot, add bacon and cook for 3 to 4 minutes until crispy.
2. Transfer bacon to a cutting board, let it cool for 5 minutes and then chop it.
3. Turn on the broiler and let it preheat.
4. Take a medium baking sheet, line it with aluminum foil, spray with oil, spread tomato slices on it, and then drizzle with vinegar and oil.
5. Season with salt and black pepper, sprinkle with cheese and bacon and then broil tomatoes for 1 to 2 minutes until cheese has melted. Serve.

502 – Egg McMuffin Sandwich with Avocado and Bacon

Serves: 2; Preparation: 10 minutes; Cook time: 15 minutes;
Nutrition facts: 355 Calories; 28 g Fats; 18.6 g Protein; 5.7 g Net Carb; 2.3 g Fiber;
Ingredients
- 2 eggs, yolks and egg whites separated
- 1/3 cup grated parmesan cheese
- 2 oz cream cheese, softened
- 2 slices of bacon
- ½ of avocado, sliced
- 2/3 tsp salt
- 1 tsp avocado oil

How to Prepare:
1. Take a medium bowl, place egg yolks in it, add cream cheese, parmesan, and salt and whisk by using an electric blender until smooth.
2. Take another medium bowl, add egg whites, beat until stiff peaks form and then fold egg whites into egg yolk mixture until combined.
3. Take a skillet pan, place it over medium heat, add oil and when hot, add one-fourth of the batter, spread it into a 1-inch thick pancake, and then fry got 2 minutes per side until golden brown.
4. When done, let sandwiches cool for 5 minutes, top two muffins with bacon and avocado slices, cover the top with another muffin, and then serve as desired.

Drinks

503 – Butter coffee

Serves: 2; Preparation: 5 minutes; Cook time: 0 minutes;
Nutrition facts: 334 Calories; 38 g Fats; 1 g Protein; 0 g Net Carb; 0 g Fiber;
Ingredients
- 2 cups brewed coffee, hot
- 4 tbsp butter, unsalted
- 2 tbsp coconut oil

How to Prepare:
1. Place all the ingredients in a food processor or blender in the order and then pulse for 1 minute until smooth.
2. Distribute coffee evenly between two cups and then serve.

504 – Ice Tea

Serves: 2; Preparation: 2 hours and 5 minutes; Cook time: 0 minutes;
Nutrition facts: 0 Calories; 0 g Fats; 0 g Protein; 0 g Net Carb; 0 g Fiber;
Ingredients
- 1 teabag
- 2 cups cold water
- 1 cup of ice cubes

How to Prepare:
1. Take a pitcher, pour in 1 cup water, add the teabag and let it steep for 2 hours in the refrigerator.
2. Then remove and discard tea bag, pour in remaining water, add ice cubes, and serve.

505 – Coconut Coffee

Serves: 2; Preparation: 5 minutes; Cook time: 0 minutes;
Nutrition facts: 230 Calories; 25 g Fats; 0 g Protein; 0 g Net Carb; 0 g Fiber;
Ingredients
- 2 cups brewed coffee
- ½ tsp ground cinnamon
- 2 tbsp coconut oil

How to Prepare:
1. Pour coffee into a blender or food processor, add oil and butter and then blend for 10 seconds until light and creamy.
2. Distribute coffee between two mugs, sprinkle with cinnamon and then serve.

506 – Coffee with Cinnamon

Serves: 2; Preparation: 5 minutes; Cook time: 10 minutes;
Nutrition facts: 140 Calories; 13.4 g Fats; 0.3 g Protein; 4 g Net Carb; 0.2 g Fiber;
Ingredients
- 2 cups brewed strong coffee
- 2 tbsp MCT oil; 1/3 tsp ground cinnamon

How to Prepare:
1. Distribute coffee between two cups, add 1 tbsp of MCT oil into each cups, and then add cinnamon. Stir until well combined and then serve.

507 – Spinach Smoothie

Serves: 2
Preparation: 5 minutes; Cook time: 10 minutes;
Nutrition facts: 162 Calories; 15.2 g Fats; 1.2 g Protein; 2.2 g Net Carb; 1.7 g Fiber;
Ingredients

- 2 oz spinach
- 1 ½ tsp ginger powder
- ¼ of lime, juiced
- 1/3 cup coconut milk, unsweetened, full-fat
- 2/3 cup water
- 1 tbsp avocado oil

How to Prepare:
1. Place all the ingredients in the order into a food processor or blender, and then pulse for 2 to 3 minutes until smooth.
2. Distribute smoothie between two glasses and then serve.

508 – Latte

Serves: 2; Preparation: 5 minutes; Cook time: 0 minutes;
Nutrition facts: 191 Calories; 18 g Fats; 6 g Protein; 1 g Net Carb; 0 g Fiber;
Ingredients
- 1 tsp pumpkin pie spice
- ¼ tsp vanilla extract, unsweetened
- 2 eggs
- 2 tbsp coconut oil
- 1 ½ cup water, boiling

How to Prepare:
1. Place all the ingredients in the order into a food processor or a blender and then pulse for 2 to 3 minutes until smooth.
2. Serve immediately.

509 – Bulletproof Coffee with Cream

Serves: 2; Preparation: 5 minutes; Cook time: 0 minutes;
Nutrition facts: 421 Calories; 47 g Fats; 1.9 g Protein; 6.9 g Net Carb; 1.7 g Fiber;
Ingredients
- 2 cups brewed coffee
- 2 tbsp coconut cream
- 2 tbsp coconut oil
- 2 tbsp butter, unsalted

How to Prepare:
1. Place all the ingredients in the order into a food processor or blender and then pulse for 1 to 2 minutes until foamy. Divide coffee between two mugs and then serve.

510 – Berries and Chocolate Milk Shake

Serves: 2; Preparation: 5 minutes; Cook time: 0 minutes;
Nutrition facts: 346 Calories; 34.17 g Fats; 2.6 g Protein; 4.8 g Net Carb; 7.4 g Fiber;
Ingredients
- ¼ cup mixed berries
- 2 tbsp cocoa powder
- ¼ tsp xanthan gum
- 1 cup coconut milk, unsweetened
- 2 tbsp MCT oil

Seasoning:
- 12 drops of stevia

How to Prepare:
1. Place all the ingredients in the order into a food processor or blender, and then pulse for 2 to 3 minutes until smooth. Distribute smoothie between two glasses, serve.

511 – Iced Latte

Serves: 2; Preparation: 5 minutes; Cook time: 0 minutes;
Nutrition facts: 180 Calories; 16.4 g Fats; 1.3 g Protein; 5.7 g Net Carb; 0 g Fiber;
Ingredients

- 2 tbsp MCT oil
- 3 cups almond milk, unsweetened
- 1/2 cup brewed coffee
- ½ cup of ice cubes

How to Prepare:
1. Place all the ingredients in the order into a food processor or blender except for ice, and then pulse for 2 to 3 minutes until smooth.
2. Distribute ice between two glasses, pour latte over it and then serve.

512 – Pumpkin Spice Smoothie

Serves: 2; Preparation: 5 minutes; Cook time: 0 minutes;
Nutrition facts: 252 Calories; 24.4 g Fats; 2.5 g Protein; 5.3 g Net Carb; 0.4 g Fiber;
Ingredients
- 1 ½ cup almond milk, unsweetened
- 1 tbsp pumpkin pie spice
- 2 tbsp erythritol sweetener
- 2 tbsp MCT oil
- 2 oz cream cheese
- ½ cup of ice cubes

How to Prepare:
1. Place all the ingredients in the order into a food processor or blender, and then pulse for 2 to 3 minutes until smooth. Distribute smoothie between two glasses, serve.

513 – Blueberry and Coconut Smoothie

Serves: 2; Preparation: 5 minutes; Cook time: 0 minutes;
Nutrition facts: 236 Calories; 22.6 g Fats; 0.6 g Protein; 5.9 g Net Carb; 1.8 g Fiber;
Ingredients
- 3 oz blueberries
- 1 tsp vanilla extract, unsweetened
- 2 tsp MCT oil
- ½ cup coconut milk, unsweetened
- ½ cup almond milk, unsweetened
- ½ cup of ice cubes

How to Prepare:
1. Place all the ingredients in the order into a food processor or blender, and then pulse for 2 to 3 minutes until smooth.
2. Distribute smoothie between two glasses and then serve.

514 – Matcha Latte

Serves: 2; Preparation: 5 minutes; Cook time: 10 minutes;
Nutrition facts: 255 Calories; 22.8 g Fats; 2.3 g Protein; 4 g Net Carb; 1.3 g Fiber;
Ingredients
- 1 tsp Matcha tea
- Stevia to taste
- 2/3 cup coconut milk, unsweetened
- 1/3 cup almond milk, unsweetened

How to Prepare:
1. Take a small pot, place it over medium heat, pour in both milk, and cook for 3 to 4 minutes until bubbles start to form around the edges of the pot.
2. Place tea and stevia in serving cups and then stir in milk until combined. Serve.

515 – Iced Hazelnut Latte

Serves: 2; Preparation: 5 minutes; Cook time: 0 minutes;
Nutrition facts: 140 Calories; 13.7 g Fats; 0.3 g Protein; 2.7 g Net Carb; 0 g Fiber;

Ingredients
- 2 tbsp hazelnut syrup, unsweetened
- 1 cup strong coffee
- 2 tbsp MCT oil
- 3 oz almond milk, unsweetened
- 1 cup of ice cubes

How to Prepare:
1. Divide ice cubes between two glasses or mugs, pour coffee over ice, then add milk, oil, and hazelnut syrup. Stir well until combined and then serve.

516 – Banana Chocolate Protein Smoothie

Serves: 2; Preparation: 5 minutes; Cook time: 0 minutes;
Nutrition facts: 340 Calories; 27.2 g Fats; 12.8 g Protein; 0.9 g Net Carb; 10.2 g Fiber;
Ingredients
- ½ of an avocado, peeled, pitted
- 2 scoops of chocolate protein powder
- ½ tsp banana extract, unsweetened
- ½ cup coconut milk, unsweetened
- 2 tbsp MCT oil
- 1 cup of water
- 4 tbsp cocoa powder
- 2 tsp erythritol sweetener
- ½ cup of ice cubes

How to Prepare:
1. Place all the ingredients in the order into a food processor or blender, and then pulse for 2 to 3 minutes until smooth.
2. Distribute smoothie between two glasses and then serve.

517 – Iced Apple Green Tea

Serves: 2; Preparation: 5 minutes; Cook time: 10 minutes;
Nutrition facts: 121 Calories; 13 g Fats; 0.6 g Protein; 0.3 g Net Carb; 0 g Fiber;
Ingredients
- 2 cups green tea, brewed, unsweetened, hot
- Stevia to taste
- 2 tbsp MCT oil
- 2 tsp apple cider vinegar
- 1 cup ice

How to Prepare:
1. Pour hot green tea in a food processor or blender, add remaining ingredients and pulse for 1 minute until smooth.
2. Distribute tea between two glasses or mugs and then serve.

518 – Chocolate, Chia and Almond Butter Smoothie

Serves: 2; Preparation: 5 minutes; Cook time: 0 minutes;
Nutrition facts: 230 Calories; 20 g Fats; 4 g Protein; 2 g Net Carb; 5 g Fiber;
Ingredients
- 1 tbsp chia seeds
- ½ of an avocado, diced
- 1 tbsp cocoa powder
- 2 tbsp almond butter
- 6 oz almond milk, unsweetened

Seasoning:
- 1 cup of ice cubes
- 2 tbsp MCT oil
- Stevia to taste

How to Prepare:
1. Place all the ingredients in the order into a food processor or blender, and then pulse for 2 to 3 minutes until smooth.
2. Distribute smoothie between two glasses and then serve.

519 – Citrus Ginger Latte

Serves: 2; Preparation: 5 minutes; Cook time: 0 minutes;
Nutrition facts: 241 Calories; 19.3 g Fats; 0.6 g Protein; 16.3 g Net Carb; 0 g Fiber;
Ingredients
- 2 sachets of ginger elixir
- 1 tbsp butter, unsalted
- 1 ½ cup water, hot
- ½ cup almond milk, unsweetened
- 2 tbsp MCT oil

How to Prepare:
1. Prepare ginger tea and for this, distribute water between two mugs, add ginger elixir and oil and then stir until mixed.
2. Take a small bowl, add butter and milk in it, whisk by using a milk frother until combined, and then evenly stir this mixture into the tea. Serve.

520 – Butter Tea

Serves: 2; Preparation: 10 minutes; Cook time: 0 minutes;
Nutrition facts: 115 Calories; 12.1 g Fats; 0 g Protein; 0 g Net Carb; 0 g Fiber;
Ingredients
- 1 ½ cup water, hot
- 2 tea bags
- Stevia to taste
- 1 tbsp butter, unsalted
- 1 tbsp MCT oil
- 1/8 tsp salt

How to Prepare:
1. Pour hot water into a bowl, add tea bags, and let them steep for 5 minutes.
2. Pour the tea into a blender, add butter, oil, stevia, and salt, and then pulse for 1 minute until foamy. Serve.

521 – Black Tea Latte

Serves: 2; Preparation: 5 minutes; Cook time: 10 minutes;
Nutrition facts: 204 Calories; 22 g Fats; 1 g Protein; 1 g Net Carb; 0 g Fiber;
Ingredients
- 2 cups brewed black tea, strong
- 2 tbsp MCT oil
- 2 tbsp almond milk, unsweetened
- 2 tsp erythritol sweetener

How to Prepare:
1. Place all the ingredients in the order into a food processor or blender, and then pulse for 2 to 3 minutes until blended. Divide tea between two mugs and then serve.

522 – Turmeric Tea

Serves: 2; Preparation: 5 minutes; Cook time: 12 minutes;
Nutrition facts: 128 Calories; 14 g Fats; 0 g Protein; 1 g Net Carb; 0.5 g Fiber;
Ingredients
- 1 tsp turmeric powder
- 2 tbsp coconut oil
- 1 tbsp whipping cream
- 3 cups of water
- ¼ tsp ground black pepper

How to Prepare:
1. Take a medium saucepan, place it over medium heat, pour in water, stir in black pepper, turmeric and oil and bring it to a boil.
2. Then switch heat to the medium low level, simmer the mixture for 7 to 10 minutes, and then distribute between two mugs.
3. Stir in whipping cream and then serve.

523 – Citrus and MCT Matcha Latte

Serves: 2; Preparation: 5 minutes; Cook time: 5 minutes;
Nutrition facts: 120 Calories; 11.2 g Fats; 1.4 g Protein; 0.8 g Net Carb; 0.1 g Fiber;
Ingredients

- 1 ½ tsp Matcha powder
- 1 ½ tbsp MCT oil
- 3 oz coconut milk, unsweetened
- 3 oz almond milk
- 1 cup of water
- ½ tsp cinnamon
- 1/8 tsp cardamom
- 1 ½ tbsp erythritol sweetener

How to Prepare:
1. Take a small saucepan, place it over low heat, add all the ingredients except for oil and Matcha powder, stir until mixed and simmer for 2 minutes.
2. Stir matcha powder for 2 minutes by using a whisker until blended, remove the pan from heat, and divide latte between 2 mugs.
3. Stir in oil by using a milk frother until combined and then serve.

524 – Mocha Milkshake

Serves: 2; Preparation: 5 minutes; Cook time: 0 minutes;
Nutrition facts: 151 Calories; 14.1 g Fats; 0.7 g Protein; 2 g Net Carb; 1.7 g Fiber;
Ingredients

- 1 tbsp cocoa powder, unsweetened
- 2 tsp instant coffee
- 2 tsp MCT oil
- 3 oz almond milk, unsweetened
- 2 oz coconut milk, unsweetened
- Stevia to taste
- ½ tsp vanilla extract, unsweetened
- 1 cup of water
- 1 cup of ice cubes

How to Prepare:
1. Place all the ingredients in the order into a food processor or blender and then pulse for 2 minutes until smooth.
2. Distribute milkshake between two glasses and then serve.

525 – Lime Ice Tea

Serves: 2; Preparation: 5 minutes; Cook time: 0 minutes;
Nutrition facts: 65 Calories; 6.5 g Fats; 0.2 g Protein; 0.3 g Net Carb; 0 g Fiber;
Ingredients

- ½ cup brewed tea, strong
- Stevia to taste
- 1/2 of lime, juiced
- 1 tbsp MCT oil
- 1 ½ cup chilled water

How to Prepare:
1. Take a large pitcher, add all the ingredients in it and stir until well combined.
2. Distribute tea between two glasses and then serve.

526 – Raspberry Yogurt Smoothie

Serves: 2; Preparation: 5 minutes; Cook time: 0 minutes;
Nutrition facts: 181 Calories; 15.8 g Fats; 2.6 g Protein; 3.8 g Net Carb; 1.9 g Fiber;
Ingredients

- 2 oz raspberries
- 1 tbsp erythritol sweetener
- 4 oz coconut milk, unsweetened
- 4 oz yogurt
- 1 cup water
- 2 tbsp MCT oil

How to Prepare:
1. Place all the ingredients in the order into a food processor or blender and then pulse for 2 minutes until smooth.
2. Distribute smoothie between two glasses and then serve.

527– Ginger Lime Tea

Serves: 2; Preparation: 10 minutes; Cook time: 5 minutes;
Nutrition facts: 82 Calories; 7 g Fats; 0.4 g Protein; 3.1 g Net Carb; 0.9 g Fiber;
Ingredients
- 2 tbsp grated ginger
- Stevia to taste
- ½ of lime, juiced
- 1 tbsp MCT oil
- 2 cups water
- ½ cup ice cubes

How to Prepare:
1. Take a medium saucepan, place it over medium heat, add water and bring it to a boil.
2. Then add ginger and lime juice, stir until mixed, remove pan from heat and let it steep for 15 minutes.
3. Stir in stevia, then strain mixture into a pitcher, add ice cubes and let tea chill completely.
4. Distribute tea between two glasses, stir in MCT oil and then serve.

528 – Avocado Parsley Shake

Serves: 2
Preparation: 5 minutes; Cook time: 0 minutes;
Nutrition facts: 201 Calories; 19.5 g Fats; 1 g Protein; 1.9 g Net Carb; 2.5 g Fiber;
Ingredients
- ½ of avocado, pitted
- 6 parsley leaves
- 3 sprigs of cilantro
- Stevia to taste
- 8 oz almond milk, unsweetened

Seasoning:
- ½ cup water
- 2 tbsp avocado oil
- 1 cup ice cubes

How to Prepare:
1. Place all the ingredients in the order into a food processor or blender and then pulse for 2 minutes until smooth.
2. Distribute smoothie between two glasses and then serve.

529 – Fat Bomb Tea

Serves: 2
Preparation: 5 minutes; Cook time: 0 minutes;
Nutrition facts: 279 Calories; 30.1 g Fats; 0 g Protein; 1.4 g Net Carb; 0 g Fiber;
Ingredients
- 2 cups hot tea
- 6 crops of stevia
- 2 tbsp whipped cream
- 2 tbsp coconut oil
- 2 tbsp butter, unsalted

How to Prepare:
1. Place all the ingredients in the order into a food processor or blender and then pulse for 1 minute until blended.
2. Distribute tea between two mugs and then serve.

530 – Cinnamon Roll Latte

Serves: 2; Preparation: 5 minutes; Cook time: 5 minutes;
Nutrition facts: 95 Calories; 8.1 g Fats; 1.3 g Protein; 2.9 g Net Carb; 0 g Fiber;
Ingredients
- 1 tsp vanilla extract, unsweetened
- ¾ cup brewed coffee
- 1 tbsp cream cheese, softened
- 4 oz almond milk, unsweetened
- 2 tbsp whipping cream
- 2 tsp cinnamon
- 2 tbsp erythritol sweetener

How to Prepare:
1. Take a small pot, place it over medium heat, add milk, stir in sweetener, cinnamon, cream cheese, and vanilla and cook for 3 to 4 minutes until cream cheese has dissolved completely, stirring frequently.
2. Then divide coffee between two mugs, pour in cream cheese mixture, and then top each mug with a tbsp of cream. Serve.

531 – Avocado, Spinach, and Chia Smoothie

Serves: 2; Preparation: 5 minutes; Cook time: 0 minutes;
Nutrition facts: 220 Calories; 20.4 g Fats; 2.2 g Protein; 1.2 g Net Carb; 4.8 g Fiber;
Ingredients
- ½ of avocado, pitted
- 2 oz spinach
- ½ bunch of collard greens
- 2 tsp chia seeds
- 2 tbsp avocado oil
- 4 oz coconut milk, unsweetened
- 2 tsp vanilla extract, unsweetened
- 4 oz of water
- ½ cup of ice cubes

How to Prepare:
1. Place all the ingredients in the order into a food processor or blender, and then pulse for 2 to 3 minutes until smooth. Distribute smoothie between two glasses, serve.

532 – Avocado, Flaxseed and Cocoa Smoothie

Serves: 2; Preparation: 5 minutes; Cook time: 0 minutes;
Nutrition facts: 215 Calories; 20.6 g Fats; 1.6 g Protein; 0.4 g Net Carb; 4.4 g Fiber;
Ingredients
- ½ of avocado, pitted
- 1 ½ tbsp cocoa powder
- 2 tbsp erythritol sweetener
- 1 tbsp flaxseeds
- 4 oz coconut milk, unsweetened
- 2 tbsp MCT oil
- ¾ cup of water
- ½ cup of ice cubes

How to Prepare:
1. Place all the ingredients in the order into a food processor or blender, and then pulse for 2 to 3 minutes until smooth.
2. Distribute smoothie between two glasses and then serve.

533 – Vanilla Latte

Serves: 2; Preparation: 5 minutes; Cook time: 5 minutes;
Nutrition facts: 202 Calories; 19.9 g Fats; 1 g Protein; 2.4 g Net Carb; 1.1 g Fiber;
Ingredients

- ¾ cup espresso
- 8 oz coconut milk, unsweetened
- 2 tbsp whipping cream
- 2 tsp vanilla extract, unsweetened
- 2 tbsp MCT oil
- 2 tbsp erythritol sweetener
- 1 tbsp cocoa powder, unsweetened

How to Prepare:
1. Take a saucepan, place it over low heat, add all the ingredients in it except for cocoa powder, whisk by using an immersion blender and cook for 3 minutes or more until hot. Divide latte between two mugs, sprinkle with cocoa powder, and then serve.

534 – Chocolate Dipped Strawberry Breakfast Shake

Serves: 2; Preparation: 5 minutes; Cook time: 0 minutes;
Nutrition facts: 141 Calories; 8 g Fats; 10.5 g Protein; 1.2 g Net Carb; 4.2 g Fiber;
Ingredients
- 3 oz strawberries
- 3 tbsp cocoa powder
- 1 scoop of protein powder
- 2 tsp avocado oil
- 6 oz coconut milk, unsweetened
- ½ cup of ice cubes; ½ cup of water

How to Prepare:
1. Place all the ingredients in the order into a food processor or blender, and then pulse for 2 to 3 minutes until smooth. Distribute smoothie among two glasses, serve.

535 – Creamy Coffee

Serves: 2; Preparation: 5 minutes; Cook time: 0 minutes;
Nutrition facts: 208 Calories; 21 g Fats; 2.5 g Protein; 2.5 g Net Carb; 1.5 g Fiber;
Ingredients
- 1 ½ cup brewed coffee
- 2 tsp erythritol sweetener
- 1 tsp cinnamon
- 1 tsp vanilla extract, unsweetened
- 4 tbsp whipping cream

How to Prepare:
1. Place all the ingredients in the order into a food processor or blender except for coffee, and then pulse for 2 to 3 minutes until smooth.
2. Distribute coffee between two mugs, and then serve.

536 – Coffee Creamer

Serves: 2; Preparation: 5 minutes; Cook time: 0 minutes;
Nutrition facts: 171 Calories; 11.6 g Fats; 10.5 g Protein; 3.3 g Net Carb; 0.3 g Fiber;
Ingredients
- 1 scoop of protein powder
- ½ tsp vanilla extract, unsweetened
- 4 oz coconut milk, unsweetened
- 2 oz whipping cream
- 1 ½ cup brewed coffee
- 2 tsp erythritol sweetener

How to Prepare:
1. Prepare the creamer and for this, place all the ingredients in the order into a food processor or blender, and then pulse for 2 to 3 minutes until smooth.
2. Distribute coffee between two mugs, add creamer, stir until mixed and then serve.

537 – Coconut Oil Coffee

Serves: 2; Preparation: 5 minutes; Cook time: 0 minutes;
Nutrition facts: 138 Calories; 13.3 g Fats; 0.7 g Protein; 3.7 g Net Carb; 0.1 g Fiber;

Ingredients
- 1 ½ cup brewed coffee
- ¼ tsp ground cinnamon
- 3 tsp coconut oil
- 4 oz coconut milk, unsweetened
- 1 tbsp whipping cream
- ¼ tsp cayenne pepper

How to Prepare:
1. Pour coffee in a blender, add coconut oil and then blend for 1 minute or more until frothy.
2. Add remaining ingredients except for cream and pulse for 20 seconds until blended. Divide coffee between two mugs, top each mug with a tbsp of whipping cream.

538 – Asparagus and Tomato Frittata

Serves: 2; Preparation: 5 minutes; Cook time: 8 minutes;
Nutrition facts: 193 Calories; 15 g Fats; 10.8 g Protein; 2 g Net Carb; 0.8 g Fiber;
Ingredients
- 1.5 oz asparagus cut, sliced
- 1-ounce grape tomatoes, halved
- 1-ounce diced tomatoes
- 2 eggs
- 1 tbsp avocado oil
- 1/3 tsp salt; ¼ tsp ground black pepper
- 1/3 tsp red chili flakes

How to Prepare:
1. Turn on the oven, then set it to 450 degrees F and let it preheat.
2. Meanwhile, take a medium bowl, crack eggs in it, add salt, black pepper, and red chili flakes and whisk well.
3. Take a medium skillet pan, place it over medium-high heat, add oil and when hot, add asparagus and cook for 1 to 2 minutes until sauté.
4. Switch heat to the low level, spread asparagus evenly in the pan, then pour egg mixture over asparagus, top with grape tomatoes and diced tomatoes and cook for 1 to 2 minutes until frittata begins to set.
5. Transfer pan into the oven and bake for 4 to 5 minutes until frittata has thoroughly cooked. When done, cut the frittata into slices and then serve.

539 – 3-Cheese Quiche with Bacon and Broccoli

Serves: 2; Preparation: 10 minutes; Cook time: 20 minutes;
Nutrition facts: 240 Calories; 16.1 g Fats; 18.7 g Protein; 3.4 g Net Carb; 0.7 g Fiber;
Ingredients
- 2 oz bacon strips, chopped
- 3 oz broccoli florets, chopped
- 1 tbsp grated parmesan cheese
- 1 tbsp grated mozzarella cheese
- 1 tbsp grated cheddar cheese
- ¼ tsp salt; 1/8 tsp ground black pepper
- 1 tbsp whipping cream
- 1 tsp sour cream
- 2 eggs

How to Prepare:
1. Turn on the oven, then set it to 375 degrees F and let it preheat.
2. Take a medium skillet pan, place it over medium heat and when hot, place chopped bacon and cook for 3 to 4 minutes until nicely browned.
3. Meanwhile, take a heatproof bowl, place chopped broccoli in it, cover with plastic wrap, and then microwave for 2 to 3 minutes until steamed.
4. When the bacon has cooked, transfer to a plate lined with paper towels, add broccoli into the pan and stir-fry for 1 to 2 minutes until golden brown.
5. Crack eggs in a bowl, add salt, black pepper, whipping cream and sour cream and then whisk until combined.
6. Add bacon, broccoli and ½ tbsp each of cheeses and then whisk until combined.
7. Take a quiche pan or a baking pan, pour broccoli mixture in it, top with remaining cheeses, and then bake for 12 to 15 minutes until cooked through and cheese has melted. When done, cut the quiche into two slices and then serve.

540 – Portobello Eggs Boats

Serves: 2; Preparation: 5 minutes; Cook time: 25 minutes;
Nutrition facts: 179 Calories; 12.6 g Fats; 9.7 g Protein; 5.2 g Net Carb; 1 g Fiber;
Ingredients
- 2 Portobello mushroom caps
- 2 eggs
- 2 tsp grated parmesan cheese

- ¼ tsp salt
- ¼ tsp ground black pepper
- 1 tbsp avocado oil

How to Prepare:
1. Turn on the oven, set it to 375 degrees F, and let it preheat.
2. Take a baking sheet, line it with parchment paper, place mushroom caps on it cup-side up, brush with oil and then crack an egg into each cap.
3. Sprinkle cheese, salt, and black pepper evenly on eggs and then bake for 20 to 25 minutes until mushroom has turned tender and eggs have cooked. Serve.

541 – Avocado and Herb Smoothie

Serves: 2; Preparation: 5 minutes; Cook time: 0 minutes;
Nutrition facts: 223 Calories; 23 g Fats; 1 g Protein; 4 g Net Carb; 1 g Fiber;
Ingredients
- ½ of avocado, pitted
- 5 leaves of parsley
- 5 leaves of cilantro
- 4 oz coconut milk, unsweetened
- 2 oz yogurt
- ¼ of lime, juiced
- ¼ tsp vanilla extract, unsweetened
- ½ cup of water; ¾ cup of ice cubes

How to Prepare:
1. Place all the ingredients in the order into a food processor or blender, and then pulse for 2 to 3 minutes until smooth. Distribute smoothie between two glasses, serve.

542 – Strawberry and Coconut Smoothie

Serves: 2; Preparation: 5 minutes; Cook time: 0 minutes;
Nutrition facts: 120 Calories; 11 g Fats; 0.6 g Protein; 2 g Net Carb; 1.5 g Fiber;
Ingredients
- 2 oz strawberries
- 2 tbsp grated coconut
- ¼ tsp vanilla extract, unsweetened
- 4 oz coconut milk, unsweetened
- 2 oz yogurt

Seasoning:
- ½ cup of water
- 1 tbsp avocado oil
- ¾ cup of ice cubes

How to Prepare:
1. Place all the ingredients in the order into a food processor or blender, and then pulse for 2 to 3 minutes until smooth. Distribute smoothie between two glasses, serve.

543 – Mocha Frozen Latte Shake

Serves: 2; Preparation: 5 minutes; Cook time: 0 minutes;
Nutrition facts: 222 Calories; 23 g Fats; 2.5 g Protein; 2.4 g Net Carb; 0 g Fiber;
Ingredients
- 4 oz almond milk, unsweetened
- 3 tbsp cocoa powder
- 3 tsp erythritol sweetener
- 3 tbsp MCT oil
- 1.5 oz whipping cream
- 1 cup ice
- ¾ cup water

How to Prepare:
1. Place all the ingredients in the order into a food processor or blender, and then pulse for 2 to 3 minutes until smooth.
2. Distribute shake between two glasses and then serve.

544 – Raspberry Protein Smoothie

Serves: 2; Preparation: 5 minutes; Cook time: 0 minutes;
Nutrition facts: 181 Calories; 10.6 g Fats; 12.8 g Protein; 4.8 g Net Carb; 2.7 g Fiber;
Ingredients

- 2 oz raspberries
- 1 tsp flaxseed
- 1 tbsp MCT oil
- 4 oz yogurt
- 4 oz almond milk, unsweetened
- 1 tsp pumpkin seed
- 1 scoop protein powder
- ½ cup water; ½ cup ice cubes

How to Prepare:
1. Place all the ingredients in the order into a food processor or blender, and then pulse for 2 to 3 minutes until smooth.
2. Distribute smoothie between two glasses and then serve.

545 – Choco Coffee Milkshake

Serves: 2; Preparation: 5 minutes; Cook time: 0 minutes;
Nutrition facts: 95 Calories; 8.5 g Fats; 0.7 g Protein; 1.5 g Net Carb; 1.4 g Fiber;
Ingredients
- 2 tsp espresso powder
- 4 tsp cocoa
- 1 tbsp avocado oil
- 4 oz almond milk, unsweetened
- 3 oz coconut milk, unsweetened
- 2 tbsp erythritol sweetener
- 1 ½ cup ice cubes; ¾ cup water

How to Prepare:
1. Place all the ingredients in the order into a food processor or blender, and then pulse for 2 to 3 minutes until smooth.
2. Distribute shake between two glasses and then serve.

546 – Vanilla Matcha Green Tea Latte

Serves: 2; Preparation: 5 minutes; Cook time: 0 minutes;
Nutrition facts: 252 Calories; 2.5 g Fats; 1.6 g Protein; 0 g Net Carb; 0.8 g Fiber;
Ingredients
- 6 oz almond milk, unsweetened
- 2 tsp matcha powder
- 2 tsp vanilla extract, unsweetened
- ½ cup of water

How to Prepare:
1. Place all the ingredients in the order into a food processor or a blender and then pulse for 2 to 3 minutes until smooth.
2. Divide latte between two mugs and then serve.

547 – Chocolate and Almond Butter Smoothie

Serves: 2; Preparation: 5 minutes; Cook time: 0 minutes;
Nutrition facts: 278 Calories; 22.5 g Fats; 6.8 g Protein; 3.4 g Net Carb; 7.5 g Fiber;
Ingredients
- ½ of avocado, pitted
- 1 tbsp erythritol sweetener
- 2 tbsp cacao powder
- 4 tbsp almond butter
- 6 oz almond milk, unsweetened
- ½ cup of water; ½ cup of ice cubes

How to Prepare:
1. Place all the ingredients in the order into a food processor or a blender and then pulse for 2 to 3 minutes until smooth.
2. Divide smoothie between two glasses and then serve.

548 – Mexican Coffee

Serves: 2; Preparation: 10 minutes; Cook time: 8 minutes;
Nutrition facts: 325 Calories; 27.8 g Fats; 0.8 g Protein; 15.6 g Net Carb; 1.3 g Fiber;
Ingredients

- ½ stick of cinnamon
- 2 whole cloves
- 3 tbsp espresso powder
- ¼ tsp vanilla extract, unsweetened
- 2 tbsp avocado oil
- 1 tbsp cocoa powder
- 1 tbsp erythritol sweetener
- 2 ½ cups water

How to Prepare:
1. Take a small saucepan, place it over medium heat, pour in water, add espresso powder, cocoa powder, cinnamon, and cloves, bring it to a boil, then switch heat to medium-low level and simmer for 5 minutes.
2. Then remove the pan from heat, add sweetener and vanilla, stir until mixed and let the coffee steep for 5 minutes.
3. Divide coffee between two mugs by passing through a coffee filter, stir in oil, taste to adjust sweetness, and then serve.

549 – Keto Broth Latte

Serves: 2; Preparation: 5 minutes; Cook time: 2 minutes;
Nutrition facts: 90 Calories; 7.7 g Fats; 2.1 g Protein; 1.3 g Net Carb; 0.2 g Fiber;
Ingredients
- 1/4 tsp salt
- 1/3 tsp turmeric powder
- 2 tsp lime juice
- 1 tbsp avocado oil
- 4 oz of chicken bone broth
- ¾ cup of water

How to Prepare:
1. Take a medium saucepan, place it over medium heat, pour in broth and water, and bring it to a simmer.
2. Pour broth into the food processor along with remaining ingredients and then pulse for 1 minute until frothy.
3. Divide the broth between two mugs and then serve.

550 – Protein Coffee

Serves: 2; Preparation: 5 minutes; Cook time: 0 minutes;
Nutrition facts: 342 Calories; 26 g Fats; 27 g Protein; 2.1 g Net Carb; 1.8 g Fiber;
Ingredients
- 12 oz brewed coffee
- 2 scoops of protein powder
- 1 tbsp coconut oil
- 1 tbsp butter, unsalted
- 2 tbsp whipping cream

Seasoning:
- 2 tbsp cacao powder

How to Prepare:
1. Place all the ingredients in the order into a food processor or blender, and then pulse for 2 to 3 minutes until smooth.
2. Distribute coffee between two glasses and then serve.

Made in the USA
Coppell, TX
18 January 2022

71858978R00109